Sanctuary and Subjectivity

T0244153

T & T CLARK STUDIES IN SOCIAL ETHICS, ETHNOGRAPHY, AND THEOLOGY

Over the last half century, there have been numerous calls for Christian theology and ethics to take human experience seriously—to delve into particular economic, socio-political, racial-ethnic, and cultural contexts from which theological and moral imagination arises. Yet actual theologies that draw upon descriptive-rich, qualitative methods— methods that place such particularity at the center of inquiry and performance—are few and scattered. **T & T Clark Studies in Social Ethics, Ethnography, and Theology** is a monograph series that addresses this gap in the literature by providing a publishing home for timely ethnographically-driven theological and ethical investigations of an expansive array of pressing social issues, ranging from armed conflict to racism to healthcare inequities to sexuality/gender and discrimination to the marginalization of persons with disabilities. The scope of the series projects, taken together, is at once global and intensely local, with the central organizing conviction that ethnography provides not only information to plug into a theology, but a valid and vibrant way of *doing* theology.

Sanctuary and Subjectivity

Thinking Theologically about
Whiteness and Sanctuary Movements

Michael Woolf

t&tclark

LONDON · NEW YORK · OXFORD · NEW DELHI · SYDNEY

T&T CLARK
Bloomsbury Publishing Plc
50 Bedford Square, London, WC1B 3DP, UK
1385 Broadway, New York, NY 10018, USA
29 Earlsfort Terrace, Dublin 2, Ireland

BLOOMSBURY, T&T CLARK and the T&T Clark logo are trademarks of
Bloomsbury Publishing Plc

First published in Great Britain 2023

Copyright © Michael Woolf, 2023

Michael Woolf has asserted his right under the Copyright, Designs and Patents Act,
1988, to be identified as Author of this work.

Cover images: AdobeStock
Cover design: Graham Robert Ward

All rights reserved. No part of this publication may be reproduced or transmitted in any
form or by any means, electronic or mechanical, including photocopying, recording,
or any information storage or retrieval system, without prior permission in writing
from the publishers.

Bloomsbury Publishing Plc does not have any control over, or responsibility for, any
third-party websites referred to or in this book. All internet addresses given in this
book were correct at the time of going to press. The author and publisher regret
any inconvenience caused if addresses have changed or sites have ceased to exist,
but can accept no responsibility for any such changes.

A catalogue record for this book is available from the British Library.

Library of Congress Control Number: 2023939088

ISBN: HB: 978-0-5677-1129-8
PB: 978-0-5677-1128-1
ePDF: 978-0-5677-1131-1
ePUB: 978-0-5677-1130-4

Typeset by Deanta Global Publishing Services, Chennai, India
Printed and bound in Great Britain

To find out more about our authors and books visit www.bloomsbury.com
and sign up for our newsletters.

CONTENTS

Introduction

Rosa crossed the border between Mexico and the United States in 1984 with the help of prominent organizers in the Sanctuary Movement of the 1980s. Months later, she would receive sanctuary from a church in Southwest. Her time there was marked by sincere gratitude for the housing, food, and accompaniment of the Sanctuary Movement, but there was tension in that gratitude. As she would tell me decades later in an interview for this book, "They just wanted me to present as a victim. A woman who had lost her children and had it not been for sanctuary I would have been killed. It was true. That was true, but I couldn't talk about what really mattered to me as a human rights activist in Guatemala." While the Sanctuary Movement provided much aid and support to recipients of sanctuary, activists also restricted the agency of recipients by cultivating recipients' identities as refugees, the preferred term that the movement used for recipients. Against this identity, recipients often reasserted their identities as activists in their home countries and utilized their status as recipients of sanctuary to ground their own further activism in the United States. For instance, Rosa was a human rights activist in Guatemala who organized for political, economic, and communal rights, where she told me she had to "literally fight for those rights to be respected and enforced." Several recipients I interviewed, including Rosa, organized vigils, support groups for victims of torture, their own organizations, or were in leadership in Central American mutual aid organizations.

A common image of the Sanctuary Movement depicts a recipient giving a *testimonio* to the press or to a gathered white community of listeners. Their face obscured by a bandana for their protection, the recipient or recipients occupy the center of the shot, framed either by clergy panelists or the back of heads. This image captures the tensions of the Sanctuary Movement. In some ways, recipients were elevated as the bearers of knowledge that the Reagan administration denied, and their *testimonios* occupied the center of the movement. In other ways, those same *testimonios* were constrained by the necessary recitations of fear and victimhood that recipients' status as refugees demanded. Their face hidden, they were marked as those who had something to fear, and that fear became the raw material out of which white religious hearers might be moved to act out of compassion, finding spiritual self-actualization. The rapt attention and symbolic centering of recipients in the *testimonio* finds its inverse in the bandana and the fear it represents.

Whiteness and white supremacy are the organizing frameworks of this book. Womanist theologian Dr. Chanequa Walker-Barnes recently tweeted that "White scholars [of religion] have one job: figuring out how to repent from and repair the White supremacist theology that pervades the US. Literally, it's the only thing they need to be doing." In many ways, this book is a response to that "one job." I argue that the Sanctuary Movement is a site of white subject formation and that the practice of sanctuary is inherently bound up with whiteness. By close analysis using interviews and autoethnographic methods, I propose that a study of sanctuary leads to a clearer understanding of whiteness and how it functions in progressive religious spaces among white allies in social movements, while at the same time arguing that the study of sanctuary can help us rethink foundational theological categories and locate, analyze, and interrogate whiteness in a social movement and practical theology. Lauren Winner's *The Dangers of Christian Practice* artfully critiques the assumed link between practices and virtues they purport to create, paying attention to the damage that the practices have created and arguing that that damage is inextricable from the practices themselves. In this book, I undertake a similar project by analyzing one practice—sanctuary—and arguing that, while it produced a social movement that accomplished much, activists were not only cultivating compassion; they were forming themselves as white subjects.

The tension between gratitude and frustration that Rosa names in her interview is in many ways the fundamental grounding of this project. As a practical theologian, my first instinct was to pay attention to the ways people cultivate excellence in particular practices, but Rosa's experience revealed the ways that the Sanctuary Movement both inhibited and enabled her practice of activism. The practice framework, it seemed, worked well for telling the stories of the mostly white activists who offered sanctuary, but it left the human complexity of the people who received sanctuary unarticulated. Most importantly, the practice framework did not help me think about power. Power differentials between activists and recipients, the power of the narratives presented by recipients in *testimonios*, and the power of the refugee framework all demanded a thoroughgoing analysis in the movement. To solve this problem, I turned to the work of Judith Butler on subjectivity. In particular, her insightful assertion that agency is "the assumption of a purpose unintended by power."[1] Such an insight helped me see more clearly the Sanctuary Movement as instantiating power that simultaneously created subjects and restricted their power, making sense of some of the tensions that I encountered in interviews and images of the movement.

---

[1] Judith Butler, *The Psychic Life of Power: Theories in Subjection* (Stanford, CA: Stanford University Press, 1997), 11.

The Sanctuary Movement of the 1980s

Most accounts of the Sanctuary Movement of the 1980s begin in Tucson with Southside Presbyterian Church's declaration of sanctuary.[2] Hanging banners that proclaimed the church a place of refuge for Central Americans, the church implored Immigration and Naturalization Services, often referred to as *La Migra* in sanctuary literature, not to profane the sanctuary of God. In these accounts, two activists at the center of that proclamation loom large—Jim Corbett and John Fife. Their conversion experiences, born of seeing the suffering of those attempting to cross the border, being detained, and having their asylum claims rejected, are well documented.[3] The spread of the Sanctuary Movement from Tucson to the rest of the United States, including activists in Chicago that would build on Tucson's conception of sanctuary to include more explicitly political work, is a central concern. Even as scholars move beyond the lionizing of prominent Tucson activists like Fife and Corbett, too often they focus on activists at other centers of the movement, while recipients' struggles for agency within the Sanctuary Movement not centered.

My analysis instead begins by asserting the complex subjectivity and agency of those who would go on to receive sanctuary. As the chapters that follow demonstrate, they were often activists in their own right, although some who received sanctuary were apolitical, fleeing home countries in chaos. Indeed, many of them came to see receiving sanctuary as a strategy for continuing that activism, seeking to give witness to the ways that the US foreign policy and history of imperialism were responsible for the state of their home countries. The problem is that much of this agency was occluded by white activists, who strived to shape narratives in ways that the American general public would sympathize with. In doing so, they cultivated recipients' identities as refugees. This term carried with it protections under the Refugee Act of 1980, but it also restricted the ways that recipients could narrate their activism and made recounting traumatic narratives and demonstrations of fear a core part of recipient *testimonios*, the evocative firsthand accounts that recipients gave that built the Sanctuary Movement. Even so, recipients' struggle for agency continued, and their contestations and strivings powerfully shaped the Sanctuary Movement in ways that few scholars center. In centering their voices in this project, a more robust vision of the Sanctuary Movement emerges, one that can provide a powerful source for

---

[2]In fact, Southside was joined by five congregations in Berkeley, CA, holding a pre-planned press conferences together.
[3]See: Jim Corbett, *Goatwalking* (New York: Viking, 1991). Miriam Davidson, *Convictions of the Heart: Jim Corbett and the Sanctuary Movement* (Tucson: University of Arizona Press, 1988). Ann Crittenden, *Sanctuary: A Story of American Conscience and the Law in Collision*, 1st ed. (New York: Weidenfeld & Nicolson, 1988).

practical theological reflection about agency, the possibilities of testimony, and new ecclesiological visions centered on fugitivity. However, in order to fully appreciate the Sanctuary Movement as a site of practical theological inquiry, new tools that pay attention to agency must be developed. This book seeks to center recipient voices, taking their critiques of the whiteness at the center of the Sanctuary Movement seriously.

The Sanctuary Movement of the 1980s was a religious and political movement that offered housing, support, and protection to Central Americans fleeing unrest in their home countries. By 1987, the Sanctuary Movement counted over 400 faith communities and around 70,000 participants among its numbers.[4] Sanctuary activists primarily organized around the offering of physical sanctuary within church buildings, but some congregations were connected to the network of activists through Bible studies, informal education opportunities, and public liturgical displays. The selection of those who would receive sanctuary varied. In Chicago, activists carefully selected sympathetic, politically minded recipients, while others had a policy of accepting whoever presented themselves and committed to the process. Activists debated the aims of the movement. Some activists were focused on changing US asylum law to be more equitable, others were explicitly anti-interventionist, and still others were focused on the humanitarian aspects of helping individual Central Americans. Oftentimes, these concerns overlapped. Perhaps the most important legacy of the Sanctuary Movement is the way it changed US refugee and asylum law through the ABC v. Thornburgh case, which forbids politicization of the asylum process, as well as the establishment of sanctuary cities. Although the New Sanctuary Movement has some important connections to the Sanctuary Movement of the 1980s, especially the practice of sanctuary, the former is focused on domestic political concerns like immigration reform and the securing of rights for the undocumented, while the latter is more concerned with foreign policy, the right of asylum, and anti-interventionism.

Conversation Partners

This book is primarily a theological inquiry—not a historical one. Recent years have seen an increase in the conversation between ethnography and theology. While some versions of this conversation emphasize the use of ethnographic tools for doing research, many theologians have begun to think more about how ethnography itself constitutes a form of theology. For instance, Natalie Wigg-Stevenson argues for a vision of ethnography as a "distinctly spiritual practice

---

[4]Hilary Cunningham, *God and Caesar at the Rio Grande: Sanctuary and the Politics of Religion* (Minneapolis, MN: University of Minnesota Press, 1995), xiii.

of religious apprenticeship," whereby ethnography becomes less "analysis of Christian practices than it is an ethnographic analysis from Christian practices."[5] Likewise, Christian Scharen argues for a vision of ethnography that "is fully theological and even an enactment of the ethics of discipleship" as opposed to "borrowed."[6] Todd Whitmore puts it succinctly, "ethnography is not simply a method that provides information to plug into our theology; rather ethnography *is* a way of doing theology."[7] This project is indebted to such perspectives as it argues not only that the Sanctuary Movement can tell us something about grace, the (im)possibilities of testimony, or atonement, but that the research itself is a theological project that involves holy moments of activism that are run through with God's grace, especially in the critical interrogations my own white supremacy as a pastor of a church in the New Sanctuary Movement. In constructing my analysis as I have, I seek to make those numinous moments visible as I yield to critique and accountability.

This project is committed to making myself visible in the work of research—most especially in Chapter 1, but throughout other chapters as well. To do so, I draw on the practice of autoethnography as well as practical theological engagement with those same methods. To do so, I draw on the work of Leon Anderson, who makes the case for "analytic ethnography,"[8] while also utilizing interactive interview methods that Carolyn Ellis, Christine E. Kiesinger, and Lisa M. Tillmann-Healy, argue is an "in-depth and intimate understanding of people's experiences with emotionally charged and sensitive topics."[9] This method is particularly important for engaging practitioners and myself in the work of understanding how whiteness constructed our ongoing work in the New Sanctuary Movement. Within practical theology, Wigg-Stevenson, Whitmore, and Mary McClintock Fulkerson serve as guiding lights for the type of inquiry that I seek to enact. Wigg-Stevenson proposes a "reflexive ethnography" that moves the researcher from practicing participant observation to "objectified participant,"[10] while Whitmore writes of how he

---

[5]Natalie Wigg-Stevenson, "What's Really Going On: Ethnographic Theology and the Production of Theological Knowledge," *Cultural Studies, Critical Methodologies* 18, no. 6 (2018): 428, 23, https://doi.org/10.1177/1532708617744576.

[6]Christian Scharen, "Theological Ethnography and World Christianity: A Response," *Journal of World Christianity* 10, no. 1 (2020): 109, https://doi.org/10.5325/jworlchri.10.1.0109, https://doi.org/10.5325/jworlchri.10.1.0109.

[7]Todd Whitmore, *Imitating Christ in Magwi: An Anthropological Theology* (London: T&T Clark, 2019), 29.

[8]Leon Anderson, "Analytic Autoethnography," *Journal of Contemporary Ethnography* 35, no. 4 (2010), https://doi.org/10.1177/0891241605280449.

[9]Carolyn Ellis, Christine E. Kiesinger, and Lisa M. Tillmann-Healy, "Interactive Interviewing: Talking about Emotional Experience," in *Reflexivity and Voice*, ed. Rosanna Hertz (Thousand Oaks, CA: Sage Publications, 1997), 129.

[10]Natalie Wigg-Stevenson, *Ethnographic Theology: An Inquiry into the Production of Theological Knowledge*, 1st ed. (New York: Palgrave Macmillan US; Imprint: Palgrave Macmillan, 2014), 49, 58.

is "always also the ethnograph*ee*,"[11] and McClintock Fulkerson's ability to render herself visible in her work as she accounts for her own social location and interactions with her participants all highlight the type of reflexivity and autoethnographic methods that I utilize throughout this project.[12] Indeed, I argue that this type of reflexivity is important not only as good scholarship but as accountability and spiritual discipline.

Whiteness, too, is a topic of increasing importance in practical theology. Mary McClintock Fulkerson deftly explicates the way that whiteness manifests as the "bodily sense of ownership of public or social space," while paying attention to the ways that the creation of white space pushes Black worshippers to enact "racialized incorporative practices of propriety" as a "protective device."[13] Moving outside of an American, congregational context, Whitmore's *Imitating Christ in Magwi* focuses on his own whiteness and how that determined the nature of his fieldwork, while also expanding understandings of whiteness outside of the American context assumed by much literature on whiteness. Within the discipline, Coutney Goto has contributed to understanding whiteness in practical theology itself by noting the ways that white practical theologians have failed to take into account the racialized character of their scholarship and have instead produced their own perspectives as objective or "central to (meaning 'well studied in') the discipline."[14] I contribute to these ongoing conversations in practical theology by analyzing white supremacy among white allies, myself included, engaged in a historical practice with deep roots in the Hebrew Bible that visually centers the narratives of recipients of sanctuary while augmenting the agency and spiritual actualization of white practitioners. In particular, this book analyzes the power-obliviousness of white activists, while also mapping the affective contours of whiteness among white allies.

This book also contributes to ongoing theoretical conversations within practical theology, especially those that seek to think beyond Alasdair MacIntyre's theories of practice.[15] While MacIntyre's definition of practice remains relevant and much of this project is in conversation with his work, recent conversations have proposed various theoretical tools to augment and replace practice as an organizing category. Of particular interest is the

---

[11]Whitmore, *Imitating Christ in Magwi: An Anthropological Theology*, 75.
[12]Mary McClintock Fulkerson, *Places of Redemption: Theology for a Worldly Church* (Oxford, New York: Oxford University Press, 2007).
[13]Ibid., 86, 87.
[14]Courtney T. Goto, "Writing in Compliance with the Racialized 'Zoo' of Practical Theology," in *Conundrums in Practical Theology*, ed. Joyce Ann Mercer and Bonnie Miller-McLemore (Boston, MA: Brill, 2016), 111. See Also: Courtney T. Goto, *Taking on Practical Theology: The Idolization of Context and the Hope of Community* (Leiden, Boston, MA: Brill, 2018).
[15]I have already mentioned Lauren Winner's *The Dangers of Christian Practice*, but her work decoupling virtue and practice is an important conversation partner for this work. Lauren F. Winner, *The Dangers of Christian Practice: On Wayward Gifts, Characteristic Damage, and Sin* (New Haven, CT: Yale University Press, 2018).

use of Pierre Bordieu's notion of habitus, which receives ample attention in Elaine Graham's *Transforming Practice*, while Christian Scharen's *Fieldwork in Theology* uses Bourdieu's notions of habitus and field to ground ethnographic, theological inquiry. In addition, Michel de Certeau's contribution in distinguishing between strategies and tactics has been a useful conversation partner in practical theology because it highlights power while paying attention to the agency of those who do not have the same access to resources (tactics).[16] My work is allied and in conversation with these scholars. In addition to these theoretical orientations in the discipline, I offer Judith Butler's notions of subjectivity as a way to help practical theologians move beyond MacIntyre and generate power-sensitive ways of paying attention to subject formation and resistance to discourse, practices, and frameworks that form the basis for that subjectivity. In particular, Butler can help practical theologians think about whiteness in ways that allow recipient experiences and critiques of whiteness to come to the fore.

Research Methods and the Researcher

For this project, I interviewed fourteen recipients and fourteen activists in Sanctuary Movement using a variety of digital methods due to Covid-19; interviews lasted between sixty and ninety minutes. Among recipients, I interviewed four men and four women from Guatemala, three of whom identified as Mayan, and three men and three women from El Salvador. Activists were part of sanctuary communities in Arizona, Washington, Texas, Illinois, Wisconsin, Vermont, Pennsylvania, Oregon, and California. While such a sample size is small, it includes indigenous voices and activists located outside of the historical centers of the movement and sanctuary scholarship—Tucson and Chicago. As such, I do not claim the sample size is representative of the entire Sanctuary Movement, but it does possess what William Firestone calls the potential for "case-to-case transfer" that empowers the reader to consider the ways that this sample might be useful for understanding other cases within the movement.[17] In addition, nearly all of the activists and recipients that I interviewed have never participated in an interview. Interviews were conducted in English and Spanish, whichever language the participant preferred. In the case of Spanish language interviews, a qualified interpreter was selected in order to ensure the accuracy of the interview.

---

[16]See: Natalie Wigg-Stevenson, "From Proclamation to Conversation: Ethnographic Disruptions to Theological Normativity," *Palgrave Communications* 1, no. 1 (2015), https://doi.org/10.1057/palcomms.2015.24, https://doi.org/10.1057/palcomms.2015.24.
[17]William A. Firestone, "Alternative Arguments for Generalizing From Data as Applied to Qualitative Research," *Educational Researcher* 22, no. 4 (1993): 16, https://doi.org/10.3102/0013189X022004016.

For Chapter 1, I also utilized autoethnographic methods in the predominantly white congregation that I pastor, which is part of the New Sanctuary Movement. For that research, I kept a detailed journal of interactions with sanctuary workers in my congregation, taking care to mark each interaction with the emotional content of the field notes in order to mark the ways that affect is an important part of white subject formation within sanctuary. I also utilized interactive interviews with between five and eight sanctuary workers, wherein we discussed whiteness, privilege, and power explicitly. This method allowed me to appear as an active participant and to name my own power as a pastor within my church context. By conducting research on the New Sanctuary Movement, I make the argument throughout this book that the practice of sanctuary has defined characteristics that can be transferred from the Sanctuary Movement of the 1980s to the New Sanctuary Movement—indeed one of the principal ways that the two are connected is the whiteness at the center of the movement, myself included.

I have already mentioned some of the identities that inform my approach to this research, but one stands out as being important to note —I am white. In many ways, this was helpful in gaining access to a movement that also centered on white allyship, as white activists found me an easy confidant. At other times it became a barrier, as recipients assumed that I was interested primarily in the trauma of their flights from their country. Recipients usually came to feel comfortable with sharing a fuller account of their experience only after I demonstrated my interest in other aspects of the Sanctuary Movement, particularly some of the complexities around race and that same white allyship. While those insights seem clear to me, what remains unclear is the ways that whiteness has constrained this my work, whether in recipients that did not feel comfortable speaking to me, my halting Spanish certainly contributing to that factor, or by my inability to properly grasp the complex dynamics of race at the heart of this movement. I began my interest in the Sanctuary Movement with the stories of white activists,[18] and this project strives to move beyond that lens to center the voices of recipients, but the continual work of reflection that the goal demands is never done. Despite my best intentions and efforts, my centering of recipient voices runs the risk of recapitulating some of the same tensions that I highlight in the following chapters—namely, the danger of a white activist or researcher telling the stories of recipients. As my research shows, good intentions are not a reliable indicator of results, and those same good intentions and their citation are inextricably linked to the project of whiteness.[19]

---

[18]Michael Woolf, "Holy Risk: Old Cambridge Baptist Church and the Sanctuary Movement," *Glossolalia* 6, no. 1 (2014).
[19]Melanie E. L. Bush, *Breaking the Code of Good Intentions: Everyday Forms of Whiteness* (Lanham, MD: Rowman & Littlefield, 2004).

Because much time has passed since the Sanctuary Movement, the ethnography that I produce here is historical ethnography, and it is bound up with memory. In some cases, distance from the events of the Sanctuary Movement produced insights that were not contemporaneous—for instance, one activist I interviewed had much to say about the movement as being about white saviors, even as she was careful to note that that was not the language the movement used or thought of in the 1980s. Recipients as well sometimes noted how time had softened or hardened their analysis of the Sanctuary Movement, producing the tension between gratitude and frustration with which I began this introduction. In that sense, I found myself grappling with whether the "event" of the Sanctuary Movement could ever be reached through this project. To help me think about that central question, I turned to two scholars to help me think about the ethnographic project and events—Kathleen Stewart and Steven Caton. While they each wrestle with different contexts and events—a near-miss accident in Stewart's case and the apparent abduction of two teenage girls in Yemen in Caton's—each came to similar conclusions about the ethnographer's ability to access events. Events are not unmediated; there is no pure event to get back to. As Stewart puts it, "events become not fixed 'objects' in the world 'out there' but fabulations always already written through with the identity of a reproduction."[20] Similarly, for Caton, the revelation that his initial understanding of the abduction he witnessed was entirely wrong forced him to confront a "terrifying breakdown in meaning, a yawning gap between our naming of the event and its being or existence" that did away with any sense that there was a "what *actually* happened" to get back to.[21] Of course, the Sanctuary Movement is somewhat different—there are historical documents, contemporaneous reports, and eyewitnesses, but dealing with memories of an event from decades ago forced me to confront similar doubts, especially when those memories are routinely in conflict with one another. The Sanctuary Movement is not a puzzle to be assembled in the right way, because as a researcher I also become part of the construction of an event in a way that solving a puzzle can never capture. In the end, I found myself at peace with my account of the event that was the Sanctuary Movement because my account strives to privilege voices that have not been fully accounted for in scholarship and because I have striven to be transparent about the ways my construction of the event is limited by my own whiteness.

Memory also played a role in those I could not speak to. Before I could speak to three recipients about their experience in the Sanctuary Movement,

---

[20]Kathleen Stewart, *A Space on the Side of the Road Cultural Poetics in an "Other" America* (Baltimore, MD: Princeton University Press, 1996), 78.
[21]Steven Charles Caton, *Yemen Chronicle: An Anthropology of War and Mediation* (New York: Hill and Wang, 2005), 64, 63.

they became ill and died, two of them of Covid-19. In one case, I had made
initial contact with a recipient and planned an interview with him, only to
find out from his son that he had passed away. In another, I called a phone
number that had been released to me by a recipient, only to find out that
she had passed before I could call it. These experiences are no accident, as
Latin communities faced disproportionately negative health outcomes from
Covid-19.[22] In still other cases, activists relayed to me that a recipient had
passed a decade ago, or a recipient relayed to me that an activist they formed
a bond with had passed recently. In many ways, my research constitutes
one of the last moments to capture experiences of the Sanctuary Movement
before they slip from the scholarly record. In others, I was haunted by the
sense that I was already too late. Because of that feeling, my recording of
interviews with recipients and activists took on a sense of urgency as we
entered further into the pandemic. During the interview and transcription
process, there were several moments that felt sacred, such as when I was
listening to someone tell their story for the first time, seeing the difficulty of
recipients and activists telling portions of their story that were painful, or
interviewing someone who referenced a friend, colleague, or companion that
had already passed before this book could be written. The work of accessing
memory, telling from memory, and the difficulty of recalling memories was
an important part of the research process, and although some were not able
to be interviewed, their loss and the memories of them are a part of this
research project in profound ways—as gaps and ellipses, certainly, but also
as inspiration, determination, and even love. The Christian story is in many
ways a story about loss and the ways that despite his death, Jesus remains
present to the church in memory, a fact most clearly articulated in Christ's
insistence that the Eucharist be celebrated as a sacred memory. Memory
became not something to be fought against or verified, but the foundation
of the entire project.

Chapter Summaries

This book's structure flows from its commitments to doing practical
theological analysis of the Sanctuary Movement. For that reason, each
chapter ends with some practical theological reflection that centers how the
Sanctuary Movement might aid in nuanced thinking about foundational
issues in theology. Likewise, this book follows a practical theological line of
inquiry, starting first with analyzing sanctuary as a practice, then turning to
how a subjectivity lens might yield additional insights into the movement,

---

[22]See: Karen S. Moore, "The Impact of COVID-19 on the Latinx Population: A Scoping
Literature Review," *Public Health Nursing (Boston, MA)* (2021), https://doi.org/10.1111/phn
.12912.

and concluding with analyzing whiteness and subjectivity in the Sanctuary Movement, and finally analyzing the key ecclesiological insights that the movement yields.

In Chapter 1, I use autoethnographic methods, in particular interactive interviewing, to put the fissures and tensions of sanctuary in personal terms, as I struggle with my dual role of pastor and researcher. In doing so, I place whiteness at the core of sanctuary and the core of my experience of it, as I lift up touchstones that have direct relevance to the research that is to come—how sanctuary feels, lack of accountability, who has ownership over a story, power, and the yearning for something that exceeds and builds upon sanctuary. Particular attention is paid to the affective production of whiteness in the practice of sanctuary, as I document how sanctuary feels, because of Eduardo Bonilla-Silva's insightful assertion that racialized emotions both deserve scholarly attention and are "ambivalent" and therefore capable of change.[23] Indeed, I spend much time contemplating what sorts of changes in sanctuary are even possible and point to some contingent futures for the practice. I argue that autoethnography is a spiritual discipline with much in common with Ignatius' examen, wherein the researcher/practitioner gains powerful insight into lived experience and future action. In relaying my personal experience with the examen, I propose an adaptation for use by white researchers and practitioners. In doing so, I seek to advance much of the recent scholarship that sees ethnography as theology by seeing my research as a type of prayer.

In Chapter 2, I analyze the practice of sanctuary in the Sanctuary Movement of the 1980s utilizing MacIntyre's theory of practice, paying close attention to the myriad of sub-practices that constitute the movement—the recruitment of recipients, activists, and communities, the offering of physical sanctuary, the *testimonio*, and caravans. I consider the standards of excellence that each sub-practice possessed, the contestations over what constituted excellence, and the ways that each practice's standards of excellence failed or succeeded in taking into account recipient agency. I argue that a close analysis of the practice of sanctuary in the Sanctuary Movement demonstrates the ways that activists were always in control of what constituted excellence, and that MacIntyre's practice framework is useful in attending to that aspect of the movement, but that account privileges the experience of white practitioners in the movement without attending to that same whiteness. In order to gain a richer perspective on the movement, I offer Bourdieu's account of habitus and de Certeau's notion of the difference between strategy and tactics, as well as their practical theological interlocutors, as a way of thinking about whiteness in the practice of sanctuary.

---

[23]Eduardo Bonilla-Silva, "Feeling Race: Theorizing the Racial Economy of Emotions," *American Sociological Review* 84, no. 1 (2019), https://doi.org/10.1177/0003122418816958, https://doi .org/10.1177/0003122418816958.

In Chapter 3, I build on those insights to propose a subjectivity model for analyzing the Sanctuary Movement through contestations over recipients' status as refugees. I demonstrate how the Sanctuary Movement cultivated recipient's identities as refugees and victims and how recipients' both adopted that moniker in order to gain sympathy from white religious liberals and pushed back on that identity through appeals to their activism in their countries of origin, ongoing activism in the United States, and thoroughgoing critiques of capitalism, imperialism, and environmental destruction. One of the clearest places this is visible is in the ways that recipients and activists differ in their use of human rights discourse. I demonstrate that recipient definitions of human rights include a more robust set of categories, favoring economic, social, and cultural rights, while white activists' use of human rights demonstrates an understanding based on civil and political rights. In particular, I argue that white activists' curtailed view of human rights is racialized, while the implicit and explicit critiques of recipients offer a vision of the rejection of white curtailment. In focusing on these contestations, I argue for a subject formation model based on the work of Judith Butler that views the Sanctuary Movement as a subjecting power and recipients' struggles to exceed the bounds of refugee identity as agency. In doing so, I argue that the Sanctuary Movement presents a challenge and opportunity for practical theological analysis and that taking seriously subject formation as theoretical lynchpin for the field allows for more robust analysis of power that a practice framework often misses.

In Chapter 4, I examine whiteness as a central category of both the Sanctuary Movement. I analyze the ways that white activists attained spiritual actualization from their participation in the Sanctuary Movement, in particular the ways they experienced themselves as sharing in the risks of recipients and in the attainment of forbidden knowledge that the Reagan administration did not want them to possess about Central America. In particular, white activists participated in a symbolic power exchange, wherein recipients theoretically held power through the *testimonio* and were said to experience free choice about the contours of their participation in the movement. This symbolic power exchange obscured the very real power differentials at the heart of the Sanctuary Movement, leading to the central aspect of whiteness that I focus on in this chapter—power-obliviousness.[24] I argue that understanding the Sanctuary Movement as a site of white subject formation is an important aspect of the movement that is oftentimes overlooked, mostly because the researchers who study it are often themselves

---

[24]I use this term as a replacement for powerblindness, in an effort to utilize less ableist and more inclusive language. That term has a distinct theoretical genealogy that this shift in language should not obscure, since I am only changing the term and not its implications. See: Charles Kurzman et al., "Powerblindness," *Sociology Compass* 8, no. 6 (2014), https://doi.org/10.1111/soc4.12161.

white. The result of this whiteness in scholarship is shown most clearly by the field's focus on white activist narratives and the cataloging of those narratives in oral history projects related to the movement. As a white researcher myself, I am not immune to this critique, and in this chapter, I also explore the ways that my own attraction to the Sanctuary Movement as a subject and my research is inexorably linked to my own whiteness. Finally, in analyzing whiteness and the Sanctuary Movement, I present a case study for understanding the white supremacy of white antiracists, an important contribution to whiteness in the study of religion.

In Chapter 5, I analyze the Biblical and medieval antecedents to the Sanctuary Movement that activists routinely cited as the foundation of the movement, demonstrating that the defining qualifier for sanctuary over time and space is fear and that sanctuary ecclesiologies produce a gordian knot of civil and religious authority. Turning to the practices of white activists, I explicate the ways that the movement's preoccupation with ideal border enforcement and asylum screening undercut activists' claims of subverting the sovereignty of the state through appeals to God's sovereignty, instead reifying the former. Drawing on Tina M. Campt's analysis of fugitivity and Giorgio Agamben's notion of inoperativity, I propose an insurgent collaborative ecclesiological model that builds on the work of Sanchez and Coutin to decenter the excellence of MacIntyrian thought and the work of activism. In doing so, I question whether the church and practical theology can see fugitivity, arguing that the church's focus on the work of the movement and practical theology's focus on practice obscure this central category of analysis. Finally, I turn to the practical, proposing methods of reading scripture and celebrating the Eucharist that can bring that vision to the fore.

1

Feeling Sanctuary

An Autoethnography of Whiteness

"Don't you research this stuff and have a PhD in it? You tell us what to do then." The question and comment make me physically step back from the encounter, surprising me, even if it shouldn't. Mark has just named one of the difficulties that I face as a white pastor of a church in the New Sanctuary Movement—I am supposed to know how to do this work well, or at least what to pay attention to. But often I find that my work as a researcher has made me equivocal—sanctuary is bound up with whiteness, but it's better to do something than to not, or is it? That open question is what motivates this autoethnography, because it is the question that I wrestle with quite a lot. In the autoethnography that follows, I put the fissures and tensions of sanctuary in personal terms, as I struggle with my dual role of pastor and researcher. In doing so, I turn to whiteness as the core of sanctuary and the core of my experience of it, as I lift up touchstones that have direct relevance to the research that is to come—how sanctuary feels, lack of accountability, who has ownership over a story, power, and the yearning for something that exceeds and builds upon sanctuary. Separated by several decades, the New Sanctuary Movement and the Sanctuary Movement of the 1980s are inexorably linked by the practice of sanctuary. Although they are concerned with different ends, they carry much of the same faults, tensions, and hope. I argue that autoethnography is a spiritual discipline with much in common with Igantius' examen, wherein the researcher/practitioner gains powerful insight into lived experience and future action. In relaying my personal experience with the examen, I propose an adaptation for use by white researchers and practitioners.

Theory and Method

Autoethnography comes from the Greek words meaning self, culture, and writing, and scholars emphasize different parts of the task depending on their discipline and the aim of their research. While autoethnography has most been associated with the evocative ethnography of Carolyn Ellis, Leon Anderson makes the case for "analytic ethnography," which contains five commitments: "(1) complete member researcher (CMR) status, (2) analytic reflexivity, (3) narrative visibility of the researcher's self, (4) dialogue with informants beyond the self, and (5) commitment to theoretical analysis."[1] I see my work as aligned with this vision for analytic autoethnography, especially its capacity for reflexivity, which is important for someone like myself—a white pastor who is not only observing or participating in a church in the New Sanctuary Movement, but wields power, makes decisions, and substantially influences the process. It offers opportunities to pay attention to affect in white subjectivity, a project that Eduardo Bonilla-Silva pays close attention to in his presidential address to the American Sociological Association, where he argues for the importance of understanding racialized emotions that are bound up with white supremacy and domination, not because these are fixed states but because "change in one's [racialized emotions] is possible" due to "ambivalence," but "there are no guarantees."[2]

That being said, I understand autoethnography broadly—and there is much in common with my work and those who do not use the term but have similar contexts. Natalie Wigg-Stevenson makes substantial use of what she calls "reflexive theology" in attending to the "hyper-belonging"[3] of being a Baptist minister and researcher in simultaneous roles at the same field site, where she moves from participant observation to "objectified participation."[4] In such a move, Wigg-Stevenson opens her experiences, emotions, failures, and slippages to theological examination in much the same way I strive to do. Likewise, other practical theologians have used the autoethnography to attend to their own whiteness in various settings. In particular, I find Todd Whitmore's ethnographic engagement with his own whiteness in the northern Ugandan and South Sudanese context especially helpful, as he wrestles not only with the "already-set expectations as to [his] own behavior" through the complex system of patronage he encounters, but also traces the complexities of how he is "always also the "ethnograph*ee*,"

---

[1] Anderson, "Analytic Autoethnography," 378.
[2] Bonilla-Silva, "Feeling Race: Theorizing the Racial Economy of Emotions."
[3] Natalie Wigg-Stevenson, "Reflexive Theology: A Preliminary Proposal," *Practical Matters*, no. 6 (Spring 2013): 15.
[4] Wigg-Stevenson, *Ethnographic Theology: An Inquiry into the Production of Theological Knowledge*, 49, 58.

analyzed by those who he encounters.[5] The result is a nuanced perspective about how whiteness plays out in global contexts often ignored by critical whiteness scholars. What is most striking to me about Whitmore's use of self-searching, reflexive ethnography is his refusal of distance and his blending of research with activism—even activism that leads to criticism from his colleagues and institution. Whitmore is not just writing about *imitatio Christi* in a particular context; he strives to make his writing, research, and ethical actions an expression of that same mimesis.

Drawing on these scholars use of autoethnographic methods, I strive to give an account of whiteness and my own white leadership in a particular context—the New Sanctuary Movement—but I also use such methods to link the New Sanctuary Movement and Sanctuary Movement of the 1980s. The issues that are raised here—power, representation, accountability, white allyship—are common to both movements, even as they address different moral issues—immigration reform and anti-interventionism, respectively. Key to this idea is my argument that sanctuary is a practice that is united across time and space, but these are issues and tensions common to white allyship generally. But this autoethnography was more than that; it also became a practice of prayer wherein I paid careful attention to my thoughts, words, and deeds and how they were bound up with white supremacy and sought amended courses of action. It is about how it feels to strive to act on your ethical commitments and find problems in that practice—it is about me, yes, but it is about so much more than that. It is about signposts pointing to something more in slippages, failures, and silences.

In order to write the following, I kept a journal of field notes and my own reflections, sometimes giving myself self-interviews and at other times responding to interaction with notes about how I reacted at the time. Within these fieldnotes, I strove to pay attention to my own emotions and coded them based on my feeling at the time—anger, sadness, fear, unease, contentment, joy, and disappointment were used and labeled. I also practiced interactive interviewing, which Carolyn Ellis, Christine E. Kiesinger, and Lisa M. Tillmann-Healy, argue is an "in-depth and intimate understanding of people's experiences with emotionally charged and sensitive topics," like whiteness.[6] Interactive interviews engage the researcher as a full participant in a group conversation where the researcher is an established collaborator and are often focused on issues arising in the group. As such, it provided a powerful research tool for sanctuary in the church context in which I serve.[7]

---

[5]Whitmore, *Imitating Christ in Magwi: An Anthropological Theology*, 166, 75.
[6]Kiesinger Ellis and Tillmann-Healy, "Interactive Interviewing: Talking about Emotional Experience," 129.
[7]Carolyn Ellis, *The Ethnographic I: A Methodological Novel about Autoethnography* (Walnut Creek, CA: AltaMira Press, 2004), 62–6.

Feeling Sanctuary, Feeling White

As I walk into the well-apportioned house of a congregant on a suburban street, the smell of arepas hits me instantly. I catch snippets of conversation from the hallway:

> The pastor just got here . . .
> > Would you like a cabernet or a pinot . . .
> > Encantada de conocerte . . .

The house is a flutter with activity as members of the sanctuary committee of the church I pastor are socializing, grabbing snacks, and glasses of wine. I feel a bit conspicuous as I decline a glass of wine, but I soon settle into a conversation about the family that has been living in an apartment in our church for several years. The congregant, a white man in his sixties, tells me: "They came from El Salvador many years ago, and none of them had any papers, but now everyone is here legally." I know this fact; everyone who is gathered here knows it. It's why the atmosphere is so jovial. The twenty or so people gathered here are excited about the success of the church's sanctuary initiative, navigating the difficult immigration enforcement environment of the Trump years and coming away with pieces of paper that guarantee the family's right to live and work in the United States.

A white man in his eighties talks about the perseverance of the family, their trials, and tribulations and says, "I've grown spiritually because of this work—seeing their faith in the midst of so many obstacles makes me rethink my own life and my response to trouble." I say, "Amen." Another congregant adds that it feels like something "tangible we can do in the face of Trump," and I say, "amen" a second time.

In the dining room, Martha sits with her daughter, Maria, at a table eating arepas and chatting in Spanish. I go up to them tentatively—while I am the pastor of the church, I am not a primary contact for our recipients of sanctuary and my spoken Spanish is not as good as I would like. I had spent the last couple of days making sure that I could communicate what I wanted to say to make them feel welcome and that they were an important part of my community.

My cheeks immediately flush with embarrassment for what I know will follow—halting conversation hamstrung by my poor language skills. Still, I muddle through. "Que bueno verte de nuevo! Todos ustedes estan en mis oraciones." She smiles at my attempts at conversation and says a sentence in Spanish.

Two seconds later, when I translate what she has said into English, I am humbled by the exchange. It is rare in my ministry context for people to say that they have been praying for me—the church I pastor is not full of the traditional displays of piety that one might expect, and I entertain for a brief moment that her prayers are likely more efficacious than mine, but fearing that I would not be understood, I settle for, "gracias." I had planned a conversation in which I offered pastoral care to a family that has been through much, but I decide my skills are not up to the task. Instead, I stick to logistics. I ask about work and English classes, but I make a mistake and know that I used a Polish word or two—a language that I am learning because my wife and daughter are Polish.

The hosts of the night interrupt us, and I am grateful, hoping that my smiles and attempts at conversation have conveyed the welcome that I had hoped for. Now it is time for prayer. We join hands—the recipients of sanctuary, the hosts, and the members of the sanctuary committee. We pray in Spanish first and then the English:

> Hoy One, we pray for this family—and thank God that you have brought them safely to their new home. We pray for their protection . . . that God will give them protection, that we will be knit together as a community. We pray for their flourishing and for their joy. We lift them up to you, who are capable of holding all of them in your hands. Amen.

In that moment I allow myself to feel the Spirit of God coursing through me in a dining room of a suburban house. It starts at the bottom of my feet and moves up to my head, and I know that it is the Spirit because I did not have any wine. In that moment, sanctuary feels uncomplicated. Here are people who have formed a community despite the obstacles of white paternalism, who are embodying a welcome that makes God welcome in this place, if only for a moment.

But the truth is moments like these are fleeting, escaping from my grasp even as I struggle to wrap my fingers around them. When I get home that night, I take out a journal and write down my thoughts about the encounter and my questions and reflections:

> Do Martha and Maria feel a part of our community? Our worship is typical of white, mainline Protestant congregations—it features European hymns, and organ, and no Spanish. Are we embodying that welcome? And then there's the matter of where Martha and Maria live—our church. It is a place to live, but it has deferred maintenance, a constant bug issue, and to be honest, I wouldn't want to live there. So much conversation is about getting the family to be independent and working, and that seems important, but what about trauma? Can we expect torture survivors to just go to work? How do we create something beyond American ideas of independence?

I jot down the Tony Benn's famous quote about power and write down my responses:

> What Power Have You Got?
> *As the white pastor of a congregation, spiritual, decision-making power (unless my decisions get me fired). The power to act or do nothing and not*

be held to account. In sanctuary, the power to determine housing, to help or to not, to welcome or to not.

Where Did You Get It From?
From the congregation, I got my pastoral responsibilities. From my whiteness, my education, my life, I have power that goes unremarked upon.

In Whose Interests Do You Exercise It?
I'd like to say in the interests of others, but often it's to benefit the institutions I serve and my own career.

To Whom Are You Accountable?
The congregation hired me and they can fire me, but when it comes to sanctuary the actions we are not accountable to Martha, Maria, or her brother, Isaac.

How Can We Get Rid Of You?
The congregation can get rid of me, but the recipients of sanctuary cannot. We are not accountable to them, but we should be.

Patricia Stuelke writes that one of the primary goals of the Sanctuary Movement of the 1980s was "feeling right," an affective move "infused by [white activists'] desire to find relief, respite, and satisfaction in communal feeling and absolution from the guilt of their complicity in US empire," with the result that "sentimental vision of person-to-person connection across the Americas superseded more materialist possibilities."[8] The moments when I, as a white pastor, feel the most at peace with sanctuary are typically these moments of personal connection coupled with a sense that I am acting out my faith by practicing sanctuary.

How sanctuary *feels* has always been at the forefront for me, as I experience the solidarity, activism, and paternalism of a movement from the vantage point of someone with real ethical commitments to immigration reform who is keenly aware of the ways that it is not fundamentally challenging the status quo. Those feelings are embodied in fundamental ways—a flush of embarrassment I can't hide, a knot in the pit of my stomach in a meeting in which I'm uncomfortable with the direction of conversation—all of these are part of the experience I have as a pastor in the movement. Some of those feelings are heightened by the fact that I feel doubly responsible as a scholar of sanctuary and as a pastor for doing this "right." At times it feels that way. As my hand grasps another in prayer over arepas in a congregant's house, it

---

[8]Patricia Rachael Stuelke, *The Ruse of Repair: US Neoliberal Empire and the Turn from Critique* (Durham, NC: Duke University Press, 2021), 108.

feels good. But those moments are far from ordinary. For me, sanctuary feels tense, like a dance on a knife's edge between real moments of transformation of interior lives and the familiar hums of charity that do not move us beyond the established power dynamic of a white congregation that has something to give, but only on our terms. What I have come to understand is that Stuelke's "feeling right" often goes hand-in-hand with whiteness—feeling right leaves whiteness unchallenged.

That is because whiteness does not react well to being challenged. Robin DiAngelo in her development of white fragility argues, "White people in North America live in a social environment that protects and insulates them from race-based stress. This insulated environment of racial protection builds white expectations for racial comfort while at the same time lowering the ability to tolerate racial stress."[9] Insulated from challenges to white supremacy, we lack the tools and accountability to pursue transformative outcomes. The moments that feel upsetting, tension-filled, and knot-in-stomach are often when sanctuary fails to live up to its capacity to move us to action and also when sanctuary begins to point to a more transformative sense of what it could be, as the next stories will show. It is upsetting because it challenges my control, my sense of what feels right, the whiteness that defines me at my very core, and points to liberation, but not how I would define it.

Whose Story to Tell?

We are all seated around tables that are in a U-shape. By all of us, I mean the white members of the sanctuary committee. We are here to talk about things we can do to weave the congregation more into the work of sanctuary. Jenny, a young white woman speaks up, "we took a vote as a congregation to become a sanctuary church, but I don't think most people even know the family is here." It's true, Martha gave a couple of interviews to local press when she came, but there was little fanfare. I offer something that might work: "how about a party? That might be nice and low stakes, but it could get people talking and we could meet each other. Maybe we could invite a few folks from town who are working on immigration, and our congressperson lives in town, maybe we can invite her?" Mark adds that he thinks that would be a good idea: "we need to keep using this as a chance to work locally and nationally on immigration." I agree, "sanctuary is a public act, and we need to keep up the pressure. How about we ask Martha to tell some of her story in worship, and we craft worship service around it?" But Elizabeth, who has perhaps the best relationship with the family

---

[9]Robin DiAngelo, "White Fragility," *International Journal of Critical Pedagogy* 3 (2011): 54.

chimes in, "I don't think she is up for telling that story anymore—there is so much trauma around it." Elizabeth is right—the trauma is real, and so is the pressure of standing in front of a congregation and bearing witness to what happened in El Salvador, so another person offers, "well, what if we tell some of her story to the congregation so that they know more about the work we are doing."

> Jenny: "but who can tell that story except the person who experienced it?"
> Sam: "surely the basic facts can be shared."
> Me: "that's true, she did give some interviews that established those facts to local news, but we should ask what she wants to share and what she wants to keep private."
> Mark: "that sounds like a good idea."

As I sit in the meeting, I try to split my attention between listening to the conversation and writing a journal entry, "I feel torn—sanctuary is public, but pastorally there has to be room not to share trauma in a church meeting, and to feel safe that it won't be shared for you. Are we a safe place for that, or do we expect a testimony that will meet our needs of doing something or being good and progressive?" The temptation to pick up someone's story and tell it to move others to activism is real in sanctuary, and so is the temptation to tell that story in order to signal to others and to yourself that we as a community are doing *something* in the midst of a broken immigration system. Those two aims bleed into one another, but I think my concern was more for the latter. As I think more about it after the fact, I start to get a little queasy at my own motivations—perhaps I have come to feel that I have some ownership over Martha and her family's story. I preach about immigration from the pulpit often, never using that story, but I would like to. I am greedy for it. I want it. I would like to use that story to make the case that our congregation is taking action, that we are not just idle talkers. I want that story for the immediacy of it, even if at the end of the day I know that it is not mine.

The *testimonio* is such an important part of sanctuary, but that testimony is always bound up in whether a white audience can hear what is being said. It is always on our terms—my terms, I should be specific as the pastor of the church. Marie E. Vargas makes the case that testimonies in contexts like mine "fit a credibility script . . . that the church members could recognize and gain something."[10] It is oriented to white transformation—to my personal and pastoral transformation. There might be good aims attached to it, but at the end of the day, I do not own that story.

---

[10]Maria Elena Vargas, "Ghostly Others: Limiting Constructions of Deserving Subjects in Asylum Claims and Sanctuary Protection," *Journal of International Women's Studies* 21, no. 7 (2020): 85.

Martha did not give me what I wanted—later on she tells me that she does not want to give that testimony, and I say that I understand. But that interaction is not one between equals, as much as I would like for it to be. Feeling as if we are collaborators, or yearning for a different power dynamic does not make it so. She had to tell the white, senior minister of the church that controls her housing, "no." Much of my research on the Sanctuary Movement of the 1980s is about the agency of recipients in giving testimonies that did not fit the script, but here was something different—agency that emerged from a refusal to tell a story, to refuse to make her resilience, struggle, and faith accessible to a white audience. The conditions for that agency arose because I wanted her story for my own. I felt entitled to it.

One of the places that whiteness shows up is in privilege, yes, but entitlement is also a way of talking about whiteness. One of the most interesting places to think about whiteness and colonialism is in library collections, which Freeda Brook, Dave Ellenwood, and Althea Eannace Lazzaro argue replicates an "imperialist desire to know and gather the cultural artifacts of marginalized cultures."[11] The entitlement to a story—a desire to possess it—is one of the hallmarks of whiteness and sanctuary, and it was certainly a part of how I navigated the situation. Sanctuary centers on the testimonio, but that testimonio also lets white hearers act as curators, assembling stories that are not their own and sometimes telling them to white audiences.

Talking about Whiteness

It's not that we don't talk about whiteness at my church. We talk about it quite a lot actually. There are sermons preached on it, book clubs, restorative justice trainings, and coffee hour conversations where whiteness is discussed prominently. In a congregation striving toward racial justice, naming and wrestling with whiteness is an important part of the work that we do. One such gathering takes place among the sanctuary committee as part of a collaborative interview, where we gather in my office to talk about the elephant in the room. Everyone is seated in comfortable chairs or a couch that threatens to swallow you whole.

> Me: I've heard when I was having a conversation with Jane, the worry is like, if it is a white savior thing, does that mean that we just can't ever do anything?

[11]Freeda Brook, Dave Ellenwood, and Althea Eannace Lazzaro, "In Pursuit of Antiracist Social Justice: Denaturalizing Whiteness in the Academic Library," *Library Trends* 64, no. 2 (2015), https://doi.org/10.1353/lib.2015.0048.

Tommy: Yeah, absolutely

Tina: We don't feel that that's the case for sure.

Me: To me, I think it probably is both. I think it's just being sort of a little honest about some stuff, and then that helps us do it better. That's my position.

Tommy: right? I think in terms of, we need to be honest with ourselves, about the power dynamics here, right. And the power dynamics are very clear. And so we have to try to be humble with that, and be willing to listen and learn and change our different ways as we go…

Tina: Exactly, I don't know, it's almost like a dilemma for white people in some ways. I don't mean that in, like, 'Oh, poor us.' But it's like, how do you do it authentically?

Me: There's just a lack of accountability. That is hard when you're when you're a white church, and you have this privilege, and you're doing this thing, and you're doing good. I'm not, I'm not saying we're not doing good, but somehow, we're not really accountable in any way to the family. And they're not really necessarily accountable in any way to us…Because ideally, it would be mutual accountability,

I shift in my chair, uncomfortable in my dual role as pastor and researcher. I feel proud of what we have done as a sanctuary church. Whether we are being white saviors, I think invariably the answer is yes, and I also think it is more complex than that—but isn't that what a white pastor of a sanctuary church would think?

One of the defining traits of white privilege is that it is invisible to those who have it. Documenting fifty examples of white privilege in her "White Privilege: Unpacking the Invisible Knapsack," perhaps the best-known essay on white privilege and invisibility, Peggy McIntosh speaks of the "invisible weightless knapsack of special provisions, maps, passports, codebooks, visas, clothes, tools and blank checks."[12] Robin DiAngelo adds, "At the same time that it is ubiquitous, white superiority also remains unnamed and explicitly denied by most whites."[13] Whiteness is not invisible or denied in my context—my congregation and I are talking about whiteness quite a lot. But if whiteness becomes visible, or at least discussed what is the next step? Just because whiteness is talked about, doesn't necessarily change the actions of white progressive liberals like myself. We/I talk a big game but do little to challenge the entrenched white privilege that we experience in our/my church. In that way, we participate in what Angie Beeman calls "liberal

---

[12]Peggy McIntosh, "White Privilege: Unpacking the Invisible Knapsack (1989)," in *On Privilege, Fraudulence, and Teaching As Learning* (Routledge, 2020), 30.
[13]DiAngelo, "White Fragility," 64.

white supremacy"—we place ourselves at the center, even as we discuss and name our own whiteness.[14]

My experience points to the fact that even when visible, whiteness restricts the imagination of people of faith—my own included. Richard Dyer speaks of this foreclosure of imagination and awareness when he writes, "White people create the dominant images of the world and don't quite see that they thus construct the world in their image."[15] There is a failure to even conceive of alternative ways of being, and a sense that one can either continue as things have been done, or do nothing. In setting up such a dichotomy, we cheapen our capacity to act. One of the key factors of sanctuary as I experience it is a lack of accountability. Faith communities largely operate autonomously, connected loosely to local New Sanctuary Movement councils or refugee organizations, but they are not accountable to them or to the recipients that inhabit church buildings. Whiteness emerges in sanctuary as a lack of clear accountability structures for people like us. Who is keeping us honest? Open and frank discussion of whiteness ought to work to undo the power-obliviousness that Charles Kurzman and others argue constitutes it.[16] But too often, discussion of whiteness is done instead of imagining new ways of practicing our faith. DiAngelo argues, "Whites who position themselves as liberal often opt to protect what they perceive as their moral reputations, rather than recognize or change their participation in systems of inequity and domination."[17] Talking is the easy part, as talking about white supremacy is both an important spiritual task but also often stops there, perhaps because talking does not require change and can even bolster the progressive credentials of white people of faith.

I write in my journal, after I have time to reflect on it:

We have to take seriously Jane's feeling that accountability and critique of whiteness eventually lead to not doing anything at all. Acknowledging that sanctuary is bound up with whiteness does not foreclose the possibility of action—it opens it. In acknowledging white supremacy, foregrounding it in our discussions, we can think beyond charity to the creation of beloved community. The possibility of such a development lies through this path, not in downplaying it, and it does not mean that the mentoring, housing, and stipends that my community has done is reduced to ashes. It simply means that those actions are bound up with whiteness, and that we will have to be creative if we want to reach beyond sanctuary to the place where God's spirit leads.

---

[14]Angie Beeman, *Liberal White Supremacy: How Progressives Silence Racial and Class Oppression* (Athens: The University of Georgia Press, 2022).
[15]Richard Dyer, *White* (New York: Routledge, 1997), 9.
[16]Kurzman et al., "Powerblindness."
[17]DiAngelo, "White Fragility," 64.

To do such work will mean more than what Stuelke calls the "ruse of repair" that is more about "settler absolution" than repair—it might look more like reparations.[18] Such a concept is not foreign in my ministry context, as the city we are located in has a municipal reparations effort that regularly receives national news attention, and it has also been applied to Central American refugees.[19] How might white Christians practice such repair within sanctuary? It might look like acknowledging the ways that America's white supremacist immigration policies benefit congregations like ours, but the tougher consideration is wrestling with the vast amount of wealth that is located in churches today. Situated on the city green, the building we have is worth some $15 million, and yet there is a culture of scarcity that dominates conversations. We do not have an endowment and money is always tight, as I am reminded every pledge season, but that does not mean that we do not have resources. We just remain unwilling to tap them. But the bigger question is, would we even be bold enough to ask recipients what reparations looks like for them and take their lead in implementing it? Such an action would take us from sanctuary to something more—something transformative.

But that is not what we do. I do not lead the conversation there. I stick to accountability, and I do that because I want to keep my job and because I do not know where it would lead us. You see, the failure of imagination is not just others—my imagination is limited by my need to access those resources from employment. Cowardice is a word for it, but practicality is another. I vacillate between the two, intermittently assigning blame and absolving myself depending on the day. But true absolution can't come from me. At least I do not kid myself about that.

A Spiritual Discipline

Originally intended to be practiced over thirty days, Ignatius of Loyola's *Spiritual Exercises* has provided a framework for discerning God's will. In it, he provides a method of prayer called the examen, which has five parts:

First Point. The first Point is to give thanks to God our Lord for the benefits received.

Second Point. The second, to ask grace to know our sins and cast them out.

Third Point. The third, to ask account of our soul from the hour that we rose up to the present Examen, hour by hour, or period by period: and

---

[18]Stuelke, *The Ruse of Repair: US Neoliberal Empire and the Turn From Critique*, 107.
[19]See: Sarah Sherman-Stokes, "Reparations for Central American Refugees," *Denver Law Review* 95 (2019): 585–634.

first as to thoughts, and then as to words, and then as to acts, in the same order as was mentioned in the Particular Examen.

Fourth Point. The fourth, to ask pardon of God our Lord for the faults.

Fifth Point. The fifth, to purpose amendment with [God's] grace.[20]

Ignatius' vision moves from thankfulness to a request for grace and asks the practitioner to make an inventory of thoughts, words, and deeds throughout the day. It then pivots to a request for pardon and an intention to amend the practitioner's interior and exterior life. As such, it first takes the practitioner on a journey inward and then leads them out again into a world in which their actions, feelings, and thoughts matter.

There are some startling similarities between the examen and my experience in autoethnographic field research. In particular, Ignatius' third point mirrors the process of journaling, taking into account thoughts, words, deeds, and emotions, and challenging the practitioner to give an account of their actions. In addition, the examen does not shy away from "faults" and "sins," even as it does not remain mired in them, offering the capacity to act and do better with the help of God's grace.[21] Like journaling, the examen works best when you are committed to an unflinching view of yourself and then documenting it.

Journaling and collecting data for autoethnography always felt prayerful to me. As someone who is ordained in a tradition that values extemporaneous prayer, it was more formal and more exacting than the prayers that I would normally pray. Within a month of my journaling, I had started to pray before and after writing because such deep, profound reflections on my own ministry had moved beyond data collection and into the realm of the holy. I would begin with a simple prayer, "Holy One, don't let me hide from myself and my own white supremacy" and end with, "Holy One, remind me I am not reducible to my faults, and that a better world is possible." Near the end of my data collection, I attended a retreat in which the topic was Ignatius' examen and I experienced a moment of enlightenment. My simple prayer that bookended my journaling had deep resonance with a sixteenth-century set of spiritual exercises. As a Baptist, this was unexpected, but it was the task of journaling that made such deep connections possible.

Some of the best theological engagement with ethnography has not only affirmed it as a toolkit for doing social science research but as theology itself. Christian Scharen and Anna Marie Vigen take up just such a project, where they make the case that ethnographic methods "can be a way to testify" and "take seriously God's incarnation in the world."[22] Likewise,

---

[20]Ignatius of Loyola, *The Spiritual Exercises of St. Ignatius of Loyola*, trans. by Elder Mullan (New York: P. J. Kennedy & Sons, Printers, 1914), 30–1.
[21]Ibid.
[22]Christian Scharen and Aana Marie Vigen, *Ethnography as Christian Theology and Ethics* (New York: Continuum, 2011), 73, 66.

Whitmore draws a direct connection between Catholic social teaching's see-judge-act model and ethnographic method, arguing that "ethnography is not simply a method that provides information to plug into our theology; rather ethnography *is* a way of doing theology."[23] James Bielo asks the provocative questions, "What would be different about recounted field notes if they took the form of a Christian confession? . . . What would be the performative force of writing ethnography as prayer?"[24] My experience of autoethnography took on the force of prayer. It was not just research, and it was not just the recounting of my own faults in leadership. Scharen and Vigen hold out the possibility that "research can be transformative—even redemptive."[25] That striving for redemption—for myself, undoubtedly, but for sanctuary as well—comes only through the naming and wrestling with white supremacy. Even then, I am not sure it can be grasped. But it is my prayer that it can be glimpsed, and it was the examen that not only taught me how to pray through my research but also to dream for that redemption. That is why I strive to figure out what is next in this chapter—how to improve my own practice of sanctuary—even as I highlight the futures that lie beyond sanctuary itself and acknowledge that as a white pastor, I am not the person to dream them.

While originally finding use mainly in Jesuit contexts, a wide variety of different Christian traditions make use of the examen. It has been adapted more recently to apply to diversity and inclusion by Xavier University, a version which focuses on "culture," while Baylor University, a Baptist institution has released an adapted version that focuses on "culture, race, ethnicity, or faith tradition."[26] While such adaptations show the examen's continued power, relevance and broad appeal, they do not go so far as to name whiteness or white supremacy. In my context, I named white supremacy as the focus of my examen and felt its power. In naming whiteness in an adapted examen, white practitioners can be powerfully shaped to focus on just what constitutes sin in America and how white practitioners might "purpose amendment."[27] The examen is a powerful tool for naming whiteness and challenging white practitioners to give an account of their thoughts, words, and deeds, but only if it is bold enough to name those identities as urgent matters to be addressed.

---

[23]Whitmore, *Imitating Christ in Magwi: An Anthropological Theology*, 29.

[24]James S. Bielo, "An Anthropologist Is Listening: A Reply to Ethnographic Theology," in *Theologically Engaged Anthropology*, ed. J. Derrick Lemons (Oxford: Oxford University Press, 2018), 155.

[25]Scharen and Vigen, *Ethnography as Christian Theology and Ethics*, 55.

[26]Debra Mooney and Cheryl Nuñez, *The Daily Examen for Diversity—Prayer Card* (Jesuit Resources, 2011); "Diversity Examen," Mindfulness BU, accessed August 20, 2022, https://blogs.baylor.edu/mindfulnessbu/simple-practice/examen/diversity-examen/.

[27]Loyola and Mullan, *The Spiritual Exercises of St. Ignatius of Loyola*, 31.

Over time, I developed my own version of the diversity examen, focused on white supremacy, which I now use as my daily prayer practice:

Begin by giving thanks: for the grace received, for my body, for the opportunities to collaborate with God

Acknowledge one's sins—the foundational sin of white supremacy, one's participation in it and benefit from it.

Make an inventory using the following questions:

How have I benefited from whiteness today?

How have I challenged whiteness by creating space for others lead, and how have I failed to do so?

How have I attended to my own power, and how have I been oblivious to it?

How have I assumed that my perspective was the only one?

How have my thoughts and feelings been bound up with white supremacy?

How have these experiences caused me to feel closer to God?

How have they made me feel farther away?

What might God be saying to me through these experiences?

How can I make use of the privilege that I have?

What will I change about my actions, thoughts, and feelings tomorrow?

Pray a prayer of confession and ask for God's forgiveness for one's faults.

Pray a prayer of commitment for how one might change tomorrow.

Preaching Sanctuary Old and New

I get up into the pulpit to preach to a congregation that is split between the pews in front of me and their screens at home. We are in the middle of a push to do more about reparations in town and confront some of our white supremacist history with a sister church, and I am sick from stress. It is one of the toughest points of my career, and I preach a sermon about coming to a decision point. I reach for the example I think most clearly makes my point, as I sweat and grip the pulpit for support, knowing that there's a growing movement of people who simply don't want to talk about this at all:

In 1984, this church had an opportunity to join the Sanctuary Movement. We heard about the horrors of US imperialism in El Salvador and Guatemala, and we were moved deeply do something. But we also heard about how it was breaking the law to house fugitives. Lawyers warned against the proposal, and we worried that we would lose our tax exempt status and that we would go to jail. We called a meeting and, by a narrow margin, we voted against joining the Sanctuary Movement of the 1980s. Fast forward to 2014, and we had the unimaginable gift of a second chance, and we took it. The same arguments were there, but this faith community did something different then. We joined the New Sanctuary Movement. We do not often get second chances—opportunities to make a different choice. That was a blessing, but we will not be so lucky again.

At the end of the day, despite my uneasiness, sanctuary still has power; that power is neither good nor bad. The decision to join the movements or not matter. It is better to do something, than nothing, but that does not give white faith communities a free pass from wrestling with their own whiteness and striving for something beyond sanctuary. There's a reason I chose sanctuary as the object lesson for coming to a decision about reparations— at its core, it still has the ability to move white audiences and is probably the best example over the past forty years of white allyship in religious social movements, even as it is also one of the best examples of white supremacy within those efforts and limits of white allyship.

Being a white pastor of a sanctuary church, I see the real transformations that can take place in sanctuary work, and I also see the ways that those personal transformations never really challenge whiteness. Let me be more specific: there are glimpses where sanctuary can reach beyond itself and lay claim to something more collaborative, but I often feel frustrated as I try to put the pieces together on how that might be. Sanctuary teases the capacity for social action—even liberation—but it fails to deliver. Sanctuary moves hearts; it moves me to compassion. It has also produced some outstanding results in the form of legal protections for asylum seekers and the development of sanctuary cities and states, but it does not fundamentally challenge white faith communities to wrestle with their own privilege and whiteness.

But because it has those glimmers of something more—I choose it as my object lesson when I get into the pulpit and look out at a white congregation that will tell you that it wants to strive for that same beloved community. But I am not sure we mean it, and I'm not sure how possible it is for us—but I still hope we can live up to our call. It is a hope that feels like a prayer—one that cries out for an answer.

2

Practicing Sanctuary

Understanding the Sanctuary Movement as Practice

Participants in the Sanctuary Movement of the 1980s often find it difficult to articulate the defining strategy of their cause. "I call it one hundred ways of doing sanctuary," one recipient told me. There is perhaps no better summation of the fluid and nimble tactics of the Sanctuary Movement, which united and divided humanitarians, anti-interventionists, and anti-Reagan activists through the practice of sanctuary. Bringing their own perspective, biases, conflicts, and meanings to sanctuary, participants presented conflicting perspectives on the movement. Viewing sanctuary as a practice helps make sense of the seemingly irreconcilable differences between activists in Tucson and Chicago as contestations over the ends, tactics, and meaning of a particular practice. Drawing on Alasdair MacIntyre's *After Virtue*, I analyze the sanctuary as a practice with several constituent parts—the recruitment of activists, recipients, and congregations to the Sanctuary Movement, the offering of physical sanctuary to recipients, the *testimonio*, and caravans. Notably, these are also acts that unite the disparate parts of the Sanctuary Movement, showcasing the power of a practice framework to highlight tension, conflict, and alignment between distinct groups.

In this chapter, I argue that the use of practice as a theoretical framework demonstrates considerable efficacy, but MacIntyre's practice framework also obscures one of the most central issues to consider in the Sanctuary Movement—power. While practice is a valuable framework for analyzing individuals with relatively equal amounts of power and helps situate the Sanctuary Movement as an object of practical theological inquiry, it struggles to account for disparities of power, which is one of the defining features of the movement, especially when it concerns the pursuit of excellence endemic to every practice within MacIntyre's framework. As I demonstrate throughout this chapter, white activists were largely in control of deciding the shape of sanctuary practice, a fact which practice frameworks render visible while failing to lead to a satisfying account of that same power. Consequently, I turn to the work of Pierre Bourdieu and Michel de Certeau on habitus, practice, strategy, and tactics, arguing that those theoretical tools might help us think in more nuanced, theological ways about sanctuary in ways that are power sensitive, while also arguing that these tools ultimately fail to account for the complexities of the Sanctuary Movement.

Defining Practice

MacIntyre's focus on action, reflection, and the internal goods produced by such actions offers a generative starting point for thinking about sanctuary. However, even if practice is the right theoretical framework, it is hardly clear that MacIntyre's theory of practice is the right choice.[1] Indeed, one of the main arguments of this book is that MacIntyre's framework does not attend to power in a convincing manner and that practical theology would do well to incorporate Judith Butler's ideas of agency and subjectivity into its theoretical underpinnings. However, practical theology's interest in practice as a category developed through engagement with MacIntyre's work, and his virtue ethics framing of practice continues to have influence within the field today. In addition, his approach also demonstrates considerable strength in the way that it outlines clear definitions of practice and showcases how conflict within a practice is natural. In doing so, MacIntyre's definition of practice—as opposed to Pierre Bourdieu's, for instance—provides the structure needed for an in-depth analysis of a practice like sanctuary.

Since my main goal is to show the inadequacies of practice as a theoretical lynchpin, I will begin by acknowledging its many strengths, beginning with MacIntyre's definition of practice:

> By a "practice" I am going to mean any coherent and complex form of socially established cooperative human activity through which goods internal to that form of activity are realised in the course of trying to achieve those standards of excellence which are appropriate to, and

---

[1]While MacIntyre's work is of foundational importance for practical theology, there are other ways of conceiving of practice that I attend to later on in this chapter—including Pierre Bourdieu's frameworks of agency, habitus, and field. For a substantial work on Bourdieu and practical theology, see: Christian Scharen, *Fieldwork in Theology: Exploring the Social Context of God's Work in the World* (Grand Rapids, MI: Baker Academic, 2015).

partially definitive of that form of activity, with the result that human powers to achieve excellence, and human conceptions to the ends and goods involved, are systematically extended.[2]

MacIntyre's work is centered on virtue and the cultivation of it through practice, focusing on the intrinsic qualities and dispositions developed as a result of participation in a practice rather than the "external goods" that accrue to certain practices like fame, money, or power. We become human through virtue, and those virtues are only available through practice, since it is through repetition that one can pursue excellence, a value that only a community of practitioners can determine. As MacIntyre puts it, "A practice involves standards of excellence and obedience to rules as well as the achievement of goods. To enter into a practice is to accept the authority of those standards and the inadequacy of my own performance as judged by them."[3]

Sanctuary clearly meets the criteria of this definition in some ways. For instance, the practice of sanctuary was certainly "cooperative human activity." But what are the internal goods realized by the movement, and what standards of excellence appropriately map onto sanctuary? In the Sanctuary Movement, the answer to that question is perhaps more varied and complex than the example of chess he gives. For example, participants in sanctuary might variously cultivate hospitality, embodied opposition to Ronald Reagan's Central America policy, closeness to God, or standing on the side of the oppressed. However, MacIntyre also lists farming and architecture as representative examples of practice, and those practices have a diverse range of goals and methods within them. Architecture has different schools within it, with different norms, while farming might have different goals depending on the crop or level of sustainability sought. In the same way, the Sanctuary Movement wrestled with the question of what its goals were, how they might be attained, and what virtues were primary within the movement. Indeed, this is a primary focus in how MacIntyre thinks of a community of practice: "For it is not merely that different participants in a tradition disagree; they also disagree as to how to characterize their disagreements and as to how to resolve them."[4] In these contestations, I contend that sanctuary emerges as a practice through which many different, competing internal goods may be realized. In fact, the realization of those internal goods was a primary concern of activists, who utilized their participation in the movement to drive their own self-actualization.

---

[2]Alasdair MacIntyre, *After Virtue: A Study in Moral Theory* (Notre Dame, IN: University of Notre Dame Press, 2007), 187.
[3]Ibid., 190.
[4]Alasdair MacIntyre, "Epistemological Crises, Dramatic Narrative, and the Philosophy of Science," in *The Tasks of Philosophy* (New York: Cambridge University Press, 2006), 11–12.

Within the practice of sanctuary there are many constitutive elements that deserve attention. In marking these, I am not saying that these constitute the entirety of the practice of sanctuary. Rather, I contend that these represent intriguing touchstones for a scholar of sanctuary to build a conception of practice. In paying attention to how activists, recipients, and communities were recruited by the Sanctuary Movement, the living arrangements of recipients in sanctuary, the *testimonio* and its relationship to trauma, and the publicity of the caravans, one can begin to more clearly understand the movements goals, tensions, and triumphs, while paying close attention to the internal goods that were cultivated by the practice of sanctuary. Perhaps most clearly, this view of sanctuary makes clear that the housing of recipients of sanctuary, which might in some ways seem like the most foundational act of the practice, is but one of a set of interlocking sub-practices that give shape to the Sanctuary Movement and sanctuary more generally. The result is an account of sanctuary as practice, albeit an account that obscures analyses of power and focuses its attention on the experience of white activists within the Sanctuary Movement. One of the places where this becomes clear is in standards of excellence, which were worked out in real-time largely by activists.

Recruiting for Sanctuary

The Sanctuary Movement recruited communities of faith, activists, and recipients in order to grow its movement, even as it developed an identity that was based around responding to a crisis at the border organically. The early movement focused on the narratives of its key founders responding to the exceptional needs of those crossing the border,[5] but soon it turned its attention to recruitment of recipients, oftentimes recruiting them while still outside of the country. In the same way, the movement attended to recruitment of activists in order to build a national movement, at times focusing on the practical needs of administration. While the narratives of early participants in the Sanctuary Movement, such as Jim Corbett and John Fife, as well as other clergy on the Tucson Ecumenical Council, have been well documented, this work is more interested in second-level participants in the movement. That is, how did activists connect with the Sanctuary Movement? If they were recruited, how? How did activists discern an affinity with the movement from their previous engagement with political activism or religious practice?

---

[5]See: "Conspiracy of Compassion: Four Indicted Leaders Discuss the Sanctuary Movement," interview by Jim Wallis and Joyce Hollyday, *Sojourners*, March 1985.

Recruitment of activists was varied, but several consistencies can be readily stated. The movement recruited many activists from established networks of communities of faith, political activism, and those that were somewhere in the middle. At the same time, through its attending to media exposure, the Sanctuary Movement also relied on activists self-recruiting by contacting other activists at the national or regional level. However, they also made direct invitations to those that were thought to be sympathetic to the cause, such as those in leadership on social justice efforts in communities of faith. As such, the sub-practice of recruitment of activists prized nimbleness and a varied approach above all else, probably because of the decentralized nature of sanctuary and various ideas of what constituted excellence in recruitment.

For those whom the motivations might be described as spiritual or religious, the story of Margaret "Peggy" Hutchison in Ann Crittenden's *Sanctuary* ably demonstrates a typical trajectory of activists. Originally interested in social work and active local justice issues in Tucson, Hutchison begins to help Salvadoran refugees navigate the legal system and apply for asylum. Frustrated at the government's overwhelming dismissal of cases that she helps to file, she faces a decision about where to put her time: "I could lobby congress; I could work for extended voluntary departure; I could educate people; I could visit the jails and the detention centers. That could be my ministry. Or I could get involved on a deeper level, with the sanctuary ministry. . . . If the values I had been brought up by meant anything, I had to get involved in sanctuary."[6] Hutchison's characterization of the practice of sanctuary as "ministry," as well as her identification of sanctuary as comprising a "deeper level" is crucial. Those who became involved, especially in the early days of the Sanctuary Movement, were connected to local religious, humanitarian networks that emphasized the need for people of faith to take action. While some did join the Sanctuary Movement as a result of a particular experience with a refugee from Central America, especially Roman Catholic priests serving parishes at the border like Father Anthony Clark, they tended to be among the earliest activists to join the movement. After the initial conversion experiences of Jim Corbett and John Fife, the second wave of activists would join the movement through humanitarian concern facilitated by their involvement with local networks. Though she was in the second wave of activists in Tucson, her zeal was nevertheless considerable. After being charged with felonies in an INS crackdown, she noted that her conviction was not shaken: "the indictments have strengthened me to work harder for peace and justice in Central America."[7] Among this group, the movement provided a "deeper level" of

---

[6]Crittenden, *Sanctuary: A Story of American Conscience and the Law in Collision*, 98.
[7]Golden Renny, "Sanctuary and Women," *Journal of Feminist Studies in Religion* 2, no. 1 (1986): 145.

religious action by challenging participants to practice discipleship in ways that challenged power and involved risk.

Those religious networks were wide and varied, as Carl's gradual movement from the Catholic Worker Movement and its emphasis on hospitality to involvement with the Sanctuary Movement demonstrates:

> I was in seminary in the early 80's in Grand Rapids, and of course Central America was one of the hot topics of the day, and several of us wanted to do more than what we were doing on campus. We ended up buying a house together and started a Catholic-worker-like house, and Central America was the focus of our work, and by 1986 we were discussing joining the sanctuary movement. We had already been doing hospitality work for the homeless and those fleeing domestic violence.

Carl joined the movement relatively late, after the trials of Tucson activists, and his primary collaboration partner was the Chicago Religious Task Force on Central America, which makes sense with his leftist political leanings and involvement with local peace movements aimed at nuclear disarmament as well as local groups demanding more robust public housing. Indeed, the practice of sanctuary would also go on to have further resonance with Carl, where he credits his involvement with the Sanctuary Movement with motivating involvement with environmental activism in the 1990s, even as he felt the "the Church's" lackluster embrace of the Sanctuary Movement necessitated his departure from seminary and the end of his engagement with organized religion.

In a similar way, the Sanctuary Movement recruited politically active activists already involved in networks of activism, some of which blurred the distinction between political and religious activism. For instance, Bob Fitch was an ordained United Church of Christ minister who played an instrumental role in launching a Sanctuary Movement for sailors in San Diego who did not want to serve or continue service on ships in the city's harbor. Drawing on many of the same organizing frameworks and techniques for generating press coverage, Fitch went on to play an important role in starting the Sanctuary Movement in the San Francisco Bay Area.[8] Indeed, many of those interviewed for the Sanctuary Oral History Project, which focused on the Bay Area, reported previous involvement with the Vietnam War Sanctuary Movement. However, this involvement was not solely limited to the Bay Area. In a previously published article, I analyze the legacies and impacts of previous Vietnam War sanctuary activism on Sanctuary Movement participation in one Boston-area congregation, demonstrating that many of the strategies, people, and rhetoric flowed from

---

[8]Bob Fitch, interview by Eileen Purcell, *The Public Sanctuary Movement: An Historical Basis of Hope* (Berkley, CA: Graduate Theological Union, 1998).

one movement to the other.[9] Both the Sanctuary Movement for Vietnam War resisters and Central Americans had some component of physical sanctuary, a combination of religious and political motivations, and a shaky legal basis that relied on creative use of the press and the government's hesitance to enter a church and forcibly remove recipients of sanctuary.[10] In seeing the resonances between the practices of sanctuary in the 1970s and 1980s, it becomes clear that sanctuary as a practice is more expansive than any one movement. The Sanctuary Movement does not have a monopoly on this practice; rather it is a particular "field," to borrow a term from Bourdieu, in which this practice can be exercised.[11]

When it comes to recruiting activists, the Sanctuary Movement drew on already established networks of compassion, hospitality, and political activism. Importantly, recruitment in this sense does not mean that individuals were approached by sanctuary leaders and asked to participate, although that did happen. For instance, one of the activists that I interviewed was active in a Unitarian Universalist parish and was asked by her minister to participate actively in a caravan, even though she had no previous involvement with the movement:

> Dana: He said, "We're planning an overground caravan from Los Angeles to Seattle" . . . And he said, "We need two people from our congregation to accompany that caravan from stop to stop, where refugees would be giving their testimony and he said, "I think you would be great. Can you do it?" And that invitation was so powerful that I said, "Yes."

In another instance, one activist—Joseph—was asked by Sanctuary leaders in Chicago to attend a meeting because he was the chairperson of the social action committee at his synagogue. Both of these activists began their activism with explicit recruitment due to a position held or previous involvement with a faith community. Another prominent avenue for recruiting activists based on their ability to speak Spanish, which was the experience of Lucy. While all these cases involve an explicit recruitment, self-recruitment based on already existing ethical, political, or religious commitments was an important way that the movement grew, as was the case with Carl's reaching out to sanctuary leaders in Chicago.

---

[9]Woolf, "Holy Risk: Old Cambridge Baptist Church and the Sanctuary Movement."
[10]For a more detailed account of some of the tactics used by religious communities to give sanctuary to Vietnam War Resisters, including the creative use of liturgies and utilization of the religious communities' social capital to generate positive press, see: Jessica Squires, *Building Sanctuary: The Movement to Support Vietnam War Resisters in Canada, 1965–73* (Vancouver, Toronto: UBC Press, 2013). And Michael S. Foley, *Confronting the War Machine: Draft Resistance during the Vietnam War* (Chapel Hill, NC: The University of North Carolina Press, 2003).
[11]Pierre Bourdieu, *Outline of a Theory of Practice* (New York: Cambridge University Press, 1977).

If the recruitment of activists primarily centered on similar networks of local activism that prepared would-be activists for sanctuary, the recruitment of recipients evolved over time and took on many different forms. No one rule can be stated for recipient recruitment. For most of the recipients I interviewed, the first point of contact with Sanctuary Movement activists was outside the United States, usually in Mexico, where international religious networks and Tucson activists provided information about the movement, ascertained preliminary fitness for public sanctuary, and gave information about how to cross the border and friendly religious communities nearby the border.[12] While seven recipients I interviewed reported some sort of contact with sanctuary activists in their country of origin or in an intermediary country like Mexico, the following three recipient narratives display the ways that recipients became connected to the movement well:

Rosa: My mom was the one that got involved with the sanctuary movement while she was in Mexico City awaiting for a political asylum decision on her case . . . She learned from the about the sanctuary movement from the Quaker group, and they were the ones that helped her get to the United States. That's how we learned about the Sanctuary Movement.

Marisol: And then a woman came to [us in Mexico] in a big van and she said she talked to the priest and she came to us and said, "I am going to take you to the border." And she was a Presbyterian woman from the Tucson Presbyterian church . . . And then So she drove us to the border, and she took us to another church, and there were two priests waiting for us.

Gloria: My brother contacted Jim Corbett and John Fife, and it was through them that we made contact with the Sanctuary Movement. Two or three people traveled to Guatemala to meet with us and to learn more about our story. They came back, and 3-4 months later we were ready to leave Guatemala with their support. We left the country at the end of 1984 . . . we traveled and entered the [United States] through the desert with the help of three sanctuary workers—two were pastors and one was a nun. From Tucson, we made it to Texas and in Texas a presbyterian church gave us sanctuary.

---

[12]While this account of the movement's methods was developed through interviews with recipients and activists, it squares nicely with Crittenden's contemporaneous description of the process used to recruit recipients: "Once a refugee in the underground railroad had made it to Hermosillo, in northwestern Mexico, he or she was usually contacted by volunteers and guided on up to the border. . . American sanctuary workers then interviewed the sojourners. If they seemed to qualify as genuine refugees, they were counseled on how to make it over the border and driven on up to Tucson." Crittenden, *Sanctuary: A Story of American Conscience and the Law in Collision*, 99.

Recipients' first point of contact with the movement was usually either activists from Tucson or international religious networks that were connected to Tucson. Being positioned on the border, Tucson took on the predominant role of initial screening for the movement either directly or through intermediaries, with Jim Corbett playing the key role in helping would-be recipients cross the border between the United States and Mexico.[13]

Most of the time, the Sanctuary Movement attempted to screen would-be recipients before they entered the United States. Although the line between a Central American refugee and an undocumented immigrant was often blurred in the 1980s, sanctuary activists sought to accompany recipients from their border crossing onward in order to separate the two issues and generate sympathy from the public.[14] One exception was Carlos, who was already in Los Angeles when he was approached by organizers for a caravan to the Pacific Northwest:

> I just got to LA. I didn't know what to do . . . And then I went to a group that they were helping Central American people. It was like a program refugees for Central America. And then I went over there and talk to them if they can help me. So from that point, I found the connection to join the caravan . . . They asked if I was interested to join because nobody was from Guatemala—it was all Salvadoran refugees and no Guatemalans . . . After the kind of question that they were asking me, I felt like I identified with the caravan. And then after a little while, I decided to come.

Instead of the typical screening process that would usually take place outside the United States through Tucson activists or their partners, Carlos connected through El Rescate to Tucson-affiliated activists in Los Angeles, indicating that the screening process was fluid and allowed for flexibility based on the needs of the current moment. In this case, a caravan from Los Angeles to the Pacific Northwest lacked a Guatemalan voice, and activists ascertained that Carlos would be a good fit for sanctuary. That flexibility, which some might characterize as a lack of organization, was both a strength and a weakness for the movement. John Fife, when considering the start of the movement,

---

[13]Crittenden, *Sanctuary: A Story of American Conscience and the Law in Collision*, 96.
[14]While the New Sanctuary Movement is focused primarily on immigration, the Sanctuary Movement of the 1980s was not interested in entangling the issues, and indeed, I would say that immigration was one of the least talked about issues among activists that I interviewed, who instead cited humanitarian concerns, anti-interventionism, solidarity, and other related values as the central motivation for their participation in the Sanctuary Movement. One parish did expand the movement to include the undocumented, however, even though that move was far from typical: La Placita in Los Angeles. The story of that congregation is covered extensively in Mario T Garcia, *Father Luis Olivares, a Biography: Faith Politics and the Origins of the Sanctuary Movement in Los Angeles* (Chapel Hill, NC: The University of North Carolina Press, 2018).

articulated that fluidity as emerging from a state of emergency: "We weren't trying to start a movement, we were just trying to do self-defense. We had no clue about starting a movement."[15] For Fife, not being a movement was central to excellence in the practice of sanctuary, as a movement would have organized, possibly political goals and would not be a purely humanitarian response to crisis. As the movement developed, both Tucson and Chicago recognized that an institutionalization process would have to occur in order to avoid pitfalls, but they disagreed on how to make that happen.[16]

However, many of those pitfalls were learning experiences that would go on to shape the nascent movement. As Coutin recounts in her *Culture of Protest,* some of the first religious communities that offered sanctuary to Central Americans witnessed alcoholism, trauma, and other "not pretty" behaviors that impeded the work of sanctuary, resulting in screening processes that worked to ensure that recipients "did not have severe emotional or social problems."[17] Even with these screening processes, some recipients did have encounters with the criminal justice system for offenses not related to immigration status.[18] Perhaps the most succinct account of a screening process for sanctuary work comes from the steering committee minutes of the East Bay Sanctuary Coalition (ESBC): "'prepared for sanctuary' means 'refugees who have no legal status and thus are in need of the protection of a congregation, who are mentally stable in spite of the persecution and dislocation they had suffered, and who are willing to speak to North American congregations about the reasons for their flight here.'"[19] Such a statement indicates that ESBC activists felt that screening was a necessary but ethically fraught part of the Sanctuary Movement, placing demands of mental stability on those who had experienced deep trauma. Even so, Tucson, with its relentless focus on the humanitarian crisis in Central America, was hesitant to reject candidates for sanctuary who were unwilling to speak publicly about their experiences. Instead, they dedicated themselves to the task of assessing whether or not a recipient fit the legal definition of refugee, a definition that excluded so-called "economic migrants" and included those who the ESBC would have deemed unsuitable for sanctuary.[20] In Tucson, the

---

[15]Quoted in: Mariana Dale, "Church Sanctuary Movement of 1980s Revived in Tucson," *The Republic*, 2014.

[16]Eventually, Chicago sought more control and institutionalization of the movement, and Tucson attempted to articulate a more horizontal, decentralized organization.

[17]Susan Bibler Coutin, *The Culture of Protest: Religious Activism and the U.S. Sanctuary Movement* (Boulder: Westview Press, 1993), 112, 13.

[18]R. Bruce Dold, "Fearful Sanctuary Fugitive Flees Child-Molesting Trial," *Chicago Tribune*, 1985.

[19]Quoted in: Coutin, *The Culture of Protest: Religious Activism and the U.S. Sanctuary Movement*, 112.

[20]Coutin, *The Culture of Protest: Religious Activism and the U.S. Sanctuary Movement*, 114.

Sanctuary Movement was about responding to a crisis, and the urgency the movement felt precluded intensive screening.

Emerging as centers of sanctuary activism, Tucson, Chicago, and, to a slightly lesser extent, the East Bay each constructed their own screening procedures for would-be recipients of public sanctuary. The major fault line that would separate the movement's networks was inherently a question of how to practice sanctuary, specifically the question of political affiliation in recipients' countries of origin. More specifically, should the movement give sanctuary to those who had been affiliated with right-wing militaries in Guatemala and El Salvador, or was sanctuary only available to those who were oppressed by those groups? Predictably, Tucson eschewed any political test, with John Fife stating: "We assist people from the whole political spectrum. We don't ask which side they're on."[21] Another sanctuary worker in the Tucson network was more blunt: "To even suggest that people be moved around on the basis of political efficacy is an obscenity."[22] As a result, Tucson did connect communities of faith with recipients that had served in the military and had committed crimes during that service, including rape and torture, so long as the recipient had a legitimate case for asylum.[23] This led to tensions, as two recipients of sanctuary might know each other from their home country's conflict, leading some recipients to question the movement's commitment to their safety.[24] Political neutrality was important for humanitarians who feared politicization of their actions and saw neutrality as an effective contrast between their actions and the United States government's discrimination against Guatemalan and Salvadoran refugees within the asylum process. In framing their actions as non-political sanctuary activists in Tucson argued that they were better enforces of the law than the government, a practice called "civil initiative" so as to distinguish it from civil disobedience.[25] As Dana put it, "it was a helping project, not a project of resistance." However, this action is also political, seeking to criticize the politicized, slanted enforcement of the Refugee Act of 1980 through a universal application of its protections.

Tucson's approach was not mirrored by the broader Sanctuary Movement; both Chicago and East Bay were comfortable screening for willingness to speak, emotional stability, and political affiliation, indicating the conflict that MacIntyre claims is a constitutive part of any practice. In effect, both Chicago

---

[21]Quoted in: Crittenden, *Sanctuary: A Story of American Conscience and the Law in Collision*, 92.

[22]Susan Bibler Coutin, "Enacting Law through Social Practice: Sanctuary as a Form of Resistance," in *Contested States: Law, Hegemony, and Resistance*, ed. Susan F. Hirsch and Mindie Lazarus-Black (New York: Routledge, 1994), 302.

[23]Crittenden, *Sanctuary: A Story of American Conscience and the Law in Collision*, 95.

[24]Coutin, *The Culture of Protest: Religious Activism and the U.S. Sanctuary Movement*, 129–30.

[25]Ibid., 109.

and East Bay gave sanctuary to left-of-center Salvadorans and Guatemalans who were prepared to speak about the conditions in their home country. Indeed, as Coutin notes, organizers from these camps "assume[d] that Central Americans were persecution from the Right, rather than the Left," with sanctuary screening procedures not even having an option to select "persecution by guerilla forces" as an option.[26] Indeed, all of the recipients that I spoke to were either leftists or at the very least not right wing. In one letter, the Chicago camp rejected two would-be-recipients because they "were not useful" due to their lack of political engagement.[27] Both Chicago and East Bay centers of sanctuary strived to connect communities of faith with those who would "appeal to liberal people in the community" as one Chicago activist put it, utilizing sympathy for Central American leftists among religious liberals.[28] This screening process makes sense for a particular pursuit of excellence in the practice of sanctuary that is based on raising the consciousness of white, religious communities. Crucially, in all cases the screening process was in the full control of activists, who made discussions about suitability of recipients for sanctuary and applied them to the individual cases of recipients.

Jim, one of the founding organizers of the Chicago Religious Task Force on Central America describes their recruitment process for recipients in this way:

> But then it became important that we create a discernment process for the refugees so that they were really clear what they were doing was their decision. So we set up safe houses and processed in Phoenix, Arizona and Los Angeles, California, and developed teams there that would spend the time—often several weeks and several months—working with refugees in what we call it the discernment process, too. So it was—They were very clear about what public sanctuary was. The risk that was there. That really enabled us to have refugees that were prepared to enter into sanctuary that we were organizing because we ended up organizing over 500 congregations in public sanctuary and getting refugees to those people who were prepared and who were clear and had decided, discerned that that was their calling with their sense of what they wanted to do, how they felt . . . And that involves kind of getting to know them better and hearing their stories and also figuring out . . . are they prepared for public

---

[26]Ibid., 113.
[27]Crittenden, *Sanctuary: A Story of American Conscience and the Law in Collision*, 91. As discussed in Chapter 2, this is likely not the whole story. These two young men were indigenous Mayans and there were other reasons why Chicago might not have wanted to work with them—language difficulties, for instance, but it is true that they were rejected because they did not meet Chicago's understanding of refugee identity.
[28]Robin Lorentzen, "Women in the Sanctuary Movement: A Case Study in Chicago" (PhD, Loyola University Chicago, 1989), 57.

role? Are they aware of that? . . . So we wanted to make sure that the refugees, if they if they weren't, uh, call to the ministry the prophetic ministry of public sanctuary that they had other ways—other options, and we helped move them to other possibilities if that was not their call.

Steeped in the religious language of ministry and discernment, Jim reveals the network of activists that worked to screen recipients for "public" sanctuary—that is, the sharing of *testimonios* publicly—and the attendant risk of deportation or harm to their families in their home countries. Like an ordination or discernment process, this was overseen by a network of volunteers who screened recipients for sanctuary as Chicago understood it.[29] Such a network was key because souring relationships between Tucson and Chicago meant that Tucson strove to not send recipients to Chicago, and Chicago had to manage its own networks of recruitment.[30] Where Tucson maintained connections in Mexico to screen recipients, Chicago focused its energy on those who had crossed the border and found themselves in cities like Phoenix, AZ, and Los Angeles, CA.

While it's true that the Chicago and Tucson centers of the Movement experienced tensions in 1984 and 1985, culminating with Chicago's refusal to share a mailing list with Jim Corbett, who was seeking to plan a symposium in Tucson, it would be a mistake to portray the boundary between the two as impermeable.[31] Although tensions between the two groups made direct collaboration more difficult, both maintained relationships with East Bay Sanctuary activists. Likewise, just because a recipient began their sanctuary in one network, does not mean that they stayed that way. Indeed, Gloria, a recipient from Guatemala, increasingly found herself more drawn to the Chicago network after receiving sanctuary in the Tucson network. After attending a national conference of sanctuary leaders as one of the only recipients present, Gloria spoke to an activist in the Chicago network: "At one of those conventions, I met Michael, and he told me that there was the possibility of coming to Chicago, and there was a progressive synagogue . . . I was very independent and I had a mind of my own, and it sounded perfect. It was a perfect match for me." In the end, Gloria concluded her relationship with a Texas faith community and received sanctuary in the Chicago network, which she discerned was a better fit for her activism. This

[29]East Bay followed a similar process, with intake and processing happening largely in the Bay Area, but with similar screening. See: Coutin, *The Culture of Protest: Religious Activism and the U.S. Sanctuary Movement*, 109–15.

[30]Crittenden, *Sanctuary: A Story of American Conscience and the Law in Collision*, 92. This doesn't mean that the networks remained independent however. They would collaborate on particular cases, and some recipients even changed networks in the middle of their sanctuary.

[31]Corbett fired back that he was proud to be labeled a heretic with regards to the "Chicago creed" in the CRTFCA's newsletter, *Basta!*, see: Davidson, *Convictions of the Heart: Jim Corbett and the Sanctuary Movement*.

story was mirrored with Luis, who was in rural Kansas before coming to the Chicago area. Likewise, it would be a mistake to assume that the concerns of activists in the Tucson network were shared by the network's recipients. Many of the recipients that I interviewed received sanctuary in the Tucson network, but did not see themselves as receiving humanitarian aid. Rather, they saw sanctuary as a platform for activism that began in their country of origin. Those tensions are analyzed in great detail in Chapter 2, which discusses recipients' struggle for agency within a movement that privileged traumatic accounts from "refugees."

Finally, another category of recruitment is worth mentioning—the recruitment of faith communities to participate in the Sanctuary Movement. While the numbers of cited "sanctuary groups" cited by the CRTFCA is over 400, including over fifty secular groups, there are reasons to think that number might be inflated.[32] In particular, there is a question of whether a community ought to count as a sanctuary group if they never actually housed a recipient, which seems at first glance like a necessary component of the practice of sanctuary. What seems clear is that with the communication breakdown between Chicago and Tucson, varying definitions of what constitutes a sanctuary group—does passing a sanctuary resolution qualify, or it the housing of a recipient?—and a lack of a centralized record-keeping mirror broader contestations over what constitutes the practice of sanctuary.

Nevertheless, how movement activists and recipients recruited congregations to join the movement remains an interesting topic, and the details of that recruitment process are thankfully more concrete than the total number of sanctuary communities. Sanctuary communities after the initial wave joined through a process that usually began with pamphlets, guides,[33] or leaflets that connected the offering of sanctuary to Biblical roots as well as contemporary resources that focused on the hiding of Jews during the Holocaust.[34] An interested faith community would then make contact with activists, and the interested party, which could be a clergyperson or a lay committee, would then schedule a time to engage with both activists and recipients with an aim of drafting a sanctuary declaration for the community of faith at an annual or business meeting.

---

[32]For a table that breaks down "sanctuary groups" reported by the CTFCA by religious tradition, see: Christian Smith, *Resisting Reagan: The U.S. Central America Peace Movement* (Chicago, IL: University of Chicago Press, 1996), 185. The number of reported sanctuary communities in scholarship range from 150 to numbers in the 200s, and finally the oft-repeated "over 400" estimate that comes from the CRTFCA.

[33]Friends Peace Committee, *Sanctuary for Refugees from El Salvador and Guatemala—A Resource Guide for Friends* (Philadelphia, PA: Philadelphia Yearly Meeting, 1985).

[34]Sanctuary communities discerning their participation often read: Philip P. Hallie, *Lest Innocent Blood be Shed: The Story of the Village of Le Chambon, and How Goodness Happened There*, 1st ed. (New York: Harper & Row, 1979).

As Eduardo's story demonstrates, obtaining this declaration took a large amount of work with intense collaboration between recipients, activists, and interested members of a faith community:

It was pretty well organized. Let's say we are working at the chapel in Berkeley, we went through a process, where we wanted to have a vote, and the goal was 2/3rds of the sanctuary to declare sanctuary. And the goal was not for the pastor to decide. We wanted them to ask the hard questions, and we would do kind of a test to see if we have the numbers. And if we didn't, we would wait, and if we didn't we would do another round of testimonies or presentation. Sometimes we did not call a vote ... In sanctuary we have the view of the lawyers, and there are lawyers for every single church, if you are found guilty of giving sanctuary, you might lose your 501c3 status, so that's the view of the lawyers. So the lawyers in the room may be conservative—that's their job, to look at the worst case scenario. So you typically get the lawyer out of the room and ask again. All due respect to lawyers—their advice would be not to do it, because you're risking too much. You might lose parishioners too. So, when you remove the lawyers from the room, you ask what does our God ask us to do? What should we do? Then the question is very straight forward.

Eduardo, an activist in his own right, demonstrates the skillful negotiation required for the movement to recruit communities of faith to formally declare sanctuary, a step which took the community to the threshold of giving sanctuary to a recipient and necessitated "get[ting] the lawyer out of the room." That next step would be handled in collaboration with movement leaders, who matched recipients based on the size of the recipient family and the housing arrangements to which a community could commit.

Sanctuary Movement activists and recipients had to consider the appropriate time to call a vote, how to structure the vote in such a way as to privilege the voices of advocates and proponents, and how to ask questions that move communities of faith toward a declaration. While a community of faith's affinity for sanctuary may have been organic, it is clear that the formal process was not, requiring deft navigation of potential difficulties. In this way, it becomes clear that rather than a gradual drift toward sanctuary, sanctuary communities, like recipients and activists, were recruited to join a movement that practiced sanctuary, an act that defined the movement and which we turn to next.

Seeing sanctuary as a practice, the recruitment of activists, recipients, and faith communities all contained standards of excellence that were contested within the movement. If one side favored self-avowed apoliticism, while the other saw sanctuary as necessarily having a political component, it might be tempting to view them as separate movements entirely. However, those tensions between the two camps reveal contestations about excellent practice within a singular movement. From a practice framework, we can instead begin to see the movements not as having contesting ideas about the urgency of the situation, but as having different views of the very practice of sanctuary. Both sought to challenge Reagan's Central American policy and enforcement of the Refugee Act of 1980, but they had different views of the form of excellence in the practice of sanctuary. What this analysis reveals is a practice that was in a state of flux, as standards for excellence were articulated through a process of trial and error. This pushes the edges of MacIntyre's practice framework, since chess as well as architecture and farming all have some established metrics for success. There are established rules and knowledges that can be applied to a particular outcome. However, in the Sanctuary Movement, the practice of sanctuary had very few recent traditions to ground the movement, and the practitioners of it worked out the standards of excellence in real-time and through contestations. Importantly, it was the activists of the movement that worked out excellence in practice, as recipient voices were conspicuously absent in discussions about who should receive sanctuary.

Offering Sanctuary

Within the practice of sanctuary, one of the actions that receives the most attention is the actual offering of physical sanctuary— that is a community coming together to provide some housing and protection from immigration enforcement. My research indicates that physical sanctuary took many forms within the movement, including the iconic and much-written-about housing of a recipient in a faith community's building itself. While several did report living in a community's basement or a converted space within a house of worship, several also reported living in an apartment owned by a member of a faith community who donated the space to the recipient, and still, others reported living with members of the faith community either in a shared domicile, a private apartment attached to a community member's home, or an intentional community that was connected to the house of worship housing the recipient. Strikingly, among the recipients I interviewed, no living arrangement encompassed a majority of recipient experiences, showcasing the malleability of the offering of physical sanctuary. Likewise, the durability of the arrangement was also highly variable. While many left sanctuary after the attainment of permanent residency, some remained in their living arrangements indefinitely, with one recipient I interviewed still residing in the house that she took sanctuary in and another reporting having lived on the grounds of a religious community for twenty-three years. Though anecdotal due to the small sample size of this study, these experiences indicate the adaptability of sanctuary living situations.

Although the living arrangements of recipients were diverse, one consistent standard of excellence in the practice of sanctuary was security for recipients in case of reprisals from Immigration and Naturalization Services (INS, *La Migra*) or an emergency response network for dealing with emergencies:

> Isabella: And we were provided food and clothing, but they also organized surveillance. So, we have members of the church that will, like every four hours stay in the Stairs. And so we looked through the little hole [in the door] and said, "oh my goodness. They're there."

> Joseph: They were amazingly self-sufficient. I don't think anybody like spent the night with them in the apartment. We had a system to alert members of the congregation if anything bad started to happen, but we were not there standing guard.

Where a recipient physically lived was not as important for the practice of sanctuary as might be thought, but protecting recipients from deportation was a common and important part of the practice. This was seen as a reciprocal arrangement. Since recipients had agreed to, in most cases, be public in their arrival and continued residence, communities of faith had a duty to provide one of the most basic elements of sanctuary—protection from authorities.

Most communities also operated using a committee structure that attempted to collaborate with recipients on the quotidian affairs of life such as food, money, living arrangements, work, language, and education. Some sanctuary committees were more solicitous of recipient feedback than others and as a result, some collaborations were successful and others failed. In those I interviewed, sanctuary committees ran the gamut from supportive, empowering spaces that prioritized recipients' goals, needs, and desires to those that placed recipients in passive roles as objects of charitable action:

> Gloria: When I just got to [the sanctuary location], they had a meeting between the church and us, and this woman gave this speech about what to expect in the US and how to behave in public. I found it so racist. What was enraging for me, was that she said that the people in Guatemala . . . the toilet paper they don't throw it in the toilet, they throw it in the basket, and she told us that was just for savages. Here in the US, we should not do that—the toilet paper went in the toilet, and she made sure we understood that. They would bring things we thought we missed. They would have Guatemalan food, according to them, and we ate beans and rice in Guatemala because we didn't have resources to eat something else. So there were cultural misconceptions that we had. Small and big things that really, really made the time in sanctuary very difficult.

> Isabella: The sanctuary committee was] very respectful, though, because, um if they had to talk about something about, you know, our living conditions, they were very respectful. They will bring the issue. And they say," What do you think?" they were not imposing. They were not . . .

everything they had to bring an issue, they had a translator at that time. They had one member who spoke Spanish, but they never said, "Oh, this is what we want!" Nothing. Nothing about the white privilege stuff . . . and they were very progressive people in 1984 . . . they treated us with dignity.

While these two recipient experiences represent two poles of sanctuary committee relationships with recipients, the majority reported more mundane interactions between the two groups.

One point of tension was work, as recipients lacked work authorization and struggled with the desire to earn income that was not donated by the house of worship that housed them. Most recipients reported that they earned income through domestic work, which relied on the generosity of community members and reified differences in status between activists and recipients, who paid for domestic work while also feeling beneficent. The words of Rosa, a recipient from Guatemala, make it clear that recipients rarely wanted to rely on donations to support them: "[Our family worked] whatever they could find so that we could try to blend in, or at least not depend so much on sanctuary, because sanctuary was a bridge, and we needed to do our part so that we could stay here and apply for political asylum and do all the stuff that we needed to do to be able to have a normal life eventually." In addition to domestic work, recipients often taught Spanish to members of the faith community that housed them. However, Isabella, a recipient from El Salvador, reported driving to a farm willing to employ refugees to pick cherries seasonally in order to earn money not directly tied to sanctuary:

My husband was getting a license. I was taking classes in the community college, and one summer, we told them "we're going Oregon, and we will drive." And they were afraid.

"You guys are driving?"

"Yeah, we are."

And they said, "OK, are you going to be okay?"

"Yeah."

"Okay." They were not. "Ah, no, no. You cannot go."

We took off to Oregon. We needed to earn money, because actually . . . Somebody told us about other Quakers who had some cherry farms and they were providing jobs for refugees. So that connection, somebody said, "You want to earn some money?" We drove down and we went and worked over there.

The desire not to be dependent on donations was not simply a desire for American-style self-sufficiency. Rather, in a situation where houses of worship controlled every resource, including housing, earning one's own money helped recipients achieve some modicum of agency and control over their own lives. As Isabella's story indicates, some sanctuary committees were more willing than others to facilitate collaborative relationships with room for recipient independence.

As a practice, the offering of physical sanctuary was highly adaptable to the circumstances of each individual faith community, and no one housing option comprised a majority of recipient experiences. The image of sanctuary recipients living in churches in the Sanctuary Movement needs to be widened to include a variety of communal living options. While ample attention was paid to matching recipients with a particular faith community, as well as to the initial process of faith communities' discernment of participation in the movement, I found little engagement with issues of power within the movement, and with the movement being decentralized, there was not a structure in place to evaluate living situations or offer corrections. Of course, individual communities were able to collaborate with recipients in ways that increased their agency, but they were also free to fail to consider recipient agency an integral part of the practice of sanctuary. If the recruitment practices of sanctuary revealed tensions over articulating the standards of excellence that comprise the practice of sanctuary, the disparity in the offering of housing and the relationships that developed reveal that the recipient agency was not an integral part of the practice of sanctuary, or, if it was, that activists had the power to decide if that agency was optional or not. Put another way, from the viewpoint of activists, excellence in the practice of sanctuary could be sought without attending to recipient power and agency. This disparity might be due to the fact that the offering of sanctuary in a church, apartment, or communal living arrangement was the least visible part of the practice of sanctuary, which might have hampered the learning in-the-moment that I highlight in the sub-practice of recruitment.

The *Testimonio* and Trauma

While the offering of physical sanctuary is important, there is perhaps no act more directly linked in the public imagination of sanctuary than the *testimonio*. Sometimes with faces obscured to protect their identities and always using pseudonyms, recipients were called upon to share their story as it connected to conflicts in their country of origin. *Testimonios* were utilized as an important counter to official American accounts of the conflicts in El Salvador and Guatemala, giving hearers in the United States a firsthand account of atrocities, violence, and suffering that forced them to discern which information source was telling the truth, especially when the United States' policy was a direct cause of the conflict that recipients were now testifying about. One activist put it this way: "The refugees themselves told why they had to flee and there was no question that we, the U.S., were causing the problem ourselves."[35] In replacing a "broad and abstract issue in the news" with a "specific, concrete reality in one's church or living room," Christian Smith argues that Sanctuary Movement activists were able to generate an "insurgent consciousness" that led to religious and political conversions and to direct, radical action on the part of hearers.[36] Indeed, care was taken by the movement to select particular recipients for specific audiences in order to make consciousness-raising and involvement in the movement more likely. For instance, a catechist or participant in a Base Christian Community might speak to a Roman Catholic parish.[37]

In an era before social media granted broad access to firsthand, unapproved accounts of events, sanctuary activists deployed recipient *testimonios* as a counterweight to official news reports, positing a different set of facts corroborated by the lived experience of recipients:

> Eduardo: I was telling my story in Arizona with John Fife's community, and my 7 year old son was with me on the way to a conference at the border and my son didn't understand everything that was happening. But he asked me, "what did you say that everyone in the church was crying?" I was telling my testimony. Everyone was breaking. That was the power of sanctuary, because people could compare with what the government was saying, and people would believe us, the refugees. What do you do with that information? Do you move on or get active? Many people decided to do something and joined the movement. Not only churches, but universities, even cities, and states.

In hearing these *testimonios*, white religious participants in the movement became bearers of "forbidden knowledge," leading to a sense of intrigue that helped activists craft their own identities and fostered a sense of commitment to the movement.[38] The meteoric growth of the early Sanctuary Movement can in large part be traced to the success of *testimonios* in moving from abstract to concrete knowledge, while also offering activists and members of sanctuary houses of worship the experience of being insiders and possessing information that the United States government did not want them to have.[39] Indeed, the secrecy of identity of recipients may have contributed to a sense of mystique in which the hearers were produced as "authentic" and their subsequent actions were heroic.[40]

---

[35]Smith, *Resisting Reagan: The U.S. Central America Peace Movement*, 400.
[36]Ibid., 183.
[37]Coutin, "Enacting Law through Social Practice: Sanctuary as a Form of Resistance," 302.
[38]Coutin, *The Culture of Protest: Religious Activism and the U.S. Sanctuary Movement*, 125.
[39]See: Smith, *Resisting Reagan: The U.S. Central America Peace Movement*, 183.
[40]Amy Villareal Garza, "Places of Sanctuary: Religious Revivalism and the Politics of Immigration in New Mexico" (PhD, University of California—Santa Cruz, 2014), 78.

As Chapter 2 demonstrates in-depth, traumatic narratives received greater attention and celebration within the movement, cementing a recipient's status as a refugee and emotionally moving white religious liberals who heard their *testimonio*. Far from solely moving them to political action and engagement with the Sanctuary Movement, *testimonios* also served as a vehicle for personal and spiritual development. For instance, one activist, Rachel, used a lack of sufficient housing provided by her sanctuary committee as a learning experience and fodder for personal reflection: "one of my early observations with these people was that they would be in a very small space and never crowded. And it never felt like . . . one of the many things, I learned about us and about them was how we require so much space and it never . . . I don't know where they all slept, but I think initially, it probably was a one bedroom." Other connections were less problematic, as in the case of Erik, who saw the pain of recipients as expressed in *testimonios* as moving him to reach out more radically to "those on the edges" and bring the Gospel message of "good news to the poor" to them. Perhaps the most interesting personal and spiritual development that emerged from *testimonios* in my research was from Martha, an activist from the Pacific Northwest, who equated the risk taken by recipients—" how brave the refugees were that they would risk arrest and deportation. They were all women who spoke, and I just always was so impressed by their courage"—with the call to risk that participation in the movement represented, a call which she would not have previously undertaken: "there were threats for providing aid and comfort to illegal aliens. I just totally believed in what we're doing, and the call—that's what Jesus surely would have done, and that's what we have to do."

In likely and unlikely ways, the *testimonio* served as a transformative moment for hearers, who inevitably made connections to their own lives and used recipient narratives to advance their own personal development. In essence, those transformative moments for activists were built on the trauma of recipients, who sometimes kept a full schedule of speaking appearances and might be expected to give their *testimonio* and answer questions throughout the week but especially on Friday, Saturday, and Sunday. Some activists, like Jim, recognized the *testimonio*'s potential for recipients to re-live the trauma of their narratives:

And because of that issue of the potential of repeating the trauma every time you tell that story. So it was always the intention that the refugee was clear that you can say I can't do it this time, or I need a month break or, you know "no, I want to do it more. I'm bored here—I came here to tell my story. Line me up." So there are a variety of different approaches. But again, trying to have each congregation, each refugee be listening to each other and being able to care.

While Jim's commitment to recipient agency is admirable, the fact that each recipient was in sanctuary with a particular faith community meant that recipients received varying levels of support and recognition of the *testimonio* as a traumatic space. In one case, Carl only realized trauma was a salient category in the Sanctuary Movement after the recipient he had been working with for years fled from a medical helicopter as it was approaching:

> That same day I was doing the translation, the very next day I was there doing the translating, and I was there with the husband and we had parked up the hill, and the parking lot we were at was right next to the helicopter pad, and all of sudden this hospital helicopter started coming, and all of sudden this guy who I was with just took off running. And I was like, "what's he doing?!"

Time and time again, recipients and activists alike reflect that a trauma-informed approach was missing from the movement and that recognizing the trauma of recipients would have yielded better results for recipients. The earlier experience caused Carl to state that the primary thing that he would have altered about sanctuary was sensitivity to trauma: "And just recognizing those sort of dynamics and being sensitive and prepared for that. If I had anything to say to the [Sanctuary Movement], it would be conversations about trauma, and re-traumatization by the state." As Juana, a recipient from Guatemala, succinctly states: "the one thing that I wish they would have provided, but the one thing is talk therapy, mental support . . . When you go through something like that, you can't not [have access to mental health support]. It's also about can you be mentally in a good place."

While white activists made use of *testimonios* to advance the cause and foster personal growth, the trauma of recipients was often only addressed well after the last *testimonio* had been shared, but the effects lingered in the recipients I interviewed. Rosa put it this way: "Let me tell you about fear. It never leaves you. It never leaves you," but that fear was a critical component of activist self-actualization, as was the otherness of recipient experiences that were shared. In the following quote from Christian Smith's *Resisting Reagan* that otherness is inexorably linked not just to trauma but to "brown faces" that relay experiences of profound trauma: "After seeing those beautiful brown faces, hearing their personal tragedies, stories of torture, brutality, tragedy so horrendous it offends love, you realize it can kill the human spirit. But the crucifixion has taken on new meaning for me; it is through suffering, I have learned from the refugees, that we learn compassion."[41] In hearing recipient *testimonios*, some hearers gained new insight into theological doctrines like the crucifixion, while others received the information needed to counter economic migrant narratives. For the Tucson camp, it was through the sharing of physical, emotional, and sexual

---

[41]Smith, *Resisting Reagan: The U.S. Central America Peace Movement*, 183.

trauma that listeners became convicted of recipients' refugee status: "I knew they were refugees because I had heard so many of their stories."[42] One might say that trauma, as expressed in the *testimonio*, was not only the sine qua non of refugee status but also of the movement. The practice of sanctuary in both the Chicago and Tucson movements is inexorably linked to trauma, creating a space where participants in the Sanctuary Movement became initiated into secret knowledge that rendered them the judge of recipients' identity and provided fodder for self-actualization.

The standards of excellence for the sub-practice of the *testimonio* were perhaps the most consistent across the Sanctuary Movement. One of the chief causes of this standardization was the repetition and public nature of the *testimonio*—a recipient could give a *testimonio* dozens of times to crowds of over a hundred listeners. The subject material differed little, as citations of trauma served as an indictment of biased news coverage and invited listeners to form community around forbidden knowledge. Part of those standards of excellence seems to have been concern over re-traumatization of recipients, although that concern seems to have manifested unevenly and from a sense of voluntary choice. Take Jim's insistence that recipients were in control of their narrative and could step back from the work of presenting *testimonios* at any time. In an ideal iteration of the practice of sanctuary this would undoubtedly be true, but the power differentials between recipients and activists render the concepts of free choice an illusion in many cases. As Chapter 2 will show in-depth, there was consistent restriction as to what could be said in *testimonios*, and the question of whether a recipient wished to give a *testimonio* at any given time was complicated by receiving food and housing from a sanctuary community. In such a context, free choice is a simplification of the dynamics at work, especially when tears and recitation of trauma were encouraged in order to build the Sanctuary Movement.

Caravans

Another aspect of the practice of sanctuary embraced by the movement was the caravan—a group of activists transporting recipients to either the house of worship they would eventually take sanctuary in or an event. In the case of the latter, the caravan was used often as a means of defiance against the government's crackdown on the movement through trials of sanctuary activists and the covert infiltration project known as Operation Sojourner.[43] Perhaps the most common use of the caravan mentioned in

---

[42]Coutin, *The Culture of Protest: Religious Activism and the U.S. Sanctuary Movement*, 116.
[43]See: Kristina M. Campbell, "Operation Sojourner: The Government Infiltration of the Sanctuary Movement in the 1980s and Its Legacy on the Modern Central American Refugee Crisis," *University of St. Thomas Law Journal* 13, no. 2 (2017): 474.

primary and secondary literature on the movement was in response to the arrests of Tucson sanctuary activists Jack Elder and Phil Conger. Worried about arrests of participants and refugees, sanctuary activists in Tucson organized a large caravan to take recipients to a Freedom Seder at Tucson's reform synagogue. As Jim Corbett reported of the "nonviolent protective response" to the federal government, the caravan had "more than seventy Salvadorans and Guatemalans . . . and the caravan that took them to Temple Emanu-El was two miles long."[44] Another source says that there were 143 passengers and drivers who signed a defiant statement contesting the Reagan administration's legitimacy in order to demonstrate that "church resistance" to prosecution of sanctuary workers was strong.[45] In effect, these caravans were used to send a message to two audiences—INS and recipients themselves—that sanctuary workers were not scared of government action and would continue the work of sanctuary. The result was largely successful, as large-scale prosecutions did not take place, and the response from sympathetic community members was overwhelming, helping the movement to recruit more workers. One activist called the prosecutions and subsequent caravans "the best media push we've ever had. It got a lot more people interested in us."[46]

This model of a defensive caravan was used throughout the Sanctuary Movement. Take, for example, Jim's retelling of a caravan in the early days of the Sanctuary Movement:

> So I was the organizer that organized them it to become the first sanctuary congregation on the public sanctuary model that then would be developed and organized across the country. And so after that we didn't know what was going to happen with that, right? I mean, would they back down? And we organized a big caravan. But first, press conference in front of the Federal Plaza, A caravan from the Federal Plaza to [the church]. And some crazy priest like Chuck, Tom and other folks were with me in the lead car with refugees and kind of an interesting accompaniment through that . . . We were a great success and *La Migra* backed down after that.

In both cases, sanctuary leaders utilize the caravan not knowing what the result will be, challenging the federal government to do something in public to a number of activists and recipients. The use of a press conference in the earlier case is particularly important, and while sanctuary activists were not above provoking the government at times, each utilized caravans in order to attract new members through media engagement and let the government

---

[44]Corbett, *Goatwalking*, 157.

[45]Renny Golden, *Sanctuary: The New Underground Railroad*, ed. Michael McConnell (Maryknoll, NY: Orbis Books, 1986), 70.

[46]Coutin, *The Culture of Protest: Religious Activism and the U.S. Sanctuary Movement*, 36.

know that the movement was not fragile enough to be dispersed by a handful of arrests.

The twin effects of caravans intended as a response to some action—building collective strength in the face of opposition from the Reagan administration and generating media engagement—were also the desired outcomes for caravans taking recipients to their sanctuary location. Because the caravan was meant to generate positive media, it was made as public as possible through the use of banners, signs, meetings with officials, and stops to give *testimonios* along the way. Moreover, the caravan was useful because it prevented isolation and made any attempts at arrest more visible and public, thereby putting pressure on INS to ignore the caravan even as they had most likely infiltrated it, as was the case with one of the recipients I spoke with.[47]

One of the best attested caravans in secondary literature was the journey of an indigenous family from Arizona to Chicago and then to a religious community in the Northeast. Coutin notes some of the signs that made sure the caravan would stand out: "when the twelve car caravan left Chicago, the cars were festooned with signs reading "Freedom Train," Refugee Express," and "INS Stop Deportations."[48] In my research, I interviewed both the architect of the caravan strategy who pioneered its use with the trip from Chicago to the Northeast and the recipients who made the trip:

> Jim: And so when the bust happened in Texas, we had the people on route, different places, kind of go underground, go to safehouses. And then . . . we decided what we have to do is just confront the state even more dramatically. And so we organized the first public caravan, which was from Chicago to Weston Priory. And we went first right to Washington, D. C. And then up to [the Northeast]. And that was a very important response to the first arrests. And rather than being intimidated, we decided we needed to just keep pushing the church to be the church and giving space or the refugee story to be told as boldly and as loudly and clearly as possible. So then after [this caravan] we you know, we have a New York Times correspondent go along with us. We have a very good coverage in the Times and television. So it was probably one of the things that increased the visibility of the Sanctuary Movement in a very dramatic way—that caravan.

---

[47]Two recipients I interviewed had experiences with sanctuary workers that turned out to be undercover agents that would go on to testify in trials. In one case, a recipient was called to testify against the workers that helped him cross the border, an extremely painful experience. In addition to the infiltration of events like the caravan, INS also attended church services to spy on the activities of sanctuary communities. See: Harvey Cox, "The Spy in the Pew," *New York Times*, Monday, March 3, 1986.

[48]Coutin, *The Culture of Protest: Religious Activism and the U.S. Sanctuary Movement*, 71.

Luis: We started our trip from Arizona to that community across the US
but with caution because we were afraid of *La Migra*. We spent several
days traveling, but also several days resting. We shared our testimony
with the press, and other churches, and people who were very interested
in their experience . . . When we got to Chicago, we got to a UCC church,
and that was when we were finally able to break our silence about what
was happening to the church in Guatemala. We were able to talk about
the caravan of people coming out of Guatemala. We wore masks on the
journey, to be careful to not let the press capture their face to not let their
face be exposed. Lots of newspapers covered our journey to Chicago, to
hear about our experience. We arrived on March 24, 1984.

Both interviews record the tenuous nature of the arrangement. It was an
intentional provocation in order to "confront the state even more drastically"
and to generate news coverage through embedded journalists and the
spectacle of the caravan. At the same time, recipients needed to keep their
specific identity hidden through the use of bandanas used to obscure the
face out of fear of reprisals from government officials in the United States
or violent actors in their country of origin. In many ways, the obscuring of
their individual identity was a necessary component of sanctuary, but it also
made it harder for recipients to articulate their agency in ways separate from
the "refugee" that activists, government officials, and others were quick to
interpret and utilize for their own project.

Caravans were also important tools for activist recruitment, helping to
elicit more concrete commitments from sanctuary activists. Dana was on the
periphery of the movement before being asked to participate in a caravan
to Seattle, an invitation that she considered "quite powerful" and which
precipitated a decade of activism on Central American issues:

[My minister] said, "we're planning an overground Caravan from Los
Angeles to Seattle." And you know, I think everybody sort of knew some
of the details about what it would look like. And he said, "we need two
people from our congregation to a company that caravan from stop to
stop, where refugees would be giving their testimony and he said, I think
you would be great. Can you do it?" And that invitation was so powerful
that I said "Yes, I just need to check and see if I could get time away from
work"—which I was able to get. And so, um, with others from the area two
or so people from the Quaker meeting also too from [the Baptist church in
town] and myself and one other women from [our Unitarian Universalist
parish]. We all flew down to Los Angeles and then traveled back to Seattle
in vans, overground, stopping periodically for talks to be given in different
churches along the way. Our last stop was in Portland. And I can't quite
remember where we stayed there. But the minister of our congregation at
the time met us there. And then he rode in the caravan to [our Unitarian
Universalist parish]. And in that time we had a police escort . . . I walked

up the aisle, sat in the front of the sanctuary, it was full of people who had been there waiting for the caravan to arrive, and among the people were also elected officials—like our city council members. It was quite powerful. And, um, people who were there remember it strongly. And I think part of the formation for me with that whole trip was really the beginnings of seeing that the movement as accompaniment.

As Dana clearly outlines, it was not just the travel from one place to another that could produce "powerful" experiences for activists and garner press, but also the arrival at the place of sanctuary, where a worship service was often held immediately to welcome recipients who had arrived on the caravan. Also of particular note is how this strategy helped to spread the impact of the movement to communities that might not have had a faith community directly participating in the movement. Isabella, who was also a part of Dana's afore-mentioned caravan, points out that speaking at churches along the way was a major part of her experience: "Then from there we did a caravan that started in California through, you know, the Pacific. And we stopped at [strong emphasis] every [strong emphasis] little church throughout the Pacific—it was a beautiful trip until we arrived in Seattle." Through caravans "every little church" became the site of a *testimonio*.

In the sub-practice of caravans, the movement built organizational power through media exposure, dared the INS to act in public, and turned "every little church" into a potential site of transformation. They also took the lessons learned about provocation and movement building from caravans and applied them to the trials of sanctuary activists. As Coutin notes, the trials too were an occasion for "spectacle," setting up alternative rituals which celebrated convictions as a "conspiracy of love."[49] In addition, they organized marches where chanters echoed the refrain "If they are guilty, so am I!" creating a sense of community and solidarity with those accused of harboring fugitives.[50] In so doing, they attracted considerable media attention, added members to their movement, and subverted the legal rituals that convicted them.

Conversation Partners for MacIntyre: Pierre Bourdieu and Michel de Certeau

While MacIntyre remains the primary theoretical interlocutor for this project, much work has been done recently to bring the work of Pierre Bourdieu into dialogue with practical theology.[51] While other authors have

---

[49]Susan Bibler Coutin, "Smugglers or Samaritans in Tucson, Arizona: Producing and Contesting Legal Truth," *American Ethnologist* 22, no. 3 (1995): 561, https://doi.org/10.1525/ae.1995.22 .3.02a00050.

[50]Ibid., 561.

[51]In addition to Scharen's previously mentioned work, *Fieldwork in Theology*, see: Adam

taken the time to carefully outline the ways that Bourdieu might be useful for the field, I would like to focus on his account of power. Bourdieu's account of practice is not individual; rather, it is made social through his development of the concept of habitus, which he defines as: "a subjective but not individual system of internalised structures, schemes of perception, conception, and action common to all members of the same group or class."[52] While that definition is suitable, Loïc Wacquant offers a concise definition that explains the way that habitus ties the individual to the social: "the way society becomes deposited in persons in the form of lasting dispositions, or trained capacities and structured propensities to think, feel and act in determinant ways, which then guide them."[53] Thus, habitus plays a role similar to tradition and community in MacIntyre, but it offers a new vocabulary for thinking about the power of the social to determine practice, with a focus on the ways that we are often unknowingly formed to act in certain ways. Habitus thus gives us language for speaking about the ways that white supremacy is present even in laudable, compassionate religious practice. Indeed, recent scholarship on racial habitus indicates that this line of questioning is intriguing to scholars of race throughout many different disciplines.

Indeed, Bourdieu's notion of habitus is especially effective at addressing a thorny issue that is at the heart of this work: how could sanctuary activists be so effective at resisting the Reagan administration's policies, which they correctly noted were oppressive, and also relatively uncritical about the ways that white supremacy structured their interactions with recipients of sanctuary? That tension is alive in Bourdieu's work, where context has a direct impact on habitus through his notion of "field," which sheds light on how we may collaborate with power on some occasions and resist in others. While all fields are socially embedded, "the feel for the game"[54] that Bourdieu argues constitutes habitus helps explain why white sanctuary activists could clearly act against Reagan in subversive ways but struggled to understand their own power and the ways that they constituted the field of sanctuary for recipients and activists alike in racialized ways.

As I wrote about in the previous chapter, that tension is not merely a historical question; whiteness plays a prominent role in both old and new sanctuary movements. I found it easy as the pastor of sanctuary church to think about ways that sanctuary could be used to symbolically stand against Trumpism, but navigating ownership of stories was complex and racialized,

Hearlson, "The Promise of Pierre Bourdieu's Social Theories of Practice for the Field of Homiletics," *Practical Matters*, no. 6 (2014): 9–26.

[52]Bourdieu, *Outline of a Theory of Practice*, 86.

[53]Quoted in: Zander Navarro, "In Search of a Cultural Interpretation of Power: The Contribution of Pierre Bourdieu," *IDS Bulletin (Brighton. 1984)* 37, no. 6 (2006): 16, https://doi.org/10.1111/j.1759-5436.2006.tb00319.x.

[54]Bourdieu, Pierre, *Practical Reason: On the Theory of Action* (Stanford, CA: Stanford University Press, 1998), 76–7.

as I sought access to narratives for ostensibly good reasons. Put another way, sanctuary invites activists like myself and many of those interviewed in this book to think of their work as compassionate and good. Undoubtedly this narrative is true, but it also elides the ways that sanctuary workers have power and deploy it in their activism.

In addition to Bourdieu, the work of Michel de Certeau has become important to practical theological inquiry, while also representing a potential point of connection to sanctuary scholarship itself. Of particular import is de Certeau's delineation between strategy and tactics. Strategy is what is available to "a subject with will and power,"[55] while tactics are determined by actors without recourse to power. Such definitions might help elucidate how sanctuary might simultaneously be symbolic resistance by those without access to power and a system of power acting upon recipients. Sanctuary can be both, and as the next chapter shows, it was both.

While placing MacIntyre in conversation with Bourdieu and de Certeau makes for a more nuanced theory of practice, it also focuses the scholar's attention on the sort of actions that are most visible—that is on the actions of mostly white activists. Recipients appear and give *testimonios*, but they most often appear in this practice framework as those who are acted upon. In the next chapter, a new conversation partner will be added to these three—Judith Butler—whose work showcases how receiving sanctuary might not count as a practice, but is nevertheless a valuable place to analyze power, agency, and the double-bind of power that the Sanctuary Movement found itself in.

Conclusion

This chapter has situated the Sanctuary Movement as a practice by looking at several constitutive sub-practices that make up the practice of sanctuary. Crucially, some of the acts that are the most ingrained in the public's imagination, particularly the housing of recipients of sanctuary, are less central and more malleable than they might first appear. Indeed, the *testimonio* truly emerges as the central component of the practice of sanctuary in my analysis. Furthermore, my research demonstrates that recruitment of recipients and activists were both key aspects of the movement, even as activists cast themselves as responding to an emergency at the border. Caravans, too, emerge as a powerful sub-practice that ought to be considered for any robust analysis of sanctuary as a practice in the Sanctuary Movement.

Throughout this chapter, I demonstrate the tensions and debates over what constitutes excellence within the Sanctuary Movement These contestations, splits, and arguments within the Sanctuary Movement do not diminish

---

[55]Michel de Certeau, *The Practice of Everyday Life* (Berkeley, CA: University of California Press, 1984), 35–6.

sanctuary's status as a practice, however, since contestations over what constitutes right practice are inevitably a part of practice itself. MacIntyre adds to this observation through his formulation of tradition within his work, which occupies a central role, since "there is no standing ground, no place for enquiry . . . apart from that which is provided by some particular tradition or other."[56] Practice is inevitably bound up in a social fabric that renders practices intelligible to other individuals and communities, as it is only members of a community or tradition that can judge which internal goods and what excellence a practice ought to cultivate. However, tradition and community are not static in MacIntyre's understanding; they are constantly contested, remade in the fires of conflict: "a tradition is a conflict of interpretations of that tradition."[57] And this conflict makes itself apparent in many different aspects, "For it is not merely that different participants in a tradition disagree; they also disagree as to how to characterize their disagreements and as to how to resolve them."[58] Though the conflict and splits were painful for participants, the disagreements about the aims and focus of the movement were fundamentally contestations about the nature of the practice of sanctuary, particularly what constitutes "excellence" within that practice.[59]

My account reveals the extent to which sanctuary was a practice-in-formation during the Sanctuary Movement, shedding light on how practices take shape in the absence of a strong tradition. Biblical precedents notwithstanding, sanctuary activists created their own standards of excellence for the practice of sanctuary in real-time, prizing flexibility. At the same time, these nascent standards of excellence oftentimes came into conflict with one another, indicating unresolved tensions in the practice of sanctuary. In such a state of flux, white activists played the determining role in deciding what constituted excellence, even if they disagreed with one another. As such, they at times named issues of recipient agency as part of excellent practice, but they were also free to omit such standards. While practice-in-formation might conceivably augment the agency of recipients more than a practice with an established tradition, in the Sanctuary Movement, that was not the case.

In many ways, the Sanctuary Movement finds its corollary in the church. Both are simultaneously the field in which practice takes place and are developed in real-time by practitioners. In both cases, contestations over excellence in particular practices are a defining characteristic that might lead one to question whether one movement or church exists or several. As such, in looking at the Sanctuary Movement, I am not only striving to gain greater

---

[56]Alasdair MacIntyre, *Whose Justice? Which Rationality?* (Notre Dame, IN: University of Notre Dame Press, 1988), 350.
[57]MacIntyre, "Epistemological Crises, Dramatic Narrative, and the Philosophy of Science," 11.
[58]Ibid., 11–12.
[59]Ibid., 11.

clarity about a social movement, but I am also endeavoring to gain a greater ecclesiological understanding of the ways that practice enables and restricts agency.

Practice is a useful category for thinking about the movement, showcasing how activists constructed a movement and utilized a practice to highlight humanitarian and public policy crises through the offering of sanctuary to recipients. In addition, from a practical theological perspective, situating sanctuary as a practice opens new avenues for practical theological reflection, a project I turn to in Chapter 4. However, while situating sanctuary as a practice is useful for analyzing the actions of white, liberal, religious activists, it leaves critical questions unanswered and perspectives unheard. As a theoretical framework, practice is extraordinarily good at analyzing the offering of sanctuary, but it is a poor framework for considering the reception of sanctuary. In MacIntyre's examples of practice, it is notable that games between people are considered along with tasks, but in both of these cases, the power relationship is either equal or nonexistent. What is one to do when power is a salient category, such as when there are vast disparities in power between parties? Obviously, sanctuary is such a case and the practice framework does a suitable job of surfacing how the shaping of standards of excellence was taken on by the powerful. However, it crucially leaves the question of how to address such questions of power unanswered, and utilizing such a framework exclusively only serves to reify the power imbalances and objectification of recipients that the Sanctuary Movement perpetuated in its quest for justice. These limitations do not render practice useless as a theoretical framework, but they do mean that something will have to be added to MacIntyre's practice theory in order to account for power and the recipient perspective. In doing so, a possibility emerges not only for analyzing the agency of recipients in the movement, but for doing theoretical analysis that aids the articulation of agencies in sanctuary and other social movements with power imbalances, a task I turn to in Chapter 3.

Theological *Excursus*: On the Possibility of Testimony

Testimony or witness plays a key role in some Christian traditions, whereby the one who testifies asserts the active will of God in their personal narrative, as well as in the Sanctuary Movement. While the process of testimony might seem relatively straightforward, my research has shown that it simultaneously highlights and obscures power differentials between speaker and hearer. It is tempting to view the speaker as possessing some power. After all, they might command the attention of a room, and attention might be focused on them. However, in the Sanctuary Movement, a far more complex dynamic arose in which the hearer played a large role in shaping acceptable testimony, while recipients strove for agency on the edges of that constriction. Thinking about testimony is a showcase of how accounts of power or the lack thereof shape theological concepts. If MacIntyre's theory of practice lacks an account of power and therefore fails to account for some key aspects of the movement, accounts of testimony are similarly stymied if they fail to consider power as a central category.

One of the great thinkers on religious testimony is Paul Ricoeur, who offered his analysis of the relationship between the speaker and hearer of religious testimony this way:

> Testimony is a dual relation: there is the one who testifies and the one who hears the testimony. The witness has seen, but the one who receives his testimony has not seen but hears. It is only by hearing the testimony that he can believe or not believe in the reality of the facts that the witness reports. Testimony as story is thus found in an intermediary position between a statement made by a person and belief assumed by another on the faith of the testimony of the first.[60]

In this complex web, the dialectic of speaker and hearer emerges, but a dialectic does not presuppose equality between the subject positions. In Ricoeur's thinking, testimony is only testimony if it is "used to support a judgment"; it is not "the mere recording of facts."[61] As such, the hearer is in a key role for judging the applicability and trustworthiness of the facts presented. One reader of Ricoeur's hermeneutics of testimony frames such a relationship as an acknowledged "asymmetry" between the two parties in which "the witness knows something the audience does not" but that the audience "invert[s]" this power dynamic by acting as a judge of the "unresolved questions" or "dispute."[62] Due to the power of the audience to settle the dispute, testimony is linked to death and the risking of it: "the witness is the man who is identified with the just cause which the crowd and the great hate and who, for this just cause, risks his life."[63]

Ricoeur's analysis of the dispute, the dialectic between the hearer and testifier, and the asymmetry between the two are all powerful frameworks for considering testimony. However, they fail to attend to a key issue—there is no pre-contextual testifying subject. Drawing on the work of Pamala Sue Anderson, Jacob D. Meyers writes, "No attention is paid, for instance, to the myriad ways that gender, sexuality, race, ethnicity, class, or ability shape

---

[60]Paul Ricoeur, "The Hermeneutics of Testimony," in *Essays on Biblical interpretation*, ed. Lewis Seymour Mudge (Philadelphia, PA: Fortress Press, 1980), 123.
[61]Ibid., 124.
[62]Esteban Lythgoe, "Ricoeur's Concept of Testimony," *Analetica Hermeneutica* 3 (2011): 3.
[63]Ricoeur, "The Hermeneutics of Testimony," 129.

the witness's testimony and its reception."[64] The lack of such locatedness obscures the differences in power that threatens to shut out the possibility of testimony entirely. While testifying subjects might speak, can they be heard?[65] As I analyze in-depth in Chapter 3, the testifying subjects of the movement were only able to be heard as refugees, reciting their trauma, because white activists could not hear them any other way.

There are more productive ways of conceiving the relationship between testifier and audience than Ricoeur presents. For example, the production of the testifying subject is fundamentally linked to the hearer in Judith Butler's work in *Giving an Account of Oneself*[66] as well as *Excitable Speech*.[67] The key to the usefulness of such accounts is the way that they construct a subjectivity in relationship that analyzes and reveals the contours of power in speech acts like testimony. Only an account that acknowledges the struggles for agency within the testimonial speech act as well as the fact that "'I' has no story of its own that is not also the story of a relation—or set of relations—to a set of norms," can delineate the limits and possibilities of testimony.[68]

The possibilities for testimony are also linked to the possibilities for self-knowledge. Ricoeur notes that testimony is not simply a simple speech act—"[it] is the action itself as it attests outside of himself, to the interior man, to his conviction, to his faith."[69] Importantly, the fundamental ground of testimony is found in desire and lack, being made possible by the twin

---

[64]Jacob D. Myers, "Bearing Witness to God: Ricoeur and the Practice of Religious Testimony," *Literature & Theology* 34, no. 4 (2020): 401, https://doi.org/10.1093/litthe/fraa018.

[65]In many ways this book and this specific argument is indebted to Gayatri Chakravorty Spivak's 1999 version of "Can the Subaltern Speak?" in which she revises her 1988 assertion to say that the subject of her writing "*has* spoken in some way," but that "all speaking, even seemingly the most immediate, entails a distanced decipherment by another, which is, at best, an interception. That is what speaking is." Hearing, decipherment, and speaking are inexorably linked. Gayatri Chakravorty Spivak, "Can the Subaltern Speak?," in *Can the Subaltern Speak? Reflections on the History of an Idea*, ed. Rosalind Morris (New York: Columbia University Press, 2010).

[66]"If I give an account of myself in response to such a query, I am implicated in a relation to the other before whom and to whom I speak. Thus, I come into being as a reflexive subject in the context of establishing a narrative account of myself when I am spoken to by someone and prompted to address myself to the one who addresses me." Judith Butler, *Giving an Account of Oneself* (New York: Fordham University Press, 2005), 15.

[67]"The listener is understood to occupy a social position or to have become synonymous with that position, and social positions themselves are understood to be situated in a static and hierarchical relation to one another. By virtue of the social position he or she occupies, then, the listener is injured as a consequence of that utterance. The utterance also enjoins the subject to reoccupy a subordinate social position. According to this view, such speech reinvokes and reinscribes a structural relation of domination, and constitutes the linguistic occasion for the reconstitution of that structural domination." Judith Butler, *Excitable Speech: A Politics of the Performative* (New York: Routledge, 1997), 18.

[68]Butler, *Giving an Account of Oneself*, 8.

[69]Ricoeur, "The Hermeneutics of Testimony," 130.

notions of original affirmation and *dépouillement* (divestment): "the act which accomplishes the negation of the limitations which effect individual destiny. It is a divestment (*dépouillement*). It is by this "divestment' that reflection is brought to the encounter with the contingent signs that the absolute, in its generosity, allows itself to appear."[70] As such, testimony is always "dual," comprising of "internal testimony."[71] Ricoeur proposes the self as the site where the absolute can be haltingly conveyed, even as this self remains hidden and obscured, necessitating its constant renewal as "indefinitely inaugural."[72] Thus, self-opacity, as in Butler's work does not obscure the possibility of testimony, or in her case ethical action, but instead acts as the grounding of its possibility. As one reader of Ricoeur puts it, "Lack is thus the philosophical ground upon which God-talk purportedly rests."[73]

My research questions the extent to which testimony can be understood outside power relations, indeed whether it is possible at all. Yet, the possibility of testimony is more resilient than these challenges. Even as I have lingering doubts, there is a rich body of Latinx literature that explicitly claims the *testimonio* as not only possible[74] but a generative site of resistance.[75] As Emma Haydée Fuentes and Manuel Alejandro Pérez forcefully articulate, "our stories are our sanctuary."[76] Such statements give me pause and hope, suggesting that testimony might be not only possible but necessary, pushing me to articulate what the conditions for testimony might be.

Theological consideration of testimony means that there are not just two parties, but three—God, the testifier, and the listener—and all powerfully shape the subjectivities of one another. Testimony might come from an individual, but my research has demonstrated the complex ways that the audience shapes and constrains the testifier's subjectivity. Testifiers might command attention, but in shaping what counts for acceptable testimony, they are not at the center of the event. Similarly, the testifier fundamentally shapes the audience's experiences of God,[77] who is revealed not in the recounting of facts, but in a

---

[70]Ibid., 120.
[71]Ibid., 142.
[72]Ibid., 120.
[73]Myers, "Bearing Witness to God: Ricoeur and the Practice of Religious Testimony," 394.
[74]See: Group Latina Feminist, *Telling to Live: Latina Feminist Testimonios* (Durham, NC: Duke University Press, 2001).
[75]See: Dolores Delgado Bernal, Rebeca Burciaga, and Judith Flores Carmona, *Chicana/Latina Testimonios as Pedagogical, Methodological, and Activist Approaches to Social Justice* (New York: Routledge, 2016).
[76]Emma Haydée Fuentes and Manuel Alejandro Pérez, "Our Stories are our Sanctuary: Testimony as a Sacred of Belonging," *Association of Mexican American Educators Journal* 10, no. 2 (2016): 1–15.
[77]"When a narrative is shared, listeners become part of the story and view the story as their own. Shared religious identity emerges when listeners identify themselves with the testifier and view who they are through their own interpretations of a shared testimonial narrative." Gabriel

telling of an experience, an account fundamentally shaped by the lack or the opacity of the self. God's power and activity are constrained by the testifier's ability to speak, perhaps mirroring Dorothee Sölle's contention that God needs "friends" in order to come into being.[78] At the same time, the possibility of testimony is not to be taken for granted—the entire act takes shape through grace, an offering of the capacity for self-revelation and even an account of God's activity in the world. In such a schema there is no one actor at the center, in many ways mirroring Jacob D. Meyers idea of moving beyond the focus of the speaking subject in testimony and toward "the in-between us of discourse" that might "open up space for the hearer to bear witness to God."[79] That "in-between us of discourse" is where the possibilities and limits of testimony are most clearly apprehended.

But the question of how to practice testimony in ways that do not merely reinscribe hierarchies, but instead allow something of God to be said remains unaddressed. Tamsin Jones articulates perhaps the best view of the potential and tenuousness of witnessing, which she grounds in the "discipline of cultivating hope," which eschews the twin dangers of quietism and the "idolatry" of "claim[ing] full control to dictate what is the object we hope for."[80] For Jones, witnessing is an act that grounds that hope, because of its account of subjectivity and openness to being "undone" and "remade in response":[81]

> Witnessing involves the act of cultivating an ability to respond to radical otherness without requiring it to be something I recognize first, in a way, moreover, that not only constitutes my own subjectivity, but which must simultaneously promote the ability of others to likewise respond. It also involves ceaselessly seeking the truth while acknowledging that such a truth will never be "mine"—can never be arrived at or possessed by me alone. Such an activity both requires and enacts a hope that must be active, non-teleological, open, responsive, and political.[82]

If there is hope for testimony as a practice is in Jones' vision of the capacity to respond to testimony that is unrecognizable. Put another way, the recipients

---

Faimau, "Religious Testimonial Narratives and Social Construction of Identity: Insights from Prophetic Ministries in Botswana," *Cogent Social Sciences* 3, no. 1 (2017): 13, https://doi.org /10.1080/23311886.2017.1356620.

[78]Dorothee Sölle, *Theology for Skeptics: Reflections on God* (Minneapolis, MN: Fortress Press, 1995), 16.

[79]Myers, "Bearing Witness to God: Ricoeur and the Practice of Religious Testimony," 402.

[80]Tamsin Jones, "Bearing Witness: Hope for the Unseen," *Political Theology: The Journal of Christian Socialism* 17, no. 2 (2016): 143, 38, https://doi.org/10.1080/1462317X.2016 .1161300.

[81]Ibid., 148.

[82]Ibid., 143.

of sanctuary that I interviewed testified to violence and trauma. In being cast as refugees, they were recognizable to mostly white activists, but this was not the extent of their identities. But the subjectivity of the testifier is not only shaped by the audience but also by the limitations of language and self-knowledge: "one speaks, all the while knowing that the narrative offered inevitably does violence to the original event. But one speaks, nonetheless, because one must."[83] Thus, the testifier, especially one testifying to traumatic acts, is not the free subject that is sometimes imagined in the act of testimony.

Even within such limitations, testimony still proved generative for hearers in the movement. In hearing testimony that contradicted news reports and government statements about Central America, they experienced an authentic revelation that caused many white activists to engage in activism and solidarity. Hearers of testimony in the Sanctuary Movement oftentimes underwent affective changes that ranged from sympathy to feelings of responsibility, as they understood that the United States had supported and financed the regimes that caused such suffering for recipients. Such shifts, even under the limited scope for what counted as testimony in the movement, demonstrate the revelatory vitality and possibilities of testimony that many experienced as being grounded in religious belief.

For listeners, an openness to counter-hegemonic testimony is the essential grounding of testimony, opening a conception of the practice that places the subjectivities of the speaker, listener, and God in a mutually constitutive relationship with one another. Thus, testimony rests on unstable ground, but that ground can cultivate the practice of hope. I would argue such hope is unfounded unless, considering God's role in testimony, we ground testimony in pneumatology. This seems natural, as the Holy Spirit and testimony have long been linked, particularly in the Pentecostal tradition. In Mayra Rivera's analysis of haunting and memory, the ghosts "exceed the conventional boundaries of theological discourse" just as dangerous memories possess "plurality and irreducible ambiguity."[84] In such a view the Holy Ghost grounds the possibility of witness/testimony by "incit[ing] those still alive to become witnesses," as a "Spirit of truth that blows from the past, appearing occasionally as/in spectral bodies to incite memory and enliven hope."[85] It is this Ghost that "dance[s] in the faults of history," and without it, there is no possibility for witnessing and therefore "no God."[86] My account of testimony rests on Rivera's multi-vocal conception of the Holy Ghost, which is irreducible to any one narrative. In the hauntings of memory, testimony

[83]Tamsin Jones, "Traumatized Subjects: Continental Philosophy of Religion and the Ethics of Alterity," *The Journal of Religion* 94, no. 2 (2014): 157, https://doi.org/10.1086/674952.
[84]Mayra Rivera, "Ghostly Encounters: Spirits, Memory, and the Holy Ghost," in *Planetary Loves: Spivak, Postcoloniality, and Theology*, ed. Stephen D. Moore and Mayra Rivera (New York: Fordham University Press, 2010), 132, 33.
[85]Ibid., 134.
[86]Ibid.

is possible through the work of the divine and perhaps other ghosts, as Rivera points out. Without such hauntings, testimony is impossible, leading only to the confirmation of previously held beliefs—the idolatry of hope that Jones critiques. Worse, it might simply reinscribe the very systems of power and oppression that the testifier *and the audience* wish to confront.[87] In a theological view of testimony, pneumatology must join hope as the fundamental grounding of testimony's possibility. Otherwise, not only testimony, but revelation, and God's presence in the world of the living fails to obtain.

In the Sanctuary Movement, the concept and tenuous possibility of testimony loom large. Recipients were expected to recount their experiences, so as to move their largely white audiences to reject what they heard in the news and trust a personal account. In doing so, trauma was placed at the center of narratives. Of course, this makes sense, since the Reagan administration denied that there was any trauma at all beyond the "economic" in El Salvador and Guatemala. In doing so, they drew on the concept of religious testimony or witness, in which a person speaks of the redemptive work of God in personal terms, and courtroom testimony, in which a witness shares information in order to sway a verdict. In centering recipient narratives through the *testimonio*, white activists claimed to place recipients at the center of the movement, but the bounds of acceptable testimony were limited. As I explore thoroughly in this chapter and Chapter 3, recipients were not in charge of their narratives. In order to be heard, they had to express themselves as refugees, citing their trauma. Such limitations point to the tenuous nature of testimony, highlighting power as a central category for consideration in the analysis of testimony. But they do not foreclose its possibility entirely. In grounding an account of testimony in Tamsin Jones' conception of hope, I articulate a path forward for considering the three actors in testimony—the testifier, the listener, and God. In the end, if testimony is possible, that possibility rests in the Holy Spirit. In Rivera's words, "May we pray to be haunted."[88]

---

[87]This is a very real issue. Lyon and Olson, writing from a rhetoric analysis perspective, note "challenges in using language and symbols to transform cultures in life-enhancing ways, including witnessing and testifying, because the systems of representation reflect the histories of domination and power within them." Arabella Lyon and Lester C. Olson, "Special Issue on Human Rights Rhetoric: Traditions of Testifying and Witnessing," *Rhetoric Society Quarterly* 41, no. 3 (2011), http://www.jstor.org.ezp-prod1.hul.harvard.edu/stable/23064463.
[88]Rivera, "Ghostly Encounters: Spirits, Memory, and the Holy Ghost," 135.

3

Becoming Refugees

Human Rights Discourse and Whiteness

The Sanctuary Movement of the 1980s is most commonly depicted in media and some academic works as a religious and political movement that worked to protect refugees fleeing Central America by offering them physical sanctuary. While not incorrect, these characterizations downplay or omit the movement's anti-interventionist, anti-imperialist, and anti-Reagan activism, which tied the practice of physical sanctuary to substantive political, moral, and religious critiques of American foreign policy, as well as the activism, agency, and subjectivity of recipients of sanctuary. As I spoke with numerous recipients of sanctuary, the complexity of refugee identity took centerstage. In fleeing from persecution, recipients qualified as refugees, but that was not the entirety of their story. Or rather, for those recipients that identified as refugees, refugee identity was not apolitical and did not preclude activism in one's country of origin or in the United States. As this chapter demonstrates, many recipients of sanctuary saw themselves as activists in their own right, in many cases utilizing the Sanctuary Movement as a platform for continuing their political work in their country of origin. These conflicting characterizations led to considerable tension between white activists and recipients, as well as within the movement. One of the places where this tension comes into the clearest focus is in the different ways that activists and recipients make use of sanctuary human rights discourse.

In this chapter, I argue that both activists and recipients of sanctuary in the Sanctuary Movement of the 1980s utilized human rights discourse and that differences in their conceptualization of the limits and power of human rights reveal different values, conceptualizations of agency, and analyses of power. In short, I argue that those conceptualizations were racialized, with white, American sanctuary workers identifying human rights that can largely be found in the United States Bill of Rights. Utilizing Judith Butler's concepts of subjectivity, power, and agency as a lens for viewing this tension between refugee and activist identity, I argue that the recipients' rejection and complexification of refugee identity and utilization of an expansive definition of human rights constitute Butlerian agency, which she defines as "the assumption of a purpose unintended by power."[1] In doing so, I illustrate the ways that practical theology's focus on practice as a category fails to account for the dynamic at work in the Sanctuary Movement, suggesting that a subjectivity framework might allow for assiduous attention to power, which will allow for a more thorough practical theological investigation of movements like the Sanctuary Movement.

Constructing Refugee Identity

The recipients I interviewed often felt pressured to participate in this particular type of narrativization and refugee identity, leading Isabella to characterize the desired response of white religious liberals as "oh *pobracito*! (poor little thing)." Indeed, Gloria recounts the dynamic between the mostly white audience and the recipient in this way: "There were times I felt that the more I cried the better it was because people felt sorry and they would donate money to our sanctuary . . . they just wanted me to present as a victim. A woman who had lost her children and had it not been for sanctuary I would have been killed." The pressure to perform an affective response through crying, coupled with pressure to focus on her losses, illustrates well how refugee identity, with its built-in definition of persecution and fear, restricted other forms of agency for recipients of sanctuary. It is worth noting that in my interviews, recipients of sanctuary would often spend the first several minutes of conversation recounting their well-rehearsed trauma narratives before the conversation moved to other topics, suggesting that recipients expected my interest as a researcher to be primarily centered on those same narratives. It is also important to note that there were also times when recipients themselves identified as a refugee in order to advance their own goals. Refugee identity excludes much of the power of activist roles in recipients' home countries and the United States, but adopting it can be a useful strategy for furthering that same activism.

In order to fully appreciate the Sanctuary Movement's construction of refugee identity, a comparison to its sister movement, the Central American Solidary Movement, is apt. The Central American Solidarity movement linked Central American (mostly Salvadoran and Nicaraguan) exiles and activists

---

[1]Butler, *The Psychic Life of Power: Theories in Subjection*, 11.

with their North American counterparts. It is important to note that within this movement, Central Americans wielded considerable agency, autonomy, and influence. Indeed, the solidarity movement began in the 1970s, with the formation of El Comité Cívico pro Nicaragua en los Estados Unidos (Civic Committee for Nicaragua in the United States) and El Comité de Salvadoreños Progresistas (Committee of Progressive Salvadorans).[2] Later, especially in the 1980s, white, North American activists became involved in the already extant work of Central Americans.[3] This involvement could also take on a religious character, especially with regard to the Committee In Solidarity with the People of El Salvador (CISPES). In my research, activists that were involved with solidarity organizations traced their involvement to religious and political concern over the assassination of Archbishop Oscar Romero on March 24, 1980, and the rape and murder of four American churchwomen in El Salvador on December 2, 1980. In these collaborative, activist spaces, Central Americans were the driving force behind activism, and their presence in high-visibility leadership roles was natural. For instance, Members of El Comité de Salvadoreños Progresistas, a student-led organization, were the first to organize a march aimed at raising awareness of human rights violations in El Salvador, and they engaged in high-profile activities like the occupation of the Salvadoran consulate.[4] Why then were recipients of sanctuary characterized most often as refugees, when one of the primary collaborators of the Sanctuary Movement favored an activist identity? And when El Comité de Salvadoreños Progresistas developed the strategy of Central Americans forming connections with religious communities for solidarity, why did the Sanctuary Movement become most firmly associated with religious activism on Central American issues?[5]

---

[2]Emily K. Hobson, "Central American Solidarity Movement," in *Global Encyclopedia of Lesbian, Gay, Bisexual, Transgender, and Queer (LGBTQ) History*, ed. Howard Chiang et al. (Farmington Hills, MI: Charles Scribner's Sons, 2019), 310.

[3]For a discussion of how activists became involved in Central American Solidarity work, including ample discussion of religious activism motivated by past engagement with mission work, see: Sharon Erickson Nepstad, *Convictions of the Soul: Religion, Culture, and Agency in the Central America Solidarity Movement* (Oxford, New York: Oxford University Press, 2004).

[4]Jessica Lavariega Monforti, *Latinos in the American Political System: An Encyclopedia of Latinos as Voters, Candidates, and Office Holders* (Santa Barbara, CA: ABC-CLIO, 2019), 108.

[5]"It is important to note that Salvadoreños Progresistas pioneered the strategy of immigrants approaching members of religious organizations to collaborate with them in an effort to mobilize the religious community, which other Salvadoran immigrant organizations would use to launch the movement. In 1981, following this strategy, members of the Santana Chirino Amaya Refugee Committee and the Southern California Ecumenical Council came together in Los Angeles to create El Rescate. The organization's stated mission was "to respond with free legal and social services to the mass influx of refugees fleeing the war in El Salvador." Perla Hector and Coutin Susan Bibler, "Legacies and Origins of the 1980s US—Central American Sanctuary Movement," *Refuge: Canada's Journal on Refugees* 26, no. 1 (October 08, 2010): 11, https://doi.org/10.25071/1920-7336.30602, https://refuge.journals.yorku.ca/index.php/refuge/article/view/30602.

While the answer to that question is multifaceted, the construction of refugee identity plays a pivotal role in answering both questions. Casting sanctuary recipients as refugees, as opposed to activists, accomplished several important goals. First, refugee identity opened up a matrix of theological and political justifications for the Sanctuary Movement, allowing activists to claim that their work was both required by God and a response to the federal government's failure to uphold international law. In a public letter to Attorney General William French Smith informing the government of Southside Presbyterian's declaration of sanctuary, John Fife stated:

> We take this action because we believe the current policy and practice of the United States government with regard to Central American refugees is illegal and immoral. We believe our government is in violation of the 1980 Refugee Act and international law by continuing to arrest, detain, and forcibly return refugees to the terror persecution, and murder in El Salvador and Guatemala.[6]

In the same letter to the attorney general, Fife asserted the congregation's "God-given right to aid anyone fleeing persecution and murder," and called the government's position "immoral" in addition to "illegal," making it clear that the offering of sanctuary was required due to "obedience from God."[7] The blending of legal, moral, and religious frameworks would become a hallmark of sanctuary activism, and to a large degree refugee identity is what allowed such a seamless fusion of diverse ethical frameworks to take place. By portraying recipients as refugees fleeing human rights violations, scriptural injunctions could be cited next to the requirements of conscience and legal frameworks. Indeed, when the sanctuary declarations of many faith communities are analyzed, one is immediately struck by the emphasis placed on legal arguments for sanctuary. While the harboring of recipients of sanctuary was illegal, activists argued it was not immoral, and they instead charged the government with violating its own laws by refusing to grant asylum to those fleeing US-backed Central American regimes.

Second, activists made a strategic decision that they could garner more support from religious, white North Americans by appealing to both their conscience and their narratives of American exceptionalism. Such exceptionalism was always a double move, as Sanctuary Movement activists possessed a razor-sharp analysis of America's failings while also holding out hope for the country to live up to its ideals. Consider John Fife's quote earlier, where he holds the government responsible for its failure to enforce its own

---

[6]Quoted in: John Fife, "From the Sanctuary Movement to No More Deaths: The Challenge to Communities of Faith," in *Religious and Ethical Perspectives on Global Migration*, ed. Elizabeth W. Collier and Charles R. Strain (Lanham, MD: Lexington Books, 2014), 259–60.
[7]Ibid.

laws, but America is also a country for people to flee *to*, not from. This dynamic of critical exceptionalism can be seen from the words of Rachel, who argued that recipients were fleeing countries where they "didn't have rights. They were just abused," while the United States was in the position to "do something about it," but was behaving "atrocious[ly]" in its failure to protect refugees. Perla Hector and Coutin Susan Bibler describe the strategic diminishment of Central American activists in this way:

> Central Americans' organizing practices also had to be adapted to dominant US norms, values, and perceptions of how North Americans saw themselves and saw Third World "others." (In essence, these practices had to appeal to liberal ideals.) The narrative con- struct of the "refugee" met these needs by simultaneously drawing on shared Judeo-Christian traditions regarding exile, oppression, and refuge while also directing political attention to human rights abuses in Central America and to Salvadoran and Guatemalan immigrants' need for safe haven.[8]

Situating themselves within white, religious liberal frameworks, recipients adopted a nonthreatening identity in order to engage in the crucial consciousness-raising work they endeavored to do. By forming relationships and bonds, and steadfastly refuting the dominant red-baiting narrative around their country's situation, sanctuary recipients hoped to move communities to the pivotal work of solidarity that they felt called to.

In the recipients and activists that I interviewed, there was a sense that refugee identity allowed bonds to form during an initial period of education that was required before the next step of activism or solidarity could be undertaken. For instance, six times in my interviews, activists and recipients noted that upon the arrival of recipients to a house of worship, the people of that faith community could not locate Guatemala or El Salvador on a map. However, after a period of time within a faith community, most reported that the bonds that developed between a sanctuary church and recipients helped connect many North Americans to solidarity work. Anibal, an indigenous Guatemalan extensively involved with Christian Base Communities in his home country, illustrated this interweaving of education, refugee identity, and deft navigation of allegations of Communist influence that comprised a part of many recipient's experiences:

> It was so important, the role of the US was so key and so many of the people didn't know anything. Some didn't even know where Guatemala was, or let alone how many indigenous there were. Through the testimony we did a lot of educating, and we shared a lot of what was happening in

---

[8]Hector and Susan Bibler, "Legacies and Origins of the 1980s US—Central American Sanctuary Movement," 12.

Guatemala. . . . We would encounter people who were counter to us, who would say we were tools of Russia or communists. . . . We said, "I don't know about communism—that didn't mean much to us. That was for intellectuals. We didn't have any Russians in Guatemala. . . . It was not a part of our reality.

In rejecting the influence of formal Communist parties, Anibal skillfully makes room for endemic leftist commitments in his community without being linked to America's Cold War adversary. Anibal's adoption of a refugee identity is perhaps uniquely successful, as he maintains a strong connection to his sanctuary community to this day, lives in community with members of the church, and has successfully led hundreds of North Americans on accompaniment trips and delegations to learn more about Guatemala. While much of his activism and religious training in his country of origin was downplayed, his *testimonio* as a refugee allowed for robust connections that might not have otherwise formed. This also demonstrates a complexity that can be missed—one of the ways that recipients were able to navigate the constraints of sanctuary was by taking on refugee identity, even if it did not encompass the entirety of their experience. Constructions of refugee identity were sometimes shared endeavors that worked for both parties, but as Anibal's narrative makes clear, that identity was not freely chosen but came about as the limitations of the host community became apparent. Even so, such examples demonstrate the extent to which refugee identity could be adopted as part of political activism.

While the construction of refugee identity was effective because it did not immediately challenge white, liberal expectations, it also led to three aspects that would come to characterize the Sanctuary Movement within the matrix of Central American Solidarity work: near-complete absence of recipients from formal leadership roles within the movement, "an extremely reduced and distorted form of agency," for recipients as they occupied the role of victim, and power dynamic imbalances that sometimes resulted in undesirable outcomes for both activists and recipients.[9] As Perla and Coutin argue, "certain relationships within the sanctuary movement were celebrated, while others were hidden," which meant that sanctuary recipients had to be "willing to stay quiet, become invisible, or abstain from taking on certain leadership roles in the movement, while, for the sake of achieving their and the movement's objectives, embracing identities that, to some, implied weakness or passivity, such as "refugees" or 'victims.'"[10]

---

[9]Simon Behrman, "Accidents, Agency and Asylum: Constructing the Refugee Subject," *Law and Critique* 25, no. 3 (2014): 249, https://doi.org/10.1007/s10978-014-9140-x.
[10]Hector and Susan Bibler, "Legacies and Origins of the 1980s US—Central American Sanctuary Movement," 9.

When asked about formal leadership for recipients within the Sanctuary Movement, many activists talked about meetings between sanctuary committees and recipients to determine housing, the giving of *testimonios*, and other activities within the host faith community. One activist noted that sanctuary recipients in the Chicago network attended meetings that gathered sanctuary communities in the Chicagoland area, but clarified that the council's leadership was comprised of white activists. Oftentimes, the leadership roles that were assumed by the recipients I spoke to were outside the Sanctuary Movement, within the networks of Central American Solidarity organizations, within established immigrant organizations, or within organizations that they themselves founded. For instance, two recipients from Guatemala (one indigenous and one not) that I interviewed started marimba groups focused on music-making, community, and children's education.[11] Even so, one recipient noted that their status as a sanctuary recipient placed them on the outside of many opportunities within local community groups, showing that even outside of the Sanctuary Movement, sanctuary status served as a marker of difference that could potentially lead to difficulty forming relationships and entering leadership roles.[12]

Focusing on recipients of sanctuary as refugees also led to what legal scholar Simon Behrman called "an extremely reduced and distorted form of agency," which is primarily derived from how the 1951 UN Refugee Convention defines refugee status with regard to persecution and victimhood. Indeed, Behrman argues that this grounding is "the most problematic" with regard to refugee agency.[13] Indeed, Serin D. Houston and Charlotte Morse demonstrate how the Sanctuary Movement focused on the trauma and persecution narratives of recipients to garner sympathy and support and help white, liberal activists make meaning: "Stories of extraordinary horror and violence inspired support for and grew the movement . . . migrants' stories of extraordinary hardship were often mobilized to give US citizens a chance to deepen their faiths."[14] Through repetition, trauma narratives

---

[11]For a detailed account of the importance of the marimba and music-making practices among Maya in the United States, see: Batz Giovanni, "Maya Cultural Resistance in Los Angeles: The Recovery of Identity and Culture among Maya Youth," *Latin American Perspectives* 41, no. 3 (2014), https://doi.org/10.1177/0094582X14531727.

[12]Gloria: "There was another family in sanctuary in [redacted], then two more, and then there was another family that was in [redacted] Church and you know, it was interesting because most of the Guatemalans in [redacted] were not in sanctuary. It was true they considered us to be privileged because we were in sanctuary and had all kinds of support; it was the truth. There was this little—it was like, for them, 'oh yeah, sanctuary,' [recipient rolls her eyes] but when those who were in sanctuary got together we were the only ones we could trust because we had experiences that a lot of people didn't have and we understood each other."

[13]Behrman, "Accidents, Agency and Asylum: Constructing the Refugee Subject," 249, 51.

[14]Serin D. Houston and Charlotte Morse, "The Ordinary and Extraordinary: Producing Migrant Inclusion and Exclusion in US Sanctuary Movements," *Studies in Social Justice* 11, no. 1 (2017): 35, 32, https://doi.org/10.26522/ssj.v11i1.1081.

came to be a key marker of a recipient's suitability for sanctuary, and public support was dependent on the recipient's ability to move white religious Americans.[15]

It was through the construction of refugee identity that the narratives and experiences of recipients could become legible. Indeed, the central practice of sanctuary—the offering of material aid and housing to recipients— reinforced familiar power dynamics to white activists and helped them relate to recipients using well-worn frameworks. The problem is that in privileging these stories of trauma that, as I have shown, are constitutive of refugee status, other identities—activist, indigenous, and non-traditional-Christian—were pushed to the background, unseen by activists who focused with laser precision on identities that would stir sympathy. Even those in the Chicago Religious Task Force on Central America, who provided a wider range of possibilities for recipient agency shaped that agency in ways that would render them legible and therefore useful to their constituencies. In a movement shaped by critical exceptionalism, the most desired recipient was one who could simultaneously share the trauma of their story in the *testimonio*, while highlighting the singular failures of the Reagan administration. In doing so, an idealized America would be preserved as a place where recipients could flee to, even as it was indicted as the cause of their persecution. Indeed, this argument is born out in a case presented by Ann Crittenden in her work, *Sanctuary*, in which she documents two Mayan teenagers who were turned away by the Chicago Religious Task Force on Central America for having "had no understanding of the political conflict in Central America."[16] The final judgment in the letter sent to Tucson was that they "were therefore not useful."[17] They were placed on a bus to Tucson and never seen again, having been presumably detained en route to their destination.

The Mayan teenagers of this story would likely have been able to formulate a powerful critique of imperialism, but it was not the type of imperialism that sanctuary activists were focused on. As Maria Vargas argues, "As this story shows, the flow of indigenous marked bodies and targets of state violence continues to embody unintelligible and unrelatable violence through the eyes of a white American faith-based audience."[18] Indeed, the Mayan teenagers were rendered illegible in more than one sense, as the Mayan teenagers did not speak Spanish, and the requirement of specialized translation support rendered their participation more difficult. Moreover, as I show in this chapter, indigenous recipients also struggled to

---

[15]Ibid., 35.
[16]Crittenden, *Sanctuary: A Story of American Conscience and the Law in Collision*, 91.
[17]Ibid.
[18]Vargas, "Ghostly Others: Limiting Constructions of Deserving Subjects in Asylum Claims and Sanctuary Protection," 83.

interject their critiques of colonialism alongside critiques of US imperialism. Such framings produced tension with activists, who wanted recipients to remain focused on the issues they found most resonant. In addition, the explicit framing of usefulness here is telling. Recipients needed to have the right story and "understanding" in order to be useful to the movement. The fear that people of faith in the movement might make the wrong meaning and therefore practice the wrong solidarity led to an instrumentalization of recipients, even when they were able to escape the orbit of refugee identity. Recipients were expected to chronicle their trauma narratives in *testimonios*, form connections with participants in faith communities, inspire solidarity, and produce moments of religious enlightenment[19] and conversion among white activists, but they had to do so according to a script that restricted their agency. To do anything else would invite conflict or charges of not "understanding" the movement or even their own country's political situation.

Thus, to answer the two questions posed at the start of this section, one can say that the cultivation of refugee identity by the Sanctuary Movement was a strategic decision designed to move a religious audience in the United States to take action—donate money, join a delegation, pressure elected leaders, make public statements, etc. Likewise, the characterization of recipients as refugees created the conditions for religious communities to participate in solidarity work in great numbers, while being relatively insulated from power-sharing and challenge, thus making the Sanctuary Movement the best-known example of religious solidarity with the people of Central America.[20] The refugee framework with its attendant power dynamics was a comfortable space for clergy and their communities of faith, and this allowed the forming of connections that would deliver many of the successes of the movement.

In hearing the trauma of recipient *testimonios*, religious liberals were challenged to act on their faith in unparallelly risky ways. And yet, for religious liberals, even that risk had an attractive aura to it. As Gustav Schultz, a Lutheran pastor and founder of the Sanctuary Movement in Berkeley, CA, framed it, risk was not a discouragement to action or affiliation with the movement: "Taking risks would be something that caused more people to respond . . . people did not want to be involved in things that didn't have some

---

[19]For a discussion of "conversion" narratives in activist narratives, which emphasize the ways that recipients were instrumentalized as having uniquely strong Christian faith that was expected to produce "authentic" religious experiences for the activists, see: Houston and Morse, "The Ordinary and Extraordinary: Producing Migrant Inclusion and Exclusion in US Sanctuary Movements," 34–5.

[20]Lucy articulates her reflection on the Sanctuary Movement after spending several decades living in Central America after her participation in the Sanctuary Movement as "we could not ever not be saviors—white saviors. We could not not do that, but we were always trying not to, and we knew we shouldn't. But we couldn't help ourselves."

sense of risk in it."[21] Refugee identity helped activists to engage in risky, that is criminal, behavior by interweaving such risk-taking with a comfortable power dynamic for white religious liberals. That risk-taking in turn helped white activists to make meaning and narrativize their own experiences in ways that placed their psychospiritual development at the forefront, while recipients were oftentimes, though not always, reduced to one-dimensional vehicles for activist self-actualization. Susan Bibler Coutin describes how white, middle-class North Americans experienced "conversion" by coming to identify with recipients in her *The Culture of Protest*:

> Christian sanctuary workers who reexamined their faith with an awareness of Central Americans' suffering went through not only consciousness-raising but also conversion. The conversions that were particular to the movement began when affluent, white, middle-class Americans crossed border by trying to identify with the Central American poor, to act in solidarity with them, and in some sense to *become* them. This desire to identify with the oppressed was caused by the belief that the persecuted were closer to God than were middle-class North Americans and hence were sources of knowledge about God, society, life, and spirituality.[22]

Conceived of as closer to God due to their suffering, white religious liberals were happy to use recipients as "sources of knowledge" for their own spiritual advancement. However, because suffering is what was useful to them, recipients were instrumentalized and their experiences flattened. Indeed, once a recipient had shared their *testimonio*, activists felt comfortable sharing that story in their absence, publicizing it, and retelling it as part of their work.[23] In a movement ostensibly about providing physical sanctuary to refugees, the refugees were optional.[24]

In my research, this phenomenon was largely corroborated by how activists handled artifacts of recipient trauma that could be displayed after the departure of a recipient. For instance, Rachel told the story of how her

---

[21]Gustav Schultz, interview by Eileen M. Purcell, *The Public Sanctuary Movement: An Historical Basis of Hope*, 1998, 70, http://callimachus.org/digital/collection/p15008coll2/id/43/rec/3.

[22]Coutin, *The Culture of Protest: Religious Activism and the U.S. Sanctuary Movement*, 71.

[23]"Failing the availability of actual Central Americans, sanctuary workers ought to publicize Central Americans' stories. Randy Silbert, a Tucson border worker concluded our interview by urging me, 'Go out and spread the word about what's happening here. Tell people about the human consequences of war. Publish the refugees' stories. Include pictures of their bullet scars and photos of the mutilated bodies.'" Coutin, *The Culture of Protest: Religious Activism and the U.S. Sanctuary Movement*, 70.

[24]"This marks another venue within which migrants became primarily symbolic and useful for what they represented through their experiences. Literally muting the voices of migrants themselves, albeit important for safety concerns, points out how othering can happen through material practices" Houston and Morse, "The Ordinary and Extraordinary: Producing Migrant Inclusion and Exclusion in US Sanctuary Movements," 32–3.

synagogue continued to tell a recipient's story after he moved to Canada through art that he produced:

> There was another family that was here for a while that we met, and the father came and spoke to people at [my synagogue]. And when he did, he drew couple pictures to show us what happened. And this one, where his wife is running out of the house, And I guess the soldiers, were coming. And she scraped her arm on some thorns or something, and her arm got cut. Anyway there's a picture of that—a couple. There was some picture, two drawings, and they were quite . . . they looked like Children's drawings, but they were very expressive. And then they decided they moved to Canada. And we asked him, I guess I don't know if we asked him. We wanted to put these drawings on the wall and that and write about them in the synagogue or something. As a way to continue to tell the story, you know?

The display of art produced by a recipient helped participating congregations to continue to tell the story of trauma even after the departure of recipients, potentially even without the permission of the recipient, although that seems unclear from Rachel's statement. Activists believed in the power of recipients' narratives to move hearers to action even in the absence of recipients to tell their story, and they felt empowered to take up that role in the absence of recipients.

While the structure and hegemonic narratives of the Sanctuary Movement reduced and distorted the agency of recipients, the Sanctuary Movement was not the only space that they inhabited. Indeed, about half of the recipients that I interviewed reported experiences, leadership positions, or collaborations with CASM organizations, as well as several who developed their own informal and formal networks of support, activism, and music-making. In many cases CASM organizations played pivotal roles at the beginning of recipient's sanctuary journey, connecting them with sanctuary activists. This was the case with Carlos, who first found a Central American refugee and solidarity organization, and was then connected to the Sanctuary Movement:

> I just got to LA. I didn't know what to do. And I was walking around . . . I was looking for some kind of help, you know, because, I didn't know what I was doing here. And then I went to a group that they were helping Central American people. It was like a program for refugees from Central America. And then I went over there and talk to them if they can help me. So from that point, I found the connection to join the caravan. Otherwise, I think I wouldn't be here.

El Rescate was founded by Salvadoran refugees and exiles and provided mutual aid and support for the influx of Central Americans arriving in places like Los Angeles.[25] As shown by Carlos' experience, these organizations played a robust role in the ecosystem of the CASM, and oftentimes provided one of the first points of contact for future recipients of sanctuary.[26]

Once in sanctuary, recipients also sought out connection and leadership roles within Central American Solidarity and mutual aid organizations. Marisol also participated in Central American Solidary Movement organizations while in sanctuary, and the roles that she played were varied:

> I was a member of . . . The Committee In Solidarity with the People of El Salvador (CISPES). And so we were protesting the military aid, and they asked us to join. . . . There was a group of mothers of the disappeared, and I asked them if I could join for my dad. And I was a member of that, and participated and was in leadership kind of. . . . And the community was really active. Sometimes we will go down to the federal building, we would have vigils with candles. Uh, and, uh, organized events.

From protester to grief group participant to leader in the movement, Marisol's narrative shows the breadth of options for participation available to recipients. In addition, her narrative highlights how recipients of sanctuary were not unaccustomed to activist and agitator roles, and how in certain contexts they could transcend the refugee role preferred by the Sanctuary Movement. In fact, it is worth noting that Marisol identified her receipt of sanctuary and work with CASM as flowing from an identity as an organizer: "For me, it's always been what can I do to organize?" Sanctuary was a part of a larger matrix of activism for Marisol, who also engaged in music-making and religious community building, where she served in leadership roles for her Roman Catholic diocese and fought to have her father's legacy remembered alongside his friend St. Oscar Romero. For those participating in the faith community in which she received sanctuary, Marisol offered opportunities to continue solidarity work through initiatives and causes that she herself organized.

While solidarity organizations offered more robust opportunities for Central American leadership, mutual aid organizations led by and serving Central Americans enabled the most diverse opportunities for the recipients I interviewed to act outside of refugee framing. Two recipients reported starting their own organizations to serve the Central American community in a formal capacity. Eduardo explicated some of the ways that recipients

---

[25]Los Angeles had and has a particularly vibrant Central American culture, with one activist going so far as to say, "In a sense, Los Angeles *was* sanctuary." Quoted in Chinchilla Norma Stoltz, Hamilton Nora, and Loucky James, "The Sanctuary Movement and Central American Activism in Los Angeles," *Latin American Perspectives* 36, no. 6 (2009), https://doi.org/10.1177/0094582X09350766.

[26]See: Susan Bibler Coutin, *Legalizing Moves: Salvadoran Immigrants' Struggle for U.S. Residency* (Ann Arbor, MI: University of Michigan Press, 2000).

played diverse roles in the community this way: "I was a refugee. I was in sanctuary. I had my own organization mobilizing Salvadorans for their basic needs—food, housing, and jobs, and at the same time we participated with the larger community." Eduardo noted that it was founding this organization and not being in sanctuary that gave him a seat at the table in community meetings with stakeholders in San Francisco and allowed him to form a robust partnership with LGBT organizations: "you have these large coalition meetings with 40-60 people. . . . That's how I got understanding. Oh my goodness these are good people. They invited us to do fundraising at the gay parade, and as the march was coming through, they were delivering donations. They became friends, and we were in solidarity." While Eduardo clearly appreciated sanctuary's ability to provide a platform, he also clearly articulated that it was through leadership of his own organization and activism within the Bay Area that he formed collaborations that yielded interpersonal and political benefit, mixing solidarity and the sharing of their children's soccer team.

While Eduardo's model focused on activism, Gloria's efforts focused on bringing those who experienced torture together for healing. Knowing that "there was not a Guatemalan community, but there was a Guatemalan population," Gloria created "a support group for Guatemalan survivors of torture, some were not in sanctuary, but there were four or five families that were in sanctuary and that was an opportunity." The fact that Gloria's organization included but was not limited to recipients demonstrates the way that recipients deftly organized the communities in which they found themselves, in this case specifically addressing trauma within a group in order to form community. This is particularly important because Sanctuary Movement activists rarely directly addressed the trauma of recipients' lived experience beyond urging them to utilize such trauma in *testimonios* for white audiences, a fact which many activists I interviewed regretted. Seeing a lack of opportunity to explore and work through trauma, recipients banded together to provide that care themselves, showcasing an agency that moves beyond the identity of a refugee.

In addition to formal Central American support organizations, recipients also banded together to create their own networks of recipients with ambitions that sometimes exceeded those of activists:

The three families together we became a community also. Also, we organize among ourselves and continue connecting the work here, and the white community knew that, and we were very clear. We're raising money for this and this organizations. And in the end, the churches are say, "which organization?" This and this, we identified which ones and they were fine and general terms they did not put any barriers because I say, "Okay, so here we doing the work and, uh, elevating the political consciousness of your own membership here, But we need to continue the work." We did that for a long time, and from there we built where was called Ah, Central American Refugee Committee. That's where we had, and we had meetings. And that committee, kind of developed into not only connecting with the struggle over there in central America. But like, you know, as a leader, I learned to go to the community college and learned how to play the system. "Oh, yeah. You going to be there? OK," I enrolled in classes, right? And then I took the other members and they came, you know? Okay, now we're doing this. Whatever.

Instead of going through official, activist-centered networks of sanctuary, Isabella created her own network of recipients. In addition to raising funds, this group of recipients explicitly stated that the consciousness-raising work of sanctuary was a benefit to white activists, which Isabella termed "your membership here." Isabella stated that sanctuary activists found it difficult to move beyond a power dynamic that emphasized white activists' ability to give, to one in which it was acknowledged that both activists and recipients were giving and receiving, but what eventually resulted was a more thorough sense of "accompaniment." Such a recognition did not come without recipients banding together and articulating their vision for sanctuary as a starting point for future activism and mutual aid.

Participation in and organizing activism should come as no surprise, as most of the recipients that I interviewed participated in some form of activism in their home countries. Recipients that I interviewed were trade unionists, student movement leaders, peasant organizers, and human rights activists in their countries of origin. Indeed, many participated in more than one movement, such as Carlos who responded to a question about whether he was politically active before receiving sanctuary with this answer: "I started my participation when I was 14 in Guatemala. As a younger guy, I joined the student movement, peasant movement, worker movement—all of them." Another area where recipients were likely to have some experience was the *Comunidades Eclesiales de Base* (Christian Base Communities or CEBs), which brought together small groups of Roman Catholic laity for worship and scriptural study and served as a primary vehicle for the spread of liberation theology throughout Central and Latin America.[27] Two recipients that I interviewed had substantial experience with CEBs, including one whose father was an associate of Oscar Romero in El Salvador and another who was trained as a catechist in Guatemala. Both received extensive training and were markedly gifted at organizing communities, experiences that they brought to their time as recipients in the Sanctuary Movement.

Of the two experiences noted earlier, participation in CEBs was celebrated as marking the "extraordinary" religiosity of recipients, which

---

[27]Kjell Nordstokke, "Christian Base Communities (CEB)," in *Encyclopedia of Latin American Religions*, ed. Henri Gooren (Cham: Springer International Publishing, 2014).

white activists time and time again used as inspiration for their own spiritual journeys, while experience in more politically motivated activism was received ambivalently.[28] Recipients were discouraged from sharing about their activism in their home country. As Isabella shared about her extensive history of activism in her home country and how that related to her work as a recipient of sanctuary, I asked her whether she felt she had space to speak about those things while in sanctuary. She responded simply: "No. Not that type of things. I should not be talking to you about that, either." Interpretations of this statement vary. For instance, the recipient could be concerned that sharing such narratives would be dangerous for her safety, while it could also indicate that it was dangerous for the movement's scaffolding of sympathy. In the moment, the indication I took was that that because I was a researcher interested in the Sanctuary Movement as well as an ordained minister serving a church in the New Sanctuary Movement, she should instead focus on the public persona that she inhabited while in sanctuary.[29]

When recipients did have an opportunity to discuss their political activism, it was to emphasize their oppression at the hands of their country of origin's government. This emphasis supported the maintenance of refugee identity grounded firmly in what some would have viewed as "implied weakness or passivity," according to Coutin and Perla.[30] For instance, a trade unionist who faced retribution for her activity fit within a narrative of trauma and oppression necessary for constructing refugee identity, while turning one's attention to recipients' strength, resilience, and unbowed fight for dignity in their home country would not, especially if it also entailed strident critiques of capitalism in ways that made white, middle-class Americans uncomfortable. What is clear is that activists self-consciously selected those parts of recipients' pasts that were most likely to lead to sympathy and engagement. Indeed, one of the primary concerns of activists was the refutation of the "economic migrant" narrative that the Reagan administration espoused.[31] In focusing on the oppression that recipients faced, even if that came directly from agential action as activists and organizers, sanctuary activists were able to challenge the Reagan administration narrative about Central Americans,

---

[28]Houston and Morse, "The Ordinary and Extraordinary: Producing Migrant Inclusion and Exclusion in US Sanctuary Movements."

[29]This was a common experience that I had during research, that recipients assumed the portions of their story that would interest me and would tailor their responses to those assumptions until I was able to make it clear that I was indeed interested in those parts of their story.

[30]Hector and Susan Bibler, "Legacies and Origins of the 1980s US—Central American Sanctuary Movement," 9.

[31]Maria Cristina Garcia, *Refugees or Economic Migrants? The Debate over Accountability in the United States* (Berkeley, CA: University of California Press, 2019). See also, for a contemporaneous discussion of contesting the "economic migrant" narrative: Colman McCarthy, "The Sanctuary Movement in America," *Washington Post* August 21, 1988.

while also creating a dynamic that white, middle-class religious practitioners would find familiar.

Noted activist Angela Sanbrano describes the relationship between the Sanctuary and Solidarity Movements as being "like sisters."[32] To some extent this is obviously correct, and yet it does not quite explicate the complex relationship between the two that emerged in my interviews with recipients. In some ways, they were partners with similar goals that engaged in rich collaboration, a point that Eduardo makes well: "The solidarity was very rich. Sanctuary was just one piece. You had the solidarity movement, the anti-intervention movement, the civil disobedience people. We participated in those activities. Each one had their own needs, and we may disagree on tactics, or we might agree on a general goal." What seems clear from my research is that the interplay between solidary and sanctuary organizations provided crucial space for recipient to exhibit more agency, engage in leadership roles, and exceed the boundaries of refugee identity. Indeed, in these spaces, recipients could lay claim to their activist and organizer identities, choosing which activists and participants they wanted to invite into a deeper relationship of solidarity. Perla and Coutin make this point as well: "There were also other spaces among the most trusted sanctuary activists, or within the broader peace and solidarity movement, such as CISPES, Comite Farabundo Marti, Salvadoreños Progresistas, and MASPS meetings or events, where the refugee identity could be moved to the background by the Central Americans in favour of a more empowered or militant persona."[33] If the movement's focus on refugee identity necessarily produced "an extremely reduced and distorted form of agency," as Berhman argues, then Central American and solidarity organizations provided alternative spaces where recipients could experience an agency not molded by the needs of white activists.[34] This is not to say that recipients were entirely free within these spaces; they found their agency restricted in many of the same ways that other immigrants experienced in the 1980s and today. Nevertheless, recipients' deft navigation of the matrix of organizations doing work with Central Americans demonstrates that recipients were rarely content with the Sanctuary Movement's framing of their identity, and instead sought ways to expand that identity by embracing activist and leadership roles.

This is also not to say that all recipients were interested in wholesale rejection of refugee identity. Much of my analysis has pointed to the power of that identity, even if that power was largely seen in how it prompted

---

[32]Quoted in: Hilary Goodfriend, "What Immigrant Rights Activists Can Learn From the Original Sanctuary Movement," *In These Times*, 2017, https://inthesetimes.com/article/a-demand -for-sanctuary-el-salvador-central-america-solidarity-trump.

[33]Hector and Susan Bibler, "Legacies and Origins of the 1980s US—Central American Sanctuary Movement," 18.

[34]Behrman, "Accidents, Agency and Asylum: Constructing the Refugee Subject," 249.

responses from white activists. Several recipients referred to themselves as refugees or exiles in their interviews, even as they adopted other identities: immigrant, activist, and organizer being the most common. For instance, Eduardo notes his refugee status as one of the identities he claims: "I was a refugee, I was in sanctuary," but he also goes on to note his organizing activities in conjunction of the sanctuary experience. The most forceful rejection of the use of refugee identity that I encountered with the recipients I interviewed occurred when Gloria decried how those in the Sanctuary Movement referred to her family as "our refugees":

> So there were cultural misconceptions that we had. Small and big things that really, really made the time in sanctuary very difficult. They were generous. They were friendly. They provided accompaniment and in a way they saved our lives. But on the other hand, we were their refugees. They referred to us as "our refugees."

While refugee identity offered strategic advantages to the Sanctuary Movement, it also limited recipient agency in ways that felt constricting, and in the case quoted earlier, controlling. The sense that refugees were "ours" from activists could, of course, stem from feelings of support and the offering of sanctuary, but it also led to feelings of possessiveness or ownership as Gloria so artfully notes. The feeling of constriction denoted by Gloria reflects the restriction of agency that the construction of refugee identity instituted for recipients.

One way to think about this is to consider a framework from practical theologian Mary McClintock Fulkerson. In her *Places of Redemption*, Fulkerson draws on postmodern place theory and political theorist Kimberley Curtis' work on a "shared space of appearance" to analyze how one congregation generates and obscures "a place to appear, a place to be seen, to be recognized and to recognize the other," which she also identifies with "being seen and heard by others, being acknowledged by others."[35] Taking this valuable practical theological contribution as a lens, one might consider how the Sanctuary Movement both created and hindered "a place to appear" for recipients of sanctuary. Surely, refugee identity enabled some form of appearance to take place for recipients, but that appearance was not complete. As Marta Caminero-Santangelo notes in her article, "Voice of the Voiceless: Religious Rhetoric, Undocumented Immigrants, and the New Sanctuary Movement in the United States," which analyzes both the Sanctuary Movement of the 1980s and the New Sanctuary Movement, sanctuary was a practice that enabled a certain type of appearing, but at a cost: "'sanctuary' . . . was a way of speaking, as the subaltern, that for

---

[35]Fulkerson, *Places of Redemption: Theology for a Worldly Church*, 21.

once could be heard by the American public. . . . It is by seeking sanctuary (by becoming 'refugees,' in the most literal and fundamental sense of taking refuge) that [recipients] gained access to a media voice."[36] Refugee identity did help recipients to find an audience, and in this way, the subaltern was able to speak in some sense. Yet, if refugee identities enabled a "place to appear," even imperfectly, other identities were foreclosed from that same possibility of appearance. As Houston and Morse note, "If their personal biographies had not been as they were, migrants might have been able to stand and tell their own stories, in the varied and multifaceted forms that a citizen enjoys."[37] There are times when a partial appearance may be worth the strategic cost, but it bears repeating that those making that decision were oftentimes not the recipients themselves—those about whom the movement purported to care the most and upon whose *testimonios* it rests. In my analysis, the "place to appear" for recipients within the Sanctuary Movement shrinks with more robust analysis of the movement.

Human Rights Discourse in the Sanctuary Movement

If the "place to appear" generated by refugee identity was limited, giving way to Behrman's "reduced and distorted form of agency," that does not mean that such limitations or distortions went unnoted or uncontested within the movement. In addition to some of the tensions over the actual housing of recipients that I note in the previous chapter, the different ways that activists and recipients deploy human rights discourse within the Sanctuary Movement serve as one locus of contestation about the aims of the movement and the agency of recipients. In focusing on the ways that human rights rhetoric was used within the movement, we see that recipients often incorporated an array of rights that activists eschewed in favor of the human rights contained in the constitution. That is to say, activists often spoke of democracy and freedom of speech in their delineation of human rights, while recipients were more likely to mention labor rights, healthcare, or indigenous rights as being key to their understanding and advocacy. Activists' conception of human rights was not fundamentally shaped by the Refugee Act of 1980, which outlines persecution based on race, religion, nationality, social groups, and political opinion as the basis of eligibility for

[36]Marta Caminero-Santangelo, "The Voice of the Voiceless: Religious Rhetoric, Undocumented Immigrants, and the New Sanctuary Movement in the United States," in *Sanctuary Practices in International Perspectives: Migration, Citizenship and Social Movements*, ed. Randy Lippert and Sean Rehaag (New York: Routledge, 2013).
[37]Houston and Morse, "The Ordinary and Extraordinary: Producing Migrant Inclusion and Exclusion in US Sanctuary Movements," 33.

asylum. Rather, the enshrinement of political rights in America's founding documents played a major role, shaping both the political imagination of activists and making those recipients sympathetic to Americans who shared that political imagination. Importantly, human rights discourse did not emerge in a vacuum, and is instead directly linked to how recipients viewed themselves, the goals of their time in sanctuary, and their preferred strategy for accomplishing those goals— that is, their context.[38] Recipients and white activists alike actively made use of their context to generate their language of human rights, and the ways that those two contexts meet and contest one another in the Sanctuary Movement is an important narrative to consider. Indeed, I argue that the scope of human rights discourse used signals the limits of recipients' "place to appear" within the movement.

Within the academic study of human rights discourse, there are tensions between those perspectives with foundations in "secular" and "religious" frameworks, to the extent that "some scholars may see religion and human rights as incompatible with one another," leading to the result that "the dominant narrative concerning human rights is not just one that favors the secular but one that necessarily excludes religion, because it suggests that religion actually opposes human rights."[39] While this perspective is doubtlessly supported by data,[40] my research with activists and recipients demonstrates an astounding ability to blend human rights discourses from both political and theological perspectives. Activists, who were oftentimes clergy, and recipients, who often had experience as political organizers and/or lay ministry in faith communities, readily connected the Universal Declaration of Human Rights (UDHR) with theological concepts like *imago dei*. This led to statements about the inherent worth of human life from both legal, political, and theological frameworks.

Indeed, many sanctuary declarations authored by churches joining the movement quote extensively from both sets of sources in their frameworks.

---

[38]Although it is beyond the scope of this chapter, it is worth noting that situating human rights discourse contextually has plenty of resonance with turns within the fields of sociology, anthropology, and philosophy. Human rights discourse has been broadly critiqued as imperialist, Eurocentric, and as a tool to enervate political movements. Yet, many scholars see some promise in contextual analyses of human rights that eschew the universalizing trend that so easily seems to take hold in human rights discourse. For a broad literature review as well as an example of contextualized, ethnographic research on human rights, See: David Landy, "Talking Human Rights: How Social Movement Activists Are Constructed and Constrained by Human Rights Discourse," *International Sociology* 28, no. 4 (2013), https://doi.org/10.1177/0268580913490769.

[39]Charity Butcher and Maia Hallward, "Religious vs. Secular Human Rights Organizations: Discourse, Framing, and Action," *Journal of Human Rights* 17, no. 4 (2018): 503, 02, https://doi.org/10.1080/14754835.2018.1486701.

[40]See: Turan Kayaoglu, "Giving an Inch Only to Lose a Mile: Muslim States, Liberalism, and Human Rights in the United Nations," *Human Rights Quarterly* 36, no. 1 (2014), https://doi.org/10.1353/hrq.2014.0004. And Thomas Banchoff and Robert Wuthnow, *Religion and the Global Politics of Human Rights* (Cary: Oxford University Press, 2011).

Dana noted that, alongside quotations from scripture, "it looked like an attorney wrote it, which I know there was some attorney contributions, but you know, very specific, um, international law references and US law references and things that the USA was signatory to." While this was doubtlessly done to manage risk of arrest and to persuade doubtful members, it also indicates the extent to which activists made human rights and its attending legal and theological sources a part of the movement. As a result, the Sanctuary Movement could mesh the UDHR's "recognition of the inherent dignity and of the equal and inalienable rights of all members of the human family is the foundation of freedom, justice and peace in the world," with theological language grounded in either the Jewish or Christian tradition concerning the obligation to act to prevent injustice.[41]

For instance, Martha, an activist from the Pacific Northwest, reported that her community quoted from international treaties, while also grounding their action this way: "Jesus stood with the poor and called for justice, and we are called to model our lives on his. People are sacred and worthy, and deserve for us to protect them." Likewise, Noam, a Rabbi, grounded his guided his community's decision to vote for sanctuary by drawing on both UDHR and "Jewish values," specifically by noting how the UDHR is grounded on "biblical principles":

> I always connect these things to Jewish values. . . . The International (*sic*) Declaration of Human Rights, which is beautiful, and I love it. You know, a lot of it is based on, as you know, biblical principles. So we talked about not standing idly by. We talked about welcoming the stranger. We talked about visiting the sick. We talked about the notion that all human beings are created in the image of God and those are the things that I think resonate. And, of course, you know, it wasn't just happenstance that I got a play about the Holocaust [to be performed in preparation for the vote] because, this hits a certain chord with Jewish peoplehood.

Noam's characterization of the compatibility between religious and secular human rights frameworks might be considered somewhat skeptically by scholars who see such formulations as antithetical to one another, especially his argument that the UDHR originates from "biblical principles," but the movement had no such qualms. Instead, it sought to marshal both frameworks in order to make the best argument for the movement within congregations and within the media, and the blending of these conceptions of human rights became a hallmark of the Sanctuary Movement.

As we saw previously in this chapter, the Sanctuary Movement's casting of recipients as refugees both enabled and hindered certain types

---

[41]United Nations General Assembly, *Universal Declaration of Human Rights* (Lake Success: United Nations Department of Public Information, 1949).

of appearance, but it is also worth noting how the physical practice of sanctuary furthered the formation of refugee identity by appealing to human rights. Activists consecrated their holy spaces to the providing of sanctuary to recipients, but the offering of sanctuary necessarily entails certain power imbalances between activists and recipients. The right to dignity, protection from harm, or food and water does not, for instance, self-evidently include the right to joint decision-making or to an equal seat at the table. Mainly white religious activists saw themselves as safeguarding essential human rights in the offering of sanctuary, but those rights were different from the human rights of which recipients spoke. Where white activists focused on protection from deportation and the provision of basic sustenance in their physical practice of sanctuary, recipients defined their understandings of human rights differently.

That is not to say there was no overlap—there was, but activists routinely framed their actions on the grounds of pity or mercy, which forecloses much agency. A poem read at the worship service declaring sanctuary at La Placita Church in Los Angeles read:

> *Ayudamos a tenera amor y*
> *Compassion hacia estos*
> *Jan Diegos Refugiados*

> Help us to love
> And to pity
> These rejected Juan Diegos.[42]

Pity and mercy are certainly powerful motivators for providing basic care and safety, moving religious participants to act in ways that they were comfortable with. However, those were rarely the sorts of needs that were discussed by recipients that I interviewed, although they were still present. Human rights discourse amplified activists' agency by framing them as defenders of human rights over and against their own government, taking bold risks to protect the human rights of and provide basic needs for refugees. Of course, this same human rights discourse leaves little room for recipients to "appear" or exercise their own agency. Faced with this prospect, recipients often struggled to create their own "place to appear" through an expanding of the scope of human rights discourse, leading to tension.

In positioning themselves as defenders of human rights for recipients, activists contested their own government, arguing that the United States

---

[42]Juan Diego was an indigenous Marian visionary whose testimony provides the basis of the veneration of Our Lady of Guadalupe. Translated by Henry Olivares, the brother of important sanctuary figure, Luis Olivares, and quoted in: Garcia, *Father Luis Olivares, a Biography: Faith Politics and the Origins of the Sanctuary Movement in Los Angeles*, 324.

was breaking its own laws by not ending its support of regimes in Central America and by denying asylum status to those fleeing US-backed regimes. This resulted in an increase in agency for white activists, who emerged as defenders and actors, in direct contrast to recipients who were characterized as lacking access to human rights. For instance, Rachel grounded her participation in recipients' lack of human rights and the movements desire "to do something about it":

> Well, yeah. I mean, I guess I feel like that they didn't have rights, right? They were just abused. . . . I would call it human rights. But I don't quite know how to articulate it except that this was atrocious. It shouldn't have been happening. These people shouldn't have been having to live in these conditions in this situation. They shouldn't have been in danger. Um, and we shouldn't be supporting that. And we should be trying to do something about it.

Likewise, Joan and Erik articulate a link of human rights to anti-interventionism, with particular emphasis on opposing "our own government" in the upholding of human rights for those in Guatemala, the country of origin of the recipient that they collaborated with:

> Joan: Human rights—that was something that was being denied in Guatemala. The innocent lives being taken.

> Erik: The very position of the Sanctuary Movement is that over and against our own government, they were denying the human rights of these people who were fleeing Central America for their lives. They came here—they should have been accepted because their lives are in danger. This is a human right, but they were not, because they were systematically being sent back to Central America. Human rights was at the heart of the sanctuary movement position.

Human rights discourse in the Sanctuary Movement was effective at moving activists and sympathetic religious practitioners to consider their own complicity with US foreign policy. The desired result was that "we shouldn't be supporting that," with "that" being US-backed regimes in Central America. While human rights discourse played an important role in scaffolding both the anti-interventionist and humanitarian camps of the movement, time and time again it also placed activists in the center of the movement's focus as those who had the power, in the words of Rachel "to do something about it." Recipient *testimonios* and their attending public consciousness-raising activities would surely qualify as action to these activists, and activist recognized those risks, but the focus was placed almost exclusively on moving white activists to, in the words of Rev. Dick Lundy, "risk penalty in the hope that the policies of our government might be changed" and to "assume some risk by and for those who have experienced such great injustice."[43]

While white activists spoke at length about human rights, they primarily preferred civil and political rights (CPR) over economic, social, and cultural rights (ESCR) models of human rights. CPR models of human rights were characterized as "the bedrock of human freedom" by the United States, and they loosely correlate with what might be called "natural rights."[44] ESCR on the other hand includes more robust focus on standards of living, the right to join trade unions, and the right to housing, clothes, and food.[45] The tension between the two has its roots in the Cold War, where the United States forcefully argued for a neoliberal adoption of "negative rights" with no fiscal implications for governments since they seek to stop state interference in individuals' rights, while eschewing the ESCR's "positive rights that have implications for state funds because they seek to oblige states to implement positive arrangements for society."[46] The human right most often referenced in my research with white activists is that of asylum seeking and refugee status, which makes sense for a movement that offered sanctuary to those fleeing Central America. Other references include— the right to democracy, freedom of speech, and freedom of expression. Persecution for political beliefs emerges often as an issue that activists decry, seeing it as an act directly supported by their government and therefore one which activists could alleviate through pressure. If sanctuary activists characterized themselves as defenders of human rights, they intended a very particular set of rights—largely CPR rights. Recipients were characterized as fleeing situations in which they lacked rights, and those rights were also the same rights that can be found in the Bill of Rights and supported by American foreign policy. In advocating for recipients' human rights as they understood them, sanctuary activists reified the government's understanding of human rights even as they simultaneously opposed their human rights abuses.

In contrast, sanctuary recipients developed a much more robust characterization of human rights. These characterizations generally include the CPRs favored by activists, but they rarely place those same CPR rights at the center of their human rights discourse, which heavily favors the ESCR framework. Indeed, the most common facet of human rights that are

---

[43]Crittenden, *Sanctuary: A Story of American Conscience and the Law in Collision*, 94.

[44]Waseem Ahmad Qureshi, "Stemming the Bias of Civil and Political Rights Over Economic, Social, and Cultural Rights," *Denver Journal of International Law and Policy* 46, no. 4 (2018): 289.

[45]Office of the United Nations High Commissioner for Human Rights, "Frequently Asked Questions on Economic, Social and Cultural Rights—OHCHR Fact Sheet No. 33" (Geneva, Switzerland, New York: Centre for Human Rights, 2008).

[46]Qureshi, "Stemming the Bias of Civil and Political Rights Over Economic, Social, and Cultural Rights," 298.

referenced in my interviews are labor rights, followed closely by indigenous rights, with references to healthcare, the environment, and housing occupying other important lynchpins to recipient articulations of human rights. In all, recipients tended to highly favor ESCR rights over CPR rights.

For example, Juana, a recipient from Guatemala, prominently features ESCR frameworks in her definition of human rights, focusing largely on workers' rights to collective bargaining and employment protection: "Human rights was about labor rights. It was about fair wages, health care, they were being abused, multiple hours and no breaks—No concept of a holiday or vacation." Likewise, Isabella forcefully articulates a vision of human rights that exceeds, but includes CPR frameworks:

> Because for me, human rights is not only the right to organize. It's the right to have a decent job. The right to have a house, the five basic needs. The right to have all of those without being killed, and every single right that we were trying to do in terms of getting a decent salaries, education, to overthrow poverty. You could not even talk about it because you get killed, right? At that time, you were subversive because you were talking about these rights. So including I mean, you talk about in the countryside, in the farm areas, but the right to access water. It's still going on.

Isabella mingles the right to free expression with rights to housing, work, a living wage, and water rights in a way that encompasses the concerns of many recipients, emphasizing that the lines between these two human rights discourses are blurry. Instead of being starkly divided, CPR and ESCR are articulated as being inexorably linked, even if ESCR concerns are highlighted more often.

Two key rights that many recipients I spoke to mentioned were the right to healthcare and indigenous rights, while only one activist mentioned indigenous rights as central to her conception of human rights and no activist mentioned healthcare rights at all. Gloria, who identified herself as a "human rights activist" in Guatemala combines these concerns into one "simple" statement:

> It's very simple—very, very simple. And I'm going to talk about Guatemala. To have access to healthcare, access to housing, access to education, access to work. Those are basic human rights. To have food on the table, to be able to go see a doctor when you or your children get sick. To have a place to live, so you don't have to be in the streets begging. In the case of Guatemala, the indigenous people have the right to their own land so they can survive. They had the right—they should be able to take their child to a doctor, if your child wakes up in the middle of the night.

Rosalina and Luis saw sanctuary as a platform to advocate for the Maya people's struggle for self-determination, and their definition of human rights focuses on the rights of North and South America's indigenous communities, as well rights of "Mother Earth":

Rosalina: It was not just about the Mayans, it was an act of solidarity between the Maya to other indigenous people in the Americas. From Alaska to South America, the continent is full of indigenous people that imperialists are mistreating.

Luis: Knowing the value of one's life, and the values that everyone deserves. Once you know that and see that, you cannot turn away from injustices, not just for your own sake, but for children that will come—to make a better place for them. Without this fight, we're never going to see equality. We're never going to see equal dignity for all people, we will never see the end of injustices against our culture. At this time, even back in that time, I used to talk about climate change, and really emphasize has the damage done to Mother Earth. . . . To be a Mayan is to be in a deep relationship with Mother Earth . . . We continue connecting people to each other to talk about the earth in a way that benefits mother air, water, earth in a way that doesn't destroy it. It's not just an option; it's a requirement. Father air gives us air everyday so we can't stop talking about it. Father air and mother earth—we have an obligation to them.

Luis' reference to the "fight" is important in this case, as both recipients and activists articulated their activism as a fight for human rights in many respects. But the human rights that recipients and activists were fighting for were different. White activists were concerned largely about CPR rights, seeing democratic society, freedom from fear of torture, and political expression as universal rights that they could push the United States to support through an anti-interventionist stance. Recipients also shared similar concerns, but they also emphasized ESCR rights that are more controversial in the United States. In the end, recipients articulated a simultaneously more robust and more tenuous vision of human rights, and they saw their receiving of sanctuary as part of a struggle to secure those rights. To be certain, recipients were also anti-interventionist and saw their efforts as consciousness-raising for white religious liberals to petition their government to cease intervention in Central America. However, recipients did not generally understand themselves as fleeing a place that did not have rights. Rather, they saw themselves as involved in a struggle to secure those rights, and sanctuary was a part of that struggle. Recipients did not see themselves as primarily receiving humanitarian care after fleeing human rights abuses, although they were oftentimes victims of torture and had at a minimum received death threats. Rather, they saw sanctuary as a platform for critiquing US imperialism, putting pressure on governmental and international organizations to act and continuing the struggle that was begun in their country of origin.

In short, most of the recipients framed their sanctuary experience in terms of consciousness-raising. Where activists focused on religious communities and leaders as possessing moral authority to act on their own government through the firsthand accounts of recipients, recipients saw themselves as building capacity for accompaniment and critique, taking on the task of educating progressive religious people. Recipients that I interviewed often stated that their primary task at the start of their sanctuary experience was to show those that came to their *testimonio* where their home country was on a map. For instance, Carlos put it this way: "Well, you know, I'm remembering that there was definitely a need for some remedial education with some of the people . . . we're talking with folks that didn't really have an idea of where Guatemala or El Salvador was." While mainly white activists constructed an active-passive dichotomy with recipients through their construction of refugee identity and focus on trauma, recipients saw themselves as educating communities of faith about geography, geopolitics, and imperialism. Victor described the relationship between activists and recipients this way: "My sense was there was a disequilibrium in the power dynamic, but it was also a place where both sides would say they were learning from each other."

The differing focuses within human rights discourse between recipients and activists was not a merely theoretical concern, instead bubbling over into tension. Rachel gave this assessment of a Mayan recipient who wanted to speak about his experience in terms of the story of his people:

He wanted to speak about the Mayan people and their culture and their people. And what happened to their people over 500 years, kind of, you know, and we felt that what people really responded to was the personal story. . . . I think this is a reason it worked is when you see a person that you can connect to and he tells you that, you know, my wife was pregnant and so and so was three and we crossed. And, you know, we fled in the middle of the night, and it's just very different. I mean, we respond differently.

According to this activist, collective, indigenous-focused activism, specifically focused on the 500-year struggle of the Mayan people, was not a strategy that made sense in a context in which people relate to the personal. However, it is revealing that what a "personal story" does in this context is relay a particular type of trauma to an audience that is formed to respond to a CPR framework of rights. ESCR definitions, especially ones that relay the trauma, strength, and dignity of indigenous populations were not as easily intelligible or comfortable for American religious liberals. In effect, white activists were highly interested in violations of human rights that affected the individual, but articulations that involved communities proved difficult to grasp. This is perhaps most clearly seen in the movement's inability to grapple with a 500-year history of Mayan persecution, which moved outside of a critique of Reagan and his Central American policy and into a broader critique of imperialism.

Tensions between human rights discourses often focused on strategy, with activists worried that recipients would alienate the audience of the movement. One Guatemalan recipient artfully displayed the tension in this way:

> This is just an example of what would happen in response to the Sanctuary Movement. I would go to a church and I would talk not only about what happened,—I wouldn't give just my testimony, but I talked about the role of the US in what was happening in my country. That was a no-no. It was difficult because they wanted me to go and tell my story. There were times I felt that the more I cried the better it was because people felt sorry and they would donate money to our sanctuary. I could not talk about what was really happening in Guatemala. By that I mean the armed conflict in Guatemala and the roots of the problem. They just wanted me to present as a victim. A woman who had lost her children and had it not been for sanctuary I would have been killed. It was true. That was true, but I couldn't talk about what really mattered to me as a human rights activist in Guatemala. Those were the kind of issues that created problems.

A human rights activist in her own country, this recipient's account of the scope of human rights abuses was restricted. Instead of being a human rights activist struggling for a free Guatemala, she was instead cast as a victim.

This is not to say that every Sanctuary Movement activist and community was solely invested in a CPR framework for human rights. While that was indeed the predominant disposition, leading to many tensions, some activists embraced and learned from their recipients' framing of human rights in ESCR terms. For instance, Rosalina told of how a monastery supported her connections with indigenous groups in the United States:

> We received a lot of support from the monastery . . . They introduced us to various indigenous groups—the Blackhawks—in the US, and building this kind of relationship helped us learn more about basic human rights and the things we could expect as an indigenous group, and without that, we wouldn't have known what we deserved. The monks took us on trips to see communities—the Cherokee, the Mohawks, the Miwok, and without that we wouldn't have known that those people and those communities exist. A lot of people came to see us, to hear our testimony and to explain that they had the ability to be proud of our identity and have flourishing communities as well. That was how we got along with the monks. That's our relationship.

In this case, activists at the monastery understood that the human rights framework proposed by Rosalina as a Maya recipient would benefit from collaboration with other indigenous groups in the United States. Indeed, they were challenged by her initially, but instead of contesting her definition of human rights, they allowed their community to be informed and changed by it. By financially and spiritually supporting Rosalina's community building, the monastery helped to equip her for further activism after the Sanctuary Movement as an indigenous rights advocate in Guatemala.

One place that activists and recipients come together, is that both sets recognized human rights discourse as an effective tool for the Sanctuary Movement. Lucy, who was heavily involved in regional planning for the movement, argued that human rights discourse was "something we can get a win on":

Well, you know, in terms of involving people who were in the pews and people who may not get on board at the vanguard of the political world, Um, one thing, Americans do understand is human rights. And if you can tell people you can tell people . . . show how what's being done to a group of people in El Salvador, Guatemala is a human rights violation . . . You're going to get more support from the average American person saying, because they understand how human rights . . . and [emphasis] individual [emphasis strong from speaker] human rights are sacred, right? In a way, so we really saw human rights as a bread and butter issue, like this is something we can win on. Yeah, If we focus on this as a human rights concern, um, we can get a lot of support. Um, I don't know if that makes sense?

No, It definitely makes sense.

Okay, um, because I think the U. S. Is . . . so one aspect of being a very individualistic country, which we understood that it was, we knew it was in comparison to El Salvador and Guatemala, which is a very communitarian country, is that well, individuals matter, Right? Um, so if you could tell an individual story, then people can understand their individual rights. Um, I would say human rights was part and parcel of everything we did.

Lucy's delineation of the movement's strategy for using human rights discourse showcases an acknowledgment that American audiences were primarily ready to engage with what she calls "individual" rights, which map onto CPR frameworks. Human rights discourse helped recipients make connections with their audience and was an effective tool at moving American religious liberals to take action in ways that made sense to them.

Eduardo expressed surprise at how readily his American audience applied a human rights framework to his *testimonio*, which demonstrated to him the power of human rights discourse for his participation in the movement:

The war in El Salvador was the continuation of a lot of repression in the 70s. The military would take them and they would disappear. Here in the

US, when you tell those stories, people would say "that's a violation of human rights.". . . . The level was so high, when we told the stories here the people were very surprised and many would get very upset. . . . What we were saying it was shocking. Not only churches but in all the sectors.

Activists and recipients alike cited human rights as an issue that they cared about and that facilitated connections to the Sanctuary Movement's audience. While both parties may have disagreed about the limits of human rights discourse, they were unified in their estimation of its effectiveness.

In conclusion, we have seen how activists' and recipients' use of human rights discourse were oftentimes in tension with one another, though not always. The cause of that tension is multifaceted and racialized. Whether oblivious to ESCR frameworks of human rights or shaped to a high degree by American discourse about human rights, white activists focused on individual, political rights as opposed to the more expansive frameworks that recipients offered. Furthermore, the critiques put forward by recipients were sometimes heard but mostly went unincorporated into the Sanctuary Movement's discourse structure. The tension between those differing human rights perspectives was, if not the cause of, a touchstone for some of the broader issues in the movement, especially revealing different analyses of power and agency that broke down along racial lines. While recipients were sometimes constrained in their *testimonios* to present a narrative that conformed to mostly white audience expectations about what human rights were, namely CPR rights, they were also effective at pushing boundaries and continuing their activism in the United States by advocating for ESCR frameworks.

Conclusion: Agency and the Sanctuary Movement

In this chapter, I have previously argued that the construction of refugee identity created a "place to appear," albeit a limited one. Likewise, the differing human rights frameworks deployed by recipients and activists showcase tensions between the two groups. On the one hand, white activists often saw themselves as safeguarding basic human rights for recipients who had none, while on the other, recipients saw themselves as advocating for a broad view of human rights and oftentimes cast themselves as activists in their own right. Now I would like to turn to an analysis of agency informed by Judith Butler's arguments about subjectivity in order to illuminate some of the dynamics that are at work in this aspect of sanctuary. This account highlights many aspects that are missed when utilizing practice as the primary theoretical framework, as I do in Chapter 2. By paying attention to agency, I argue that one can more clearly account for the tensions regarding identity, human rights, and the Sanctuary Movement in general that I have showcased in this chapter. In doing so, I argue for subjectivity and agency's place as an analytical framework in practical theology.

Judith Butler's account of subjection is particularly useful in accounting for power within the Sanctuary Movement. Butler uses the term "subjection" to get to the heart of how power and subject formation are linked: "'Subjection' signifies the process of becoming subordinated by power as well as the process of becoming a subject."[47] Subject formation is then always linked to power by virtue of the subject being "subordinated" in order to become a subject: "No individual becomes a subject without first becoming subjected or undergoing 'subjectivation.'"[48] But what is the subject? For Butler, "The 'subject' is sometimes bandied about as if it were interchangeable with 'the person or 'the individual.' The genealogy of the subject . . . however, suggests that the subject, rather than being identified strictly with the individual, ought to be designated as a linguistic category, a placeholder, as structure in formation. Individuals come to occupy the site of the subject (the subject simultaneously emerges as a 'site')."[49] Within the Sanctuary Movement, recipients "come to occupy the site of the subject" through the process of refugee identity that I outline previously, but I have also shown the limits of that identity and the constraints it places on recipients.

However, that is not the final word on recipients. As I have shown, they are not simply instantiated by the power that generates subjectivity—they also come to utilize it. As Butler puts it, "subjection is nevertheless a power *assumed by* the subject, an assumption that constitutes the instrument of that subject's becoming."[50] Within that assumption of power there are limits, but I have shown recipients' resilience and capacity to move beyond the frameworks that the Sanctuary Movement placed them in. Even if imperfectly recognized by white activists, recipients staked their claim as activists in their own right, pushed back on CPR human rights frameworks favored by the movement, and fought to become more than "our refugees" or "*pobracito*." In effect, recipients' articulation of new identities and frameworks, as well as their cultivation of solidarity and power within the movement constitute agency in a Butlerian sense. For Butler, "the real task is to figure out how a subject who is constituted in and by discourse then recites that very same discourse but for another purpose. For me that's always been the question of how to find agency the moment of that recitation or that replay of discourse that is the condition of one's own emergence."[51] While activists and recipients might both utilize human rights discourse, they clearly articulate different

---

[47]Butler, *The Psychic Life of Power: Theories in Subjection*, 2.
[48]Ibid., 10.
[49]Ibid.
[50]Ibid., 11.
[51]V. Bell and J. Butler, "On Speech, Race and Melancholia. An Interview with Judith Butler: Performativity and Belonging," *Theory, Culture & Society* 16, no. 2 (1999): 165.

meanings within that same discourse. Likewise, although activists and recipients both valued the *testimonio* to raise consciousness among a white, religious liberal audience, I have demonstrated that recipients strove to build the capacity for critique in ways that exceeded refugee identity associated with weakness and vulnerability.

For Butler, "agency exceeds the power by which it is enabled. . . . To the extent that the latter diverge from the former, agency is the assumption of a purpose unintended by power."[52] Within the Sanctuary Movement, recipients often took up roles that exceeded the purpose intended by power, thereby achieving some sense of agency. If, for Butler, the slippage in citation constitutes the possibility for agency, recipients' "constitutive failure for performance" provided the possibility of "a consequential disobedience" of the movement's preference for trauma, which white activists made use of for their own spiritual and ethical development.[53] In the slippage of recipient citation and action within the movement, the possibility for resignification and agency occurs. Building on Butler's framework, Amy Hollywood names those possibilities in a particularly salient way: "misfiring looks less like a danger than a possibility, one that opens room for improvisation and resistance within the very authoritarian structures (e.g., of child-rearing, education, and religion) in which subjects are constituted."[54] Practical theology, in attending to subjectivity and agency, ought to focus its analysis around these slippages and "misfiring[s]," not as a failures in the pursuit of excellence in a particular practice but as a generative grounding for resignification and possibility.

However, that agency had its limits, which are directly tied to how Butler thinks about melancholia, which she terms as "uncompleted grief" that marks "the limits of subjectivation."[55] Although recipients assumed agency, that agency was incomplete. They were not free to tell their own stories or pursue all of the activism that they wished, as the process of subjectivation and iteration is not one that allows unrestricted agency. The melancholia of recipients echoes throughout the literature and my interviews, pointing to the limits of agency within the movement. Gloria, a human rights activist in Guatemala and forceful critic of US imperialism who manifested considerable agency, gave this delineation of the melancholia of the ends of agency: "They were generous. They were friendly. They provided accompaniment and in a way they saved our lives. But on the other hand, we were their refugees. They referred to us as 'our refugees.'" One of the most

---

[52]Butler, *The Psychic Life of Power: Theories in Subjection*, 15.
[53]Judith Butler, *Bodies that Matter: On the Discursive Limits of "Sex"* (New York: Routledge, 1993), 82.
[54]Amy Hollywood, "Performativity, Citationality, Ritualization," *History of Religions* 42, no. 2 (2002): 115, https://doi.org/10.1086/463699.
[55]Butler, *The Psychic Life of Power: Theories in Subjection*, 22, 29.

concrete ways that a subjectivity lens enables practical theological reflection in ways that a practice framework obscures is by making melancholia a site of theological reflection. In *Acute Melancholia*, Hollywood deftly outlines the stakes of avoiding such theological reflection: "to disavow the subject's melancholic constitution is to disavow the complex constellation of others who make us who and what we are. It is to disavow our losses and our grief as well as that which supports and enables our subjectivity, our agency, and, paradoxically, our responsibility."[56] In grounding theological and ethical reflection in melancholia, the complex webs of power, agency, and subjection are clarified by attending to their edges, and melancholia emerges as more than a failure of practice—as if recipients of sanctuary somehow failed in their practice of sanctuary.

In Chapter 2, I argue that there are clear benefits to analyzing sanctuary as a practice, but in this chapter, I have shown how that theoretical framework is particularly weak in its account of power. In essence, practice allows for detailed accounts of white activists within the movement, but it obscures the experiences, agency, and resilience of recipients. In a movement like the Sanctuary Movement, analysis of power is not optional; it is essential. Utilizing Butlerian accounts of agency reveals insight into the Sanctuary Movement that cannot be gained by utilizing the category of practice. In paying attention to slippages as sites of possible resignification and agency, power and subjectivity emerge as categories of analysis that can help elucidate difficult to parse dynamics within the movement. As we will see in future chapters, these analyses provide fertile territory for building practical theological reflection on the categories of trauma, grace, and, indeed, practice itself.

Theological *Excursus*: Grace and Agency

The account of recipients' struggles for agency and the limits of those struggles is a fertile ground for theological reflection on key issues of Christian doctrine—namely, agency, grace, and the relationship between the two. What does the will of God have to do with the struggle for agency of recipients? I extend the incarnational grounding of what Kevin Timpe calls a "cooperationist" model of the union of divine and human wills to broader struggles for agency beyond the salvific. In the end, if grace is to serve as a grounding for recipient agency, it has to account for multiple human wills, which allows for an account of melancholia to emerge.

---

[56]Amy Hollywood, *Acute Melancholia and Other Essays: Mysticism, History, and the Study of Religion* (New York: Columbia University Press, 2016), 86.

The extent to which human beings participate in God's salvific action is a hotly contested topic in Christian history, one which Timothy Rosendale argues continues to "haunt us and have done so, in various forms, for thousands of years,"[57] but as Mayra Rivera notes such hauntings can be generative, even sites of the holy or the Holy Ghost.[58] Perhaps the most haunted aspect of the tension between divine and human agency is the specter of Pelagius, who defended the goodness of human nature and the effectiveness of human will. Due to Augustine's caricature of Pelagius in order to secure his positions as orthodox, even today the mere accusation of Pelagianism or semi-Pelagianism is enough to mark an argument as outside the bounds of orthodoxy.[59] The question of whether the will is "bounded," or "free"[60] is important outside of its implications for the debate between Calvinist and Arminian thought, since it forms the possibilities and limitations of human cooperation with the divine. While much of these debates are centered around salvation—the capacity to will the good in collaboration with or independently of God is primarily an argument about salvation[61]—I argue they extend more broadly to human cooperation with the divine in politics, social movements, and everyday life.

One of the more nuanced perspectives on this perennial debate is from Kevin Timpe. Although he too takes strong precautions against being labeled a Pelagian, he puts forth a collaborative model of divine and human wills based on the incarnation. Through the hypostatic union of Christ, human and divine will are united, and in seeking to understand it, Timpe argues that we can better understand cooperative agency in general. However, this is a problem because the incarnation is "ineffable," which threatens to make the project untenable. Ultimately dispensing with the "stronger" version of this objection, he expresses some sympathy with a "weaker" version that is summed up as, "we're attempting to understand something more common (namely, cooperative agency in general) via something considerably less common, indeed singular (namely, the Incarnation)."[62] Drawing on J. David Vellemen's work on intention and plural subjects[63], Timpe argues for the importance of "conditional desire," which makes a distinction between "desire for a good without having, simpliciter, a good desire," a necessity

---

[57]Timothy Rosendale, *Theology and Agency in Early Modern Literature* (Cambridge: Cambridge University Press, 2018).

[58]Rivera, "Ghostly Encounters: Spirits, Memory, and the Holy Ghost."

[59]See: Ali Bonner, *The Myth of Pelagianism*, 1st ed. (Oxford: Oxford University Press, 2018).

[60]The classic exchange between Martin Luther and Erasmus is particularly important here, with Martin Luther writing "On the Bound Will" in response to Erasmus' "On Free Will."

[61]Indeed, Bonner argues that Augustine's denouncement and caricature of Pelagius was instrumental in the ascendancy of Augustine's soteriology as orthodox.

[62]Kevin Timpe, "Cooperative Grace, Cooperative Agency," *European Journal for Philosophy of Religion* 7, no. 3 (2015): 237, https://doi.org/10.24204/ejpr.v7i3.113.

[63]See: J. David Velleman, "How To Share An Intention," *Philosophy and Phenomenological Research* 57, no. 1 (1997), https://doi.org/10.2307/2953776.

to avoid the "anti-Pelagian constraint" at the heart of his argument.[64] In doing so, he centers quiescence as the necessary component of cooperative grace, whereby "the agent and God thus are working together to bring about a single volition in the agent, thereby genuinely cooperating."[65] In doing so, Timpe argues that he formulates "an account of how we humans can participate with God—in a very real sense—in bringing about [God's] Kingdom, both in our own wills and also in the larger world."[66]

There is much to like in Timpe's account, and I wish to build on it in three ways: by expanding his attention to a plurality of subjectivities, by centering melancholia within an account of grace and agency, and by questioning whether satisfaction of the anti-Pelagian constraint is a useful standard from which to argue about the contours of human and divine agency. Timpe's conception of cooperative agency and grace accounts for two subjectivities that work together to form one volition, but similar to my argument in Chapter 1 in my account of testimony, grace, and agency might be better thought of on a communal level, with God, an individual, and a community forming the constitutive elements. In some ways, this point merely awaits explicit formulation in Timpe's article. He quotes Vellemen's account at length, but seems to skip over Vellemen's articulation of a plurality of subjects containing "two or more subjects."[67] The alignment of wills is not merely an individual affair. As I have demonstrated in this chapter, the frameworks that shape the possibility and limits of agency are not negotiated at the individual level. Indeed, recipients were rarely free to make their own decisions about their narratives—their choices were not unbounded or free. Therefore, it stands to reason that for there to be true cooperation and agency, especially with regard to the Sanctuary Movement, there would also have to be a desire, intention, or quiescence on the part of the community to seek the good. While Timpe imagines an individual coming into alignment with God's will, the Sanctuary Movement clearly portrays the need for that same account on a communal or movement level. We are never individuals; our subjectivities are powerfully shaped by others, both divine and human.

In expanding Timpe's account to move beyond the individual, a theological engagement with melancholia also becomes possible. While it makes sense for Timpe to not spend much time delineating the ways that subjects might fail to unite their will with God's, I remain interested in those slippages, especially as a way of understanding how the three participants in my schema affect one another's wills. If we understand God as in some way grounding the good, the other two parties in my model of cooperation

---

[64]Timpe, "Cooperative Grace, Cooperative Agency," 241. It ought to be clear by now that I think this constraint is unnecessary and hampers the possibilities of argument.
[65]Timpe, "Cooperative Grace, Cooperative Agency," 241.
[66]Ibid., 242.
[67]Ibid., 240.

can fail to align their wills, or, as is more the case with sanctuary, they can imperfectly align their wills. The task of discernment of the good or of God's will is paramount, but that discernment is necessarily shaped by context. In many ways this continues to be related to my argument about witnessing in the previous chapter; the capacity for transformative testimony rests on the ability to have one's expectations violated. Otherwise, it merely confirms what one already knows. Likewise, the capacity for cooperative grace and the sharing of volition with the divine rests on the willingness of a community to decenter their own will. Slippage, imperfect alignment in the wills of all three parties, results in limits in agency on other parties, both divine and human. As I named in the previous part of this chapter, we might characterize these strivings at the edge of agency as melancholy, and now we have a theological lens through which to view it—the slippage of alignment between a tripartite system of cooperation that builds on Timpe's work.

I wish to return to my contestation that slippages between the human parties also affect God's agency. Indeed, this need not be a controversial statement, as prayer is both a key part of the Christian tradition and an acknowledged way that God might align God's will differently based on compassion, mercy, or justice.[68] Thus, there already exists a lens through viewing a changing will and capacity of God's action in the world. Likewise, Timpe excludes coercion as a mode of divine action outright, positing that there are actions or desires that God wishes to act upon but cannot due to unalignment. One way of making sense of my earlier arguments is by adopting a process theology frame that abandons omnipotence altogether, and there is much alignment here between what I am proposing and Alfred North Whitehead and Charles Hartshorne's thought.[69] I believe Dorothee Sölle's vision of divine friendship may also be of some use here, wherein God needs "friends," perhaps best understood as those who share an intention and volition with God, in order to act in the world.[70] However, I remain unconvinced that such arguments are necessary for this argument about God, who, unlike human beings, possesses an absolute unity of will and ability. Whether one adopts a nuanced view of omnipotence, a process theology frame, or otherwise accounts for God's inability and unwillingness to coerce, the result is the same—melancholy necessarily becomes an attribute of the divine, as divine agency is limited by the other actors in this schema.

---

[68]For an approach that I particularly like, see: Flora A. Keshgegian, *God Reflected: Metaphors for Life* (Minneapolis, MN: Fortress Press, 2008).

[69]There are of course many similarities here—God's self-limitation, the ability for God to be influenced by the world, and one could even ground the relationships I discuss in terms of prehensions. However, while I am no great defender of omnipotence, I think the concept properly understood excludes the possibility of coercion due to the unity of God's will and action. God does not will to coerce, therefore God does not.

[70]Sölle, *Theology for Skeptics: Reflections on God*, 16.

So far, my arguments about God have started from the assumption that only God can will the good, and humans necessarily must base their wills to the good on God's grace. Such conceptions eschew charges of Pelagianism, but they also limit ideas about agency and how the divine and human wills interact. Is such a heavy limitation worthwhile? It ought to be apparent by now that I am chafing at such constriction. Surely depictions of prayer in scripture that result in more merciful and compassionate action from God move God's will toward a more perfect application. One way of grounding such a model might be in God's passability, which Linda Zagzebski has recently put forward as omnisubjectivity. Zagzebski argues, "It is the property of consciously grasping with perfect accuracy and completeness every conscious state of every creature from that creature's first-person perspective."[71] Such a conception is not without its issues.[72] However, its possibilities outweigh its problems. Adam Green expounds on omnisubjectivity, linking it to the incarnation in a way that I find particularly helpful: "even an omnisubjective God would learn some new things through the experience of being incarnated."[73] Such ideas move closer to what I am arguing—human experiences, not just of suffering, but of struggles for agency have the capacity to change and expand God's knowledge and therefore God's will and agency. Is it proper to say that all such human experiences are flawed and therefore could not expand on God's knowledge of the good? If so, the project of omnisubjectivity might not be useful, since there would be very little change in our model for God. However, if one accepts that certain knowledge is experiential and that God shares in some capacity with those experiences, then it stands to reason that the concern of Pelagianism ought to be discarded.

That does not mean that grace is not the starting point. Grace is also present in creation[74], in the embodied experiences of life,[75] and in this case, the melancholia and struggles for agency of recipients of sanctuary.

---

[71]Linda Trinkaus Zagzebski, *Omnisubjectivity: A Defense of a Divine Attribute* (Milwaukee, WI: Marquette University Press, 2013), 10.

[72]Mullins helpfully takes on emotional states that might not advance an image of God that one might find helpful, imagining some constraints on omnisubjectivity that are useful. While Mullins quotes Hartshorne, it is curious to me that he does not draw further on his ideas of God's empathy and the difference between feeling what one feels and how one feels. Perhaps I too am guilty of not documenting my debts to him. R. T. Mullins, "Omnisubjectivity and the Problem of Creepy Divine Emotions," *Religious Studies* (2020), https://doi.org/10.1017/S0034412520000220.

[73]Adam Green, "Omnisubjectivity and Incarnation," *Topoi* 36, no. 4 (2017): 700, https://doi.org/10.1007/s11245-016-9391-2.

[74]See: Sallie McFague, *The Body of God: An Ecological Theology* (Minneapolis, MN: Fortress Press, 1993).

[75]See: Marcus Bussey and Camila Mozzini-Alister, *Phenomenologies of Grace: The Body, Embodiment, and Transformative Futures* (Cham: Springer International Publishing AG, 2020). And David Brown, *God and Grace of Body: Sacrament in Ordinary* (New York: Oxford University Press, 2007).

Placing recipient accounts at the center of this project also means doing some of the theological work that I take on in this section of Chapter 2. Importantly, what is centered in this theological reflection is *not* suffering, but the theological issues, which I take up in the next chapter. In struggles for agency, a vision of God emerges that not only struggles alongside them, or suffers alongside them, but also perhaps grows and learns as well.

At first glance, it might appear that the Sanctuary Movement and its conceptions of agency and human rights have little to do with salvation, but practical theology makes it clear that in one learning about one, it is possible to learn about the other. Practice, with its focus on excellence, conceives of slippage as a failure that affects whether or not individuals are able to obtain the internal goods they seek. Butler's account of subjection moves us closer to the reality that misalignment between multiple individuals, communities, and God has a profound effect on God's ability to act in the world. If only God can will the good, then the possibilities for cooperative grace dissipate, and human beings become more passive in their relationship with God. Such theological beliefs rarely stay theoretical; they ossify, taking on real form in our world. Comfort with power disparity, passivity, and diminished agency are the building blocks of the very real tensions that I document in the Sanctuary Movement, and they are the driving force for my skepticism of the Pelagian constraint. If there is anything that is clear about sanctuary, it is that discursive frameworks have a real impact on agency, and God-talk is no different. How one talks about God, making room for agency in relationship or not, creates the conditions for political and spiritual agency. If grace is the aim, then one's frameworks must be ready to receive, wrestle with, and grasp it.

4

Feeling Equal

Whiteness and Affect in the Sanctuary Movement

The Sanctuary Movement was understood by both recipients and activists as a white movement aimed at solidarity with Central Americans.[1] At the same time, whiteness and its attending power dynamics were not the central preoccupation of white activists. At a national Sanctuary Movement convention at the height of the movement, women in the movement clearly articulated their contribution to sanctuary and demanded that their voice be treated as important as "macho males," exemplified by John Fife and Jim Corbett.[2] In their struggle for equality, women in the movement articulated a clear analysis of power, situating it as an important category of analysis in the movement.[3] While power dynamics between activists were debated, contested, and analyzed, those same activists consistently failed to attend to power differentials between white activists and recipients. Activists consistently interpreted the symbolic empowerment of the *testimonio*, in which a largely white audience listens intently to a recipient, as creating an equal power distribution between activists and recipients. They did so because this powerful image of power inversion feels as if power imbalances have been eliminated, which leads to the central claim of this chapter—whiteness and affect are co-constitutive.

As I have argued in Chapters 2 and 3, sanctuary activists utilized the experiences of recipients in order to advance their own spirituality and achieve some measure of self-actualization, as well as to stir the compassion

---

[1]Coutin, *The Culture of Protest: Religious Activism and the U.S. Sanctuary Movement*, 11.
[2]Cunningham, *God and Caesar at the Rio Grande*, 129.
[3]See: Robin Lorentzen, *Women in the Sanctuary Movement* (Philadelphia, PA: Temple University Press, 1991).

of religious liberals and critique the Reagan administration's Central America policy. Patricia Stuelke argues that the work of solidarity activists in the 1980s was focused on "constructing affective connections across difference" with the intent of developing "a sense of commonality with Central American subjects that might repair the violence of US imperialism in Central America."[4] She surmises that in addition to constructing a forceful critique of Reagan's policy, these movements instead relied on "performances of virtuous, sacrificial Central American victimhood" that offered a "vehicle for redeeming the guilty US nation and its citizens" through an affective promise of "feeling right."[5] This theoretical frame resolves much of my difficulties with the movement, as I argue that that "feeling right," a useful shorthand for the redemption and self-actualization of white, religious liberals, is the primary internal good generated by the practice of sanctuary. However, such a framework is, by itself, insufficient for a thoroughgoing analysis of the movement. In this chapter, I argue that sanctuary cannot be understood without assiduous attention to whiteness, and that whiteness cannot be understood in the movement without understanding how affect and whiteness are co-constitutive.

This argument has four stages. First, I consider why the category of whiteness is important for this project, outlining some recent scholarship on whiteness in religious studies and theology and arguing for the Sanctuary Movement as a site of white subject formation. Second, I map the contours of whiteness within the movement utilizing data from interviews I conducted in conversation with secondary sources, placing my research in conversation with Lauren Berlant and Steven Strick's work on sentimentality in the American political imagination. Third, I present an account of white subjectivity that can serve as a basis for ongoing practical theological inquiries on whiteness as well as answering some fundamental questions about whiteness' simultaneous hypervisibility and invisibility within the movement. Finally, I analyze white activists' theological imaginings within the Sanctuary Movement, arguing that their theological reflections demonstrate the need for a substantive engagement with suffering, particularly the suffering of others.

Wrestling with Whiteness—A Personal Journey and Some Definitions

The following pages are not meant to be an indictment of the Sanctuary Movement, but they do wrestle with the whiteness that constituted the

[4]Stuelke Patricia, "The Reparative Politics of Central America Solidarity Movement Culture," *American Quarterly* 66, no. 3 (2014): 768, https://doi.org/10.1353/aq.2014.0058.
[5]Ibid.

movement. Indeed, in drawing on the work of Stuelke, Strick, and Berlant, my intention is to show that the whiteness that the sanctuary variously saw, elided, or avoided is a central issue for solidarity movements that are white-led. Also, the type of whiteness that I catalog here is not the type of white supremacy that often garners the most attention from scholars of religion. Rather, I believe there is value in also analyzing racism and white supremacy among those who are engaging in antiracist, anticolonial work. The Sanctuary Movement demonstrates the ways that allyship, symbolic power exchange, and solidarity are used by white activists as the raw material for conversions and the creation of new spiritual selves. Using whiteness as an analytical frame can demonstrate both how white antiracists center their own encounters with difference and how scholarship can easily replicate that same centering.

That broader argument is also bound up with my identity as a white researcher and ordained minister that leads a church participating in the New Sanctuary Movement. I first became attracted to the Sanctuary Movement in 2012 while doing research for a Congregational Studies course that would eventually become an article. What I would have said then was that the solidarity that congregations were able to exhibit through their willingness to engage in practices of risk excited me and showed me that people of faith were capable of outstanding acts of courage. What I would say now is that my passion for engaging with the Sanctuary Movement of the 1980s was inexorably bound up with my own whiteness. Those two statements are not in conflict with one another, but rather the latter explains and elaborates on the first. In my initial analysis of the movement, I was interested in the journeys of white activists, how they made connections to previous moments of activism in their individual and communal lives, and what lessons people of faith might carry into the present. What was conspicuously absent were the narratives of recipients, an oversight which was due to my privilege and whiteness. As a white minister and researcher, I was looking for examples of solidarity that I could use to move the church in positive directions, and so I interviewed people who looked like me. I was focused on building capacity for the church to ally itself with those who experienced racism, colonialism, and imperialism, but in my desire to build a theological model to address those concerns, I could not see those same people in the Sanctuary Movement.

I give such an account to say that this chapter in particular is inseparable from my personal journey in relating to my own whiteness as a researcher, ordained minister, and theologian. I also give it as a note of caution about the insidiousness of white supremacy among those who seek to be antiracist. Whether it was the case that I could not *see* recipients in the Sanctuary Movement, or whether I saw them, but my whiteness prevented me from valuing their narratives appropriately, this chapter has attempted to place recipient contributions at the forefront of its argument. It was only by wrestling with my own whiteness and reflecting on it that a more robust account of the movement could be written. My hope is that, in marking the contours of whiteness in the Sanctuary Movement, that initial project of building capacity for collaboration can be more deftly engaged. The questions raised here do not invalidate the Sanctuary Movement's contributions. Certainly, they complicate them, but if I complicate that movement, I am also complicating my own commitments and seeking to understand the ways that whiteness has constrained my own work. I take George Yancy's account of whiteness seriously, in attempting to not place myself at a "moral distance" from the whiteness I explicate in the Sanctuary Movement: "Whiteness . . . because of its taken-for-granted reality, is not the sort of thing from which you can assume a stance of moral distance; you are that site."[6] If this chapter is a critique, it is also a self-critique.

That can be most clearly seen in Chapter 1, which focuses on my own experiences pastoring a New Sanctuary Movement church, while trying and failing to account for the ways I perpetuate white supremacy. That is to say—I am not someone who knows better and can call out a historical movement; I am someone who knows better and yet often failed to act out those commitments. That failure, though separated by decades, says something about how sanctuary functions and its lack of accountability structures for white clergy and activists like myself. Sanctuary's structures do not mean that all white activists perpetuate white supremacy or that that perpetuation is inevitable, but it does mean that sanctuary has certain characteristic pitfalls associated with its practice and that those pitfalls are most appropriately understood in terms of whiteness.

But what is whiteness? There are a variety of different groundings for a discussion of whiteness, some of which focus on whiteness as an embodied orientation and habit,[7] or as the normative or assumed universal experience.[8] Two perspectives on whiteness have proved particularly useful for analysis of the Sanctuary Movement are Karen Teel's and J. Kameron Carter's. Karen Teel defines whiteness as an "attitude" in an attempt to navigate affective, performative, and socio-historical definitions of whiteness: "The attitude of whiteness, then, manifests in discernible thought patterns that correspond to, and arise along with, the feeling that to be white is to be normal or

[6]George Yancy, *Backlash: What Happens When We Talk Honestly about Racism in America*, ed. Cornel West (Lanham, MD: Rowman & Littlefield, 2018), 57.
[7]"Whiteness could be described as an ongoing and unfinished history, which orientates bodies in specific directions, affecting how they 'take up' space, and what they 'can do' . . . whiteness functions as a habit, even a bad habit, which becomes a background to social action." Sara Ahmed, "A Phenomenology of Whiteness," *Feminist Theory* 8, no. 2 (2007), https://doi.org/10.1177/1464700107078139.
[8]See: George Yancy, "Is White America Ready to Confront Its Racism? Philosopher George Yancy Says We Need a 'Crisis,'" interview by Alex Blasdel, 2018. And Yancy, *Backlash: What Happens When We Talk Honestly about Racism in America*.

neutral. . . . Whiteness is powerblind (*sic*) Eurocentrism."[9] In addition, J. Kameron Carter articulates a definition of whiteness grounded in *oikonomia*: "Hence, the world was recreated from the colonial conquests from the late fifteenth century forward in the image of white dominance, where 'white' signifies not merely pigmentation but a regime of political and economic power for arranging (oikonomia) the world."[10] In some sense, of course, the Sanctuary Movement was not power-oblivious. They certainly understood the power of the United States government and formulated strong critiques of that power. Likewise, they knew and understood well the power of a religious movement based on solidarity with the people of the Sanctuary Movement. However, within the movement, the Sanctuary Movement was, if not oblivious, unable to fully account for the imbalances of power at the heart of the movement as well as the power that recipients held in their own countries as activists. Likewise, that power-obliviousness bled into white activists' *oikonomia* of the movement, where they arranged the standards of excellence for the practice of sanctuary in such a way that was power-oblivious.

I contend there are manifest benefits to looking at whiteness in progressive, activist spaces like the Sanctuary Movement. Indeed, having given an in-depth view of the practice of sanctuary, I now turn my attention to how the practice of sanctuary reinforced whiteness, even while it simultaneously produced solidarity, an awareness of whiteness and privilege, and a politics and theology that was critical of the state. Making whiteness central to a practical theological account should not be limited to explorations of communities and theologies that are self-avowedly racist, or the sorts of practices that one might attend to on the political right. Whiteness as a category is an equally powerful framework for analyzing theology and practice among self-identified progressives, radicals, and humanitarians. In my analysis, there are three key sites where sanctuary produced white subjects. First, a power-obliviousness[11] that obfuscated the racialized power imbalances between recipients and activists, both in philosophical understandings of the movement and its daily operations. Second, an instrumentalization of recipient experiences through the *testimonio* for the

---

[9]While I quote powerblindness here, I will be using a less ableist term to describe what power-blindness denotes. Although the terms are different, power-obliviousness is intended as a substitute for powerblindness, with all of its theoretical grounding intact. Karen Teel, "Whiteness in Catholic Theological Method," *Journal of the American Academy of Religion* 87, no. 2 (2019): 411, https://doi.org/10.1093/jaarel/lfz023.

[10]J. Kameron Carter, *Race: A Theological Account* (New York: Oxford University Press, 2008), 35.

[11]In this analysis, I primarily mean power-oblivious egalitarianism, which is defined as "belief that all groups are equal in power," but to a lesser extent also power-oblivious identity, which is defined as "failure to notice that one belongs to a privileged group." Kurzman et al., "Powerblindness."

purposes of white activist spiritual, political, and emotional development, centering white activist experiences and agency. Third, through the symbolic and ritual activity of the Sanctuary Movement and solidarity movements, white activists cultivated identities that performed humility in ways that reinforced their power and standing and even came to see themselves as sharing in the identities and risks of nonwhite recipients. Crucially, the movement enabled white activists to claim different white subjectivities, with the adoption of NorteAmericano identity being the most explicit, and centered whiteness even as it practiced solidarity.

Mapping the Contours of Whiteness in the Sanctuary Movement

White activists operated in a power-oblivious manner by failing to attend to the unequal power distribution between Central American recipients and white religious liberals. Part of the reason this is the case is that the movement centered the narratives of recipients through the *testimonio*, which gave the appearance of power. However, in Chapter 3, I demonstrated that this power was limited and frustrated by the de facto requirement of recipients to play the role of traumatized victim. Even though power differential was a constitutive part of the Sanctuary Movement at every level, as my research has documented assiduously, white activists emphasized the consensual nature of the arrangement, emphasizing that a recipient "could always say no," as Jim put it. In such an arrangement, the characterization of recipients and activists in an equal power relationship, wherein recipients, who depended on sanctuary communities for protection, housing, and other necessities in a country in which they faced deportation, would feel empowered to "say no" to white activists is not only misguided, it serves to reinforce white control. Indeed, this power-obliviousness becomes a way for white activists to achieve more agency and control. Having symbolically positioned themselves as learners from recipient *testimonios*, white activists felt as if equality was not only possible but already achieved. That is because, to white activists, the playing field *felt* fair.

Consider this story told about a national meeting of the National Sanctuary Movement, a group that was attempting to centralize the movement and more associated with Chicago than Tucson:

Gloria: Coming to Chicago, the Sanctuary Movement had once a year a national convention, where refugees, sanctuary workers, rabbis, there were all denominations. And most of the people that attended those gatherings once a year were of course white people. All white people from the Sanctuary Movement. The refugees—maybe ten or fifteen of us. The rest were white people, and we tried to have a voice and there would be big debates about where the movement should go, about what the role of the refugees would be, and we the refugees, even though we were a small group, we had a sense of urgency that the Sanctuary Movement people did not have. Every point would take hours to discuss. I was getting kind of fed up with that . . .

On the national level it was a little more difficult, the vast majority at the conventions—like 90 to 95% were white people—I am talking specifically this 50/50 rule. 50% men, 50% women. And we were people who were forced to leave our country, and we—once, I remember I got so upset because there was this discussion because the whole group was in this huge room and people decided at this point to discuss why there wasn't 50% women, and 50% men and that men were talking more than women and that wasn't fair. We were upset about it. We knew what happened in Guatemala. We knew why we had to leave our country. We knew what the US was doing, but this was not important to us. What mattered to us was that these people who were there was focused on the real issues—issues of life and death. I was booed by some woman because I said it was life and death issues—they were important. Everything had to be 50/50 . . .

For me and my brothers and sisters—yes, we understand, but leave us out of this discussion, because this is a discussion that you need to have yourselves. When you're finished, we'll join you, because this is not our priorities.

In subsequent conversation it was revealed that the group of women who booed the recipient for stating the urgency of the situation were nuns. While the concern that women receive equal representation within the Sanctuary Movement's activist community is in some ways laudable, this unfortunate episode clearly centers a primary focus for the movement. Namely, while the Sanctuary Movement ostensibly centered recipient voices, nuns booing recipients reveal that the true focus of the movement was white activists. In a strange way, Sanctuary Movement activists were more concerned about power and representation among white activists than they were about the power differential between activists and recipients, highlighting the fact that power was a salient category of analysis for activists. However, that analysis of power never led to concrete, formal roles of leadership within the Sanctuary Movement. In a room with 200 activists debating how recipient voices would be used by the movement, only ten to fifteen recipients were in attendance, and their voice was discounted.

It is important to note that the recipient booed in this anecdote is a woman herself. Gloria denounced the focus on gender in order to focus on what she considered "life and death issues," and nuns attempted to silence her concerns. Perhaps they would have done so with any woman who opposed the focus on equal time for men and women at the meeting.

If so, the anecdote only serves to highlight the power-obliviousness of the movement, in which nuns booed recipients who disagreed with them, presumably because the power between them was considered to be equal. The motivations of activists, in this regard, need not be nefarious. Sanctuary activists felt as if the movement was essentially a collaboration among equals. In many ways that was true—activists needed recipients in order to act, and recipients needed sanctuary workers in order to build the platform for their message. That reciprocity produced feelings of equality. In many important ways, however, the Sanctuary Movement reinforced hierarchies and reified white supremacy. My research on the Sanctuary Movement indicates that many activists *wanted* a movement in which recipients and activists wielded equal power, and in imagining such a movement, acted as if it were true. However, the previous chapters' documentation of power disparities in the movement, as well as the fact that recipients had little voice in a room of hundreds of white people, show that this does not reflect reality but the whiteness that was at the center of the Sanctuary Movement.

When I asked white activists about formal roles for recipients within the movement, their responses can be sorted into two groups. First, activists would tell me that there were no formal roles for recipients within the movement, but that was largely because things were done by consensus or that recipients did have some role in the community committees that managed the daily affairs of the living arrangement with recipients. As Jim put it, "So there are a variety of different approaches. But again, trying to have each congregation each refugee be listening to each other and being able to care." That ethic of care did not extend to formal leadership roles within the movement, perhaps because of the sentiment that Jim articulates of equal partners listening to each other. In such a view, recipients are already empowered to speak up and out, shaping their sanctuary experience in unrestricted ways. As this book has shown, such power-obliviousness did not reflect reality.

That same informal approach that resulted in the exclusion of recipients in the Sanctuary Movement of the 1980s carried over into my experience with the New Sanctuary Movement. At several points, I was involved in meetings with white sanctuary workers at my church that did not include the recipients that lived in our church. Decisions were made without their input. Some of them were small—the purchase of appliances for instance—but others were important—such as discussions about whether or not we should have a time limit on our hospitality. Always couched in terms of the church having "a game plan" order before approaching the recipients, they were nevertheless absent. As pastor, that is a dynamic that I could have altered, but I did no more than mention it a few times in a halfhearted way. While I am always careful to adopt a hermeneutic of charity with the white activists that I analyze in this work, I think I can be more forthright about myself. In most cases I was worried about how discussion among the group would affect their feeling of welcome—I was embarrassed, but excluding recipients from participation ostensibly for their own benefit is the definition of white paternalism. In reality, it placed my emotional needs ahead of the sanctuary family of the church I serve. I share this story because it demonstrates how white supremacy functions, in what feels like benevolent ways, and that benevolent white supremacy is the bedrock of the practice of sanctuary.

Because I interviewed activists decades after their involvement with the Sanctuary Movement, the possibility for deep reflections about race and power that was not present at the time emerged:

> Lucy: Yeah, We viewed this movement through the lens of accompaniment. Um and, uh, did not. We were . . . we could not ever not be saviors—white Saviors. We could not not do that, but we were always trying not to, and we knew we shouldn't. But we just couldn't help ourselves. It's just . . ., But the voice that we tried to have once we return to the U. S. Was to say, um, we are trying to give a voice to the voiceless, but it's not our voice. We don't want it to be our voice. And so, of course it was our voice, right? . . .

> We were coming out of a time when white paternalism was just the way to effect change. And we were really just the very beginning group of people saying allies, we want to be allies for other people to have their own voice and their own destiny. And that was pretty new. But we made a lot of mistakes in that and, um, we had one idea in our head and we really didn't live it out in many . . . and we kept saying "Oh doh, doh doh doh doh." so that's a reflection I have on the Sanctuary Movement too— Is we had an idea. We really did our best to create that idea and it's probably for the next generation to carry that forward.

Over twenty years removed from the events of the Sanctuary Movement, Lucy is able to articulate that the movement was defined by white identity in crucial ways. In attempting to be a "voice for the voiceless," white activists spoke with their own voice, reinforcing and reinscribing whiteness and white supremacy through "white paternalism" and "white Savior[ism]." The repetitive reliance on a power-oblivious ethic that privileged white voices even while purporting to lift up recipients' narratives, meant that the Sanctuary Movement's project was fundamentally reliant on whiteness. As Lucy notes, "we just couldn't help ourselves." And yet that realization at least hints at and motions toward the possibility of realization and therefore redemption—that what was not seen can be seen, even as it elicits a "doh, doh, doh" response that is not dissimilar from my own sense of repentance as I can reflect and name my own white supremacy as a pastor in the New Sanctuary Movement.

While Lucy may be correct about the use of the term "ally," the dynamic that she explicates is not an innovation of the Sanctuary Movement. Rather, the tensions named by her find an important antecedent in the tensions between well-meaning white supporters of abolition and the civil rights movement. Perhaps the most resonant example for the Sanctuary Movement is the case of Frederick Douglass, who recounts being told "tell your story, Frederick" by an ally, but the story that Douglass wanted to tell was different from narration: "It did not entirely satisfy me to narrate wrongs; I felt like denouncing them."[12] Nolan Bennett characterizes the difference between the two in this way: "Whereas to narrate wrongs encouraged readers to judge Douglass' story alongside popular criteria of justice, to denounce wrongs is to implicate readers within the structures that create antebellum subjects on and off the plantation, by revealing the coercions and conditionings of society that make not simply slaves but slaveowners, sympathizers, and abolitionists."[13] The differences between the two forms of argumentation, the white audience that was positioned as judge, and the attending pressures by white participants create a powerful parallel to the Sanctuary Movement, where similar dynamics over what could be said took place. Indeed, in the civil rights movement, similar contestations over the role of white supporters of the movement were held.[14] As a result, I would argue that the model employed by the Sanctuary Movement has a long genealogical history and some of the problems and tensions that were expressed in the past continued to be replicated in the Sanctuary Movement.

One story that I was told from a recipient gives more concrete meaning to Lucy's reflection that while white activists purported to give voice to recipients, it was their own voice that was speaking:

> Gloria: I remember one time I went to a church and there were a lot of people, and there was a person—this was a source of big conflict—there was a woman who was my translator. She would translate from Spanish. But I had some knowledge of English, and I knew what I was saying, and she would say, "what Gloria really means is this." And I would say no— what I said is what I meant.

Recipients often gave their *testimonios* in Spanish and Mayan languages, leading translation to be necessary. In this case, Gloria relied on a translator in giving a *testimonio* but found that here words were being edited by the white translator in order to convey a particular message. While Gloria immediately shifts to another difficult story about her time in sanctuary

---

[12]Frederick Douglass, *Autobiographies*, ed. Henry Louis Gates (New York: Library of America: Distributed to the trade in the United States by Penguin Books USA, 1994), 367. Quoted in Nolan Bennett, "To Narrate and Denounce: Frederick Douglass and the Politics of Personal Narrative," *Political Theory* 44, no. 2 (2016): 240, https://doi.org/10.1177/0090591714549075.
[13]Bennett, "To Narrate and Denounce: Frederick Douglass and the Politics of Personal Narrative," 240.
[14]See: Megan Ming Francis, "The Price of Civil Rights: Black Lives, White Funding, and Movement Capture," *Law & Society Review* 53, no. 1 (2019), https://doi.org/10.1111/lasr .12384.

in this interview and therefore does not elaborate, she had stated earlier in the interview that her sanctuary congregation was less forthrightly critical of US foreign policy than her desire to "talk about the role of the US in what was happening in my country." As discussed previously in a previous chapter, recipients were asked to perform victimhood by white activists, who then in turn used those narratives to generate theological reflections, self-actualization, and foster new identities. In fact, Gloria's story reveals that perhaps those narratives, constrained as they were by the movement's focus on trauma and victimhood, were mediated by white translators before being utilized by white hearers for a project of self-actualization and realization. In other words, while the *testimonio* is clearly mediated by whiteness through its thoroughgoing curation to address white concerns and foster white meaning, it was also, at least some of the time, mediated more directly by translation from white activists who straightforwardly edited the content of the *testimonio* to meet their needs. The instrumentalization of recipient narratives, the centering of white psychospiritual development, and the ownership over those same narratives all indicate that the Sanctuary Movement was not only characterized by whiteness; it produced and reified it, serving as a site of liberal white identity formation.

In participating in what Stuelke calls "sentimental reparativity," white activists were crafting identities for themselves that relied on the trauma narrative of recipients.[15] Utilizing sentimentality and reparativity, we can tie together the way that affect, whiteness, and subjectivity are intimately related to one another in the Sanctuary Movement. As Simon Strick argues in *American Dolorologies*, "sentimentalism, though arguing on behalf of the recognition and inclusion of subaltern bodies, is thus situated within hegemonic systems of differentiation and objectification: it always potentially reiterates and reinscribes the hierarchies of race and gender."[16] While white activists viewed themselves as fighting against the powerful, they failed to account for the ways that they too wielded power and the ways that their challenge to power served to reinforce their own agency. As Lauren Berlant, one of the foremost scholars of sentimentality argues, "as a force for the conversion of the politically privileged, sentimental politics had had powerfully transformative effects . . . But . . . sentimentality always

---

[15]Patricia, "The Reparative Politics of Central America Solidarity Movement Culture," 773. It is important to note that these concepts are derived from the work of noted queer theorist Eve Kosofsky Sedgwick. For reparativity, see: Eve Kosofsky Sedgwick, "Paranoid Reading and Reparative Reading or, You're So Paranoid, You Probably Think This Introduction is About You," in *Novel Gazing: Queer Readings in Fiction*, ed. Eve Kosofsky Sedgwick (New York: Duke University Press, 1997). For sentimentality, see: Eve Kosofsky Sedgwick, *Epistemology of the Closet*, Updated ed., preface by the author ed. (Berkeley, CA: University of California Press, 2008).
[16]Simon Strick, *American Dolorologies: Pain, Sentimentalism, Biopolitics* (Albany, NY: State University of New York Press, 2014), 7.

traffic[s] in cliche, the reproduction of a person as a thing," which provides "the privileged with heroic occasions of recognition, rescue, and inclusion."[17] In instrumentalizing the experiences of recipients, white activists found new identities in which they were "cutting edge" or awakened.[18] Indeed, part of the project of such sentimental reparativity was the critique of white identity,[19] while simultaneously reinscribing it. In becoming aware of the complicity in US foreign policy, white activists became aware in some ways of their privilege, adopting identities like "NorteAmericano." Adopting such an identity places the activist in relationship with Central Americans, even connoting a performative humility fostered by the activists' learning from recipients, and yet it also marks the activist *and their community* as radical, empathic, and consciousness raised, enhancing prestige among other activists.[20] In other words, while outwardly critical of North American identity and even possessing a capacity to recognize white privilege, the reparative sentimentality of the Sanctuary Movement served to reinscribe power and hierarchy.[21] Recipient experiences were used to achieve cache through conversion to a new way of thinking, and that instrumentalization is a key part of how the movement produced and reinforced liberal, white identity.

In analyzing how white activists utilized the category of risk to make sense of their participation in the movement, especially after the high-profile indictments of nearly a dozen sanctuary activists in Tucson, an account of the pervasive effects of sentimentality on the Sanctuary Movement becomes possible. To be sure, there were risks—activists were charged with and convicted of felonies for a variety of activities related to sanctuary work. There were other risks too—the government employed a network of spies and informants that infiltrated the movement and churches were threatened with loss of their tax-exempt status for participating. Showcasing the power of the Tucson sanctuary trial in the sanctuary community, Carl related one of his experiences with law enforcement to the trial of Tucson sanctuary workers:

> One day I happened to be upstairs on the second floor, and then one of Guatemalan guys came up to get me. So, I went downstairs, there were

---

[17]Lauren Gail Berlant, *The Female Complaint: The Unfinished Business of Sentimentality in American Culture* (Durham, NC: Duke University Press, 2008), 35.

[18]"Sanctuary Update—November 1, 1983," *Basta: Newsletter of the Chicago Religious Task Force on Central America* (Chicago, IL, 1983).

[19]See: Renny Golden, "The White Way, the Native Way," in *Dangerous Memories: Invasion and Resistance since 1492* (Chicago, IL: Chicago Religious Task Force on Central America, 1991).

[20]Recall that many activists claim that they experienced a boon in attendance and engagement through their participation in the Sanctuary Movement. See: Coutin, *The Culture of Protest: Religious Activism and the U.S. Sanctuary Movement*, 160–80.

[21]See: Marilyn Chilcote, "Interview with Reverend Marilyn Chilcote," interview by Eileen Purcell, *The Public Sanctuary Movement: An Historical Basis of Hope*, 1998. "We were the ones, we North Americans with our white faces who walked into war time's situations, and we were safe."

two guys in suits, inside the house, standing by the front door. It was two guys from the FBI, and they introduced themselves, and so right away they were going: "so, what's going on here?" I asked them to leave if they didn't have a warrant. They did leave and we never saw or heard from them again. I don't really know what that was all about, if it was just an intimidation tactic. I share that story, for people who are going to be doing sanctuary, I think it's important to have robust legal support. Obviously, this was nothing like what the people in Tucson had faced, but it certainly could have gone that way. It was a lesson of like, of the power and the reach of the state. It was a very sobering wake-up call for me. Getting beyond my ideological reasons for doing the work, to a very visceral, "wow" kind of moment. It was the first time in a real emotional way that I realized how serious it was and how serious the risk was.

In exposing themselves to risk, many sanctuary workers found a powerful link to recipients, coming to view themselves as sharing in that risk. Indeed, in border crossing narratives, Susan Bibler Coutin has pointed out that the risky nature of the experience helped activists "place themselves as fully as possible in the positions of persecuted Central Americans," an experience which led them to conclude that their experience was "more authentic than their own lives."[22]

Yet the weight of that risk was borne differently by white activists than it was by recipients. For all the identification with recipients through shared risk, the risks for white activists turned out to be limited. No churches lost their tax-exempt status, despite the fastidious attention the issue was given in interviews with activists and sanctuary materials from the time. The Tucson sanctuary workers were convicted and their appeals were denied, but they received a sentence of probation and even convinced the judge to alter the terms of their probation to allow sanctuary activists to continue to work with one another after the trail.[23] Only about a dozen sanctuary activists ever ended up in a courtroom.[24] Moreover, claiming risk-taking as a part of its identity, while costing white sanctuary activists nothing, greatly enhanced the movement's numbers.[25] Risk was an attractive part of sanctuary work, leading more people to commit to the movement. Gus Schultz, a leader of the East Bay Sanctuary Coalition described the appeal of risk-taking this way: "And I think that those, those were the things that caused people to respond

---

[22]Coutin, *The Culture of Protest: Religious Activism and the U.S. Sanctuary Movement*, 59.

[23]Coutin, "Smugglers or Samaritans in Tucson, Arizona: Producing and Contesting Legal Truth," 562.

[24]Sophie H. Pirie, "The Origins of a Political Trial: The Sanctuary Movement and Political Justice," *Yale Journal of Law & the Humanities* 2, no. 2 (1990): 284–5.

[25]The CRTFCA newsletter *Basta!* claimed that the number of sanctuary communities doubled during the trail, Coutin, "Smugglers or Samaritans in Tucson, Arizona: Producing and Contesting Legal Truth."

. . . taking risks would be something that caused more people to respond. That people, people did not want to be involved in things that didn't have some sense of risk in it."[26] Ultimately, white activists found risk attractive not only because it gave meaning to their participation in the movement, but because it gave access to new, "complex identities" that helped them "leave the familiar behind."[27] I myself have labeled the church I pastor's decision to become a sanctuary congregation "very punk" in conversation—by which I mean risky, refusing to adhere to rules, and, yes, cool. Sanctuary was an effective practice for sanctuary workers, myself included, who derived spiritual satisfaction and progressive bona-fides from participation in the New Sanctuary Movement. Many of those that I interviewed looked back at the risks faced with nostalgia, noting how "alive" or connected to their faith they were. While the actual risk ended up being quite low for the average white activist, the ability to claim a risk-taking identity proved powerful.

While white activists connected their risk-taking to the risks taken by recipients and sought to share in that risk-taking, the difference between white risk and Central American risk was vast. Convicted of felonies, white activists receive amended probationary sentences, favorable press coverage, and the ability at any time to stop. Thus, the Sanctuary Movement had an attenuated relationship to risk. In some ways, activists put recipients in the role of victims, as those who perpetually experienced risk. In others, they cultivated ways to share in that risk in ways that produced enlightenment and grew the movement. While on the surface these strategies might appear to be in tension with one another or mutually exclusive, the opportunity to jump between the two strategies, depending on which generated the most agency, self-actualization, or feelings of solidarity and repair is indicative of the way that whiteness worked within the movement.

As much as the Sanctuary Movement became a part of the identity of white activists, it was a voluntary commitment. This is precisely what made it powerful—its voluntariness—and yet the consequences of those risks paled in comparison to risks voluntarily and involuntarily taken on by recipients. To some extent, this is true in any solidarity-based movement, where some are asked to voluntarily take on risks they might have otherwise eschewed precisely because whiteness shields the risktaker from consequences. And yet, because of the sentimentality deployed by the Sanctuary Movement, white activists used such risk-taking to reach spiritual heights and claim "heroic occasions of recognition, rescue, and inclusion" that typify sentimental politics. I would argue something further—the sentimentality around risk practiced by white activists positioned recognition of the Other as a tool of self-actualization and social advancement. In recognizing the risk of the Other and even coming to identify with and co-opt the stories and trauma of

---

[26]Schultz, interview.
[27]Coutin, *The Culture of Protest: Religious Activism and the U.S. Sanctuary Movement*, 56, 60.

recipients, the white activist "not only reiterates and reinscribes the hierarchies of race and gender" they cultivate a white subjectivity that is based on the bodies of recipients. In identifying with the Other and performing risk, they came to occupy the center of the movement, reinscribing and reinstating the very domination structures they sought to disrupt. This is the double-edged sword of sentimentality; while it can move people to action, those actions are damaging and, in this case, white.

White Practical Theology, Judith Butler, and White Subjectivity

Doubtlessly, some white activists would protest against the Sanctuary Movement as a white project or a site where white identity is produced. And yet, Susan Bibler Coutin has noted that activists "regarded the sanctuary movement . . . as North American"—in other words, white.[28] According to Coutin, recipients had important roles, but "sanctuary itself . . . remained a movement about, rather than of, Central Americans."[29] While Lloyd Barba and Tatyana Castillo-Ramos make the case that the whiteness of the movement has been overstated because it focused overly much on the activism within the US to the exclusion of the networks of activists in Mexico and Central America, it still ought to be relatively uncontroversial to analyze the movement as a site of white subject formation.[30] However, whiteness as a category was not embraced as a topic of reflection by the movement itself, making whiteness both a clear organizing framework and one that often lurks just below the surface.

In my interviews, one activist, unprompted declared: "I don't think we were white saviors," but the spontaneous reference to race in the Sanctuary Movement while discussing the impact and legacy of the movement ought to give some pause. One of the central characteristics of whiteness is its assumedness and therefore invisibility, and yet here it seemed to dwell just below the surface of Carl's experience of the Sanctuary Movement.[31] Perhaps in saying so, Carl names the ways that speech shapes reality. Coutin recounts a story of an activist who became so paranoid of surveillance and infiltration that he said, "sanctuary is legal" repeatedly as a sort of shield against prosecution due to the legal system's sympathetic view of white

---

[28]Ibid., 11.
[29]Ibid.
[30]Lloyd D. Barba and Tatyana Castillo-Ramos, "Latinx Leadership and Legacies in the US Sanctuary Movement, 1980–2020," *American Religion* 3, no. 1 (2021), https://doi.org/10.2979/amerreli.3.1.01.
[31]Dyer, *White*, 9–13.

activists and their claims to be acting in good faith.[32] She uses an interesting phrase, "like a talisman," to describe the action. Such talismans occasionally litter my interviews, which is of course natural. After giving many years of one's life to a cause, there is undoubtedly the desire when speaking to a researcher to make a defense of one's participation. However, the natural use of a phrase like "white savior" indicates that race is an organic category within the movement. Why else would activists, with the exception of Lucy, spend time distancing themselves from whiteness, if it was invisible? Occasionally whiteness directly interrupts my interviews and places itself front and center.

In Chapter 3, I argued that utilizing Judith Butler's work was better suited than a MacIntyrian model for thinking about power in the Sanctuary Movement and practical theology and that it is an especially useful way of centering the experience of recipients of sanctuary. Now, I would like to add an addendum: Butler's work can also yield better insights into the sanctuary as a site of white identity formation for activists, a conclusion which commends a subjectivity and performativity lens for practical theology broadly and practical theological consideration of whiteness specifically. While Butler's work has focused on gender, there are some resonances between her arguments and the account of whiteness and the Sanctuary Movement that I have presented here. However, I do not argue that my engagement with Butler's work produces a final or even polished account of whiteness, but I do contend that it can help generate some ideas about the simultaneous omnipresence and hiddenness of whiteness.[33]

For Butler, "performativity must be understood not as a singular or deliberate 'act,' but, rather, as the reiterative and citational practice by which discourse produces the effects that it names."[34] In this framework, gender is always a "do-ing"[35] through a "stylized repetition of acts,"[36] then is not something as stable is it might seem: "If gender is instituted through

---

[32]Coutin, "Smugglers or Samaritans in Tucson, Arizona: Producing and Contesting Legal Truth," 563.

[33]In fact, Judith Butler makes the connections between performativity and whiteness explicit in George Yancy and Judith Butler, "What's Wrong With 'All Lives Matter'?," *The New York Times*, 2014. Yancy asks: "In 'Gender Trouble: Feminism and the Subversion of Identity,' you discuss gender as 'a stylized repetition of acts.' Do you also see whiteness as 'a stylized repetition of acts' that solidifies and privileges white bodies, or even leads to naïve, 'post-racial' universal formulations like 'all lives matter'?" and Butler responds, "Yes, we can certainly talk about 'doing whiteness' as a way of putting racial categories into action, since whiteness is part of what we call 'race,' and is often implicitly or explicitly part of a race project that seeks to achieve and maintain dominance for white people." Indeed, as Yancy's engagement with Butler's work shines much light on how the conversation between performativity and whiteness might move forward.

[34]Butler, *Bodies that Matter: On the Discursive Limits of "Sex,"* xiii.

[35]Judith Butler, *Gender Trouble: Feminism and the Subversion of Identity* (New York: Routledge, 1990), 25.

[36]Ibid., 192.

acts which are internally discontinuous, then the appearance of substance is precisely that, a constructed identity, a performative accomplishment which the mundane social audience, including the actors themselves, come to believe and to perform in the mode of belief."[37] This repetition is compulsive, but it always citational, as subjects are "compelled to 'cite' the norm in order to qualify and remain a viable subject."[38] Power too plays a role, especially in the role of subjection, wherein the instantiating power of the subject becomes hidden, or, as Butler argues in *Giving an Account of Oneself*, "opaque." Subjects are formed by power acting on them, but they come to utilize that power—"subjection is nevertheless a power *assumed by* the subject, an assumption that constitutes the instrument of that subject's becoming"—and in the moment of that utilization it appears as if the subject was not in fact formed by power in the first place.[39] This process does not happen in a vacuum, and the self's relation to others has an important role to play in Butler's work, but that relationality becomes "irrecoverable," rendering the subject opaque as opposed to transparent.[40]

The opacity of the subject is one of the most important arguments of George Yancy's *Look, A White!*. In *Black Bodies, White Gazes*, Yancy develops the concept of whiteness' ability to "ambush" white would-be antiracists through self-concealment and refusal to fully "examine aspects of their own white subject position."[41] For Yancy, ambush is inescapably linked to Butler's notion of opacity: "my sense is that this opacity places a limit on self-knowledge regarding one's own white racism. the experience of ambush interrupts and undermines a form of white epistemic arrogance to give a full account (a belief held by so many of my white students) of the complex dimensions of one's white racist self."[42] Building on Butler's contention that the body is "given over from the start to the world others," Yancy argues that whiteness is constituted socially, paying close attention to whiteness' "embeddedness" and the constant striving by whites to "elide their racist constitution and by extension their vulnerability."[43] Yancy argues that "vulnerability and racial constitution/subjection are coextensive," but

---

[37]Ibid., 191, 92.
[38]Butler, *Bodies that Matter: On the Discursive Limits of "Sex,"* 232.
[39]Butler, *The Psychic Life of Power: Theories in Subjection*, 11.
[40]"Moments of unknowingness about oneself tend to emerge in the context of relations to others, suggesting that these relations call upon primary forms of relationality that are not always available to explicit and reflective thematization. If we are formed in the context of relations that become partially irrecoverable to us, then that opacity seems built into our formation and follows from our status as beings who are formed in relations of dependency." Butler, *Giving an Account of Oneself*, 20.
[41]George Yancy, *Black Bodies, White Gazes: The Continuing Significance of Race* (Lanham, MD: Rowman & Littlefield Pub., 2008), 229.
[42]George Yancy, *Look, A White! Philosophical Essays on Whiteness* (Philadelphia, PA: Temple University Press, 2012), 170.
[43]Ibid., 166.

"there is no preexisting, stable, vulnerable white self that is exposed to white racism. Moreover, there is no ahistorical material 'white' vulnerable body that is the starting point of the white self."[44] Thus, we can understand more clearly how subjection works with regards to whiteness, especially with the power that marks the conditions of white subjectivity and their subsequent elision and then wielding by whites, who also strive to deny the power that marks their emergence as white subjects. To Butler, "power emerges as what belongs exclusively to the subject (making the subject appear as if it belonged to no prior operation of power)," and this is perhaps particularly well attested to with regards to white subjection, where the self's opacity is bound up with whiteness.[45] White subjects do not experience themselves as being constituted from relationality with others; they are autonomous and independent, able to adopt new identities at will. They *feel* independent.

Yancy's understanding of white subjection, as well as whiteness' capacity to "ambush," can help make sense of whiteness in the Sanctuary Movement. Simultaneously everywhere and yet rarely explicitly stated, white activists experienced themselves as autonomous individuals who were able to freely adopt new identities that were more "international" than American, like NorteAmericano.[46] They adopted strategies within the Sanctuary Movement that were directly relational, deriving their white subjectivity from their "context in relation to the other," but then rendering that relationality "irrecoverable" through symbolic power exchange that did not materially change power imbalances.[47] This can perhaps give light to the interview in which a defense of the movement is formed by one activist I interviewed—"I don't think we were white saviors." In some occasions, whiteness is known, but it is also rejected by white activists, who refuse to "tarry," as Yancy puts it, with their own whiteness.[48] When it is mentioned by activists, whiteness is instantly pushed away in favor of more nuanced identities, but denying one's whiteness by seeking other identities does not make it so—it is a signifier of that whiteness.[49] In another, as with Lucy, it is clearly stated: the Sanctuary Movement is bound up with "white paternalism." With regards to Gloria, it is again forcefully articulated in a scene in which white nuns boo a recipient who strived to shape the conversation within the movement. Clearly, whiteness had much to do with that exchange, both explicitly and

---

[44]Ibid.

[45]Butler, *The Psychic Life of Power: Theories in Subjection*, 15.

[46]Coutin, *The Culture of Protest: Religious Activism and the U.S. Sanctuary Movement*, 56.

[47]Butler, *Giving an Account of Oneself*, 20.

[48]Yancy, *Look, A White! Philosophical Essays on Whiteness*, 166.

[49]See: Tamara Nopper, "The White Anti-Racist Is an Oxymoron: An Open Letter to 'White Anti-Racists,'" 2003. And Yancy, *Backlash: What Happens When We Talk Honestly about Racism in America*, 71: "It is so easy for white people to retreat to a form of individualism designed to nullify their group status. But I get it, you don't want to be associated with a group. Sorry but that resistance is a function of whiteness, white privilege."

implicitly, but few white activists were eager to reflect on the lack of recipient voice in decision-making of the movement.

In many other interviews, whiteness never even comes up at all, no doubt due to my own whiteness and inability to center it in conversation effectively, but also because it simply was not part of the conscious experience of many white activists. Whiteness was simultaneously everywhere in the Sanctuary Movement and nowhere, denied even its acknowledgment, and it is my hope that by engaging with questions of performativity and subjectivity, the Sanctuary Movement can be placed into context as a Foucauldian "technology of the self," allowing white activists to "transform themselves" through a "sentimental reparitivity" and "feeling right," but also to reinscribe their whiteness in the myriad of ways that I have outlined in this chapter. The feelings of equality that the symbolic *testimonio* produced ultimately allowed for the establishment of hierarchies that is the sine qua non of whiteness.

An analysis of whiteness and the Sanctuary Movement must also extend beyond the movement itself to include scholarship on the movement, which centers white activist experiences and spiritual development. Many of these works are foundational, nuanced, and exceptional, but they oftentimes omit entirely recipient experiences, while giving detailed accounts of activist origin stories and theological reflection.[50] Recipient experiences, if recounted, usually comprise a small section within the work, with some rare exceptions.[51] Oral histories of the Sanctuary Movement are also only comprised of activist narratives, an even greater concern since, with the passage of time and consequent death of participants, these oral histories will shape future scholarship about the movement in ways that omit recipient struggles for agency within the movement.[52] Outside of scholarship, journalistic and theological accounts often lionize male activists, prominently featuring men like Jim Corbett and John Fife, while sensationalizing the trauma of recipients.[53] This too seems to be about whiteness, a critique from which an analysis of my work is not excluded. My first work on the Sanctuary Movement did not interview recipients and spent considerable time on the origin stories of activists, which was because

---

[50]For example, see: Lorentzen, *Women in the Sanctuary Movement*. The analysis fills a critical gap in scholarship by paying attention to women activists in the Sanctuary Movement, but it centers their origin stories and narratives in ways that reinscribe whiteness.

[51]Probably the best use of recipient experiences, although it comprises a slim amount of the fieldwork of the monograph is in Coutin, *The Culture of Protest: Religious Activism and the U.S. Sanctuary Movement*.

[52]In some ways, this critique is unfair, as Eileen Purcell had said she intended to interview recipients, but was interrupted by a life-threatening illness from which she recovered. See: Eileen Purcell, *The Public Sanctuary Movement: An Historical Basis of Hope* (Graduate Theological Union, 1998).

[53]See: Davidson, *Convictions of the Heart: Jim Corbett and the Sanctuary Movement*.

of my own unexamined whiteness.[54] Of course, this was also due to the fact that recipients are difficult to make contact with, and I did seek to interview the recipient in that case, but I did not seek to center her experience, and I did not find it objectionable to publish an article that did not interview a recipient. I related to, even admired, the white liberal religious activists that I interviewed, and so my analysis reflected that unexamined whiteness. Unfortunately, my unexamined whiteness is not aberrational; it is the norm.

Within practical theology that norm is perpetuated by use of theoretical tools that elide power and focus on individual faith formation in ways that are bound up with whiteness. Simply put, MacIntyre's practice framework is devastatingly effective at analyzing how practice forms individuals, but it is woefully ineffective at analyzing power. It imagines everyone as individuals and on equal footing in ways that do not map onto religious life in the United States, or indeed the world, and perhaps most devastatingly, it pushes analysis toward unquestioned agents, individuals who do not experience power disparities, and those whose theological inquiries are intelligible both within a practice framework and to the researcher. If obliviousness to one's own racialized power is one of the most important aspects of whiteness, then MacIntyre's practice framework buttresses a white theological project.

In some ways, the field of practical theology has already begun reckoning with this problem. in an important essay in *Opening Practical Theology* titled "White Practical Theology," Tom Beaudoin and Katherine Turpin articulate the defining features, theological focuses, and theoretical frameworks of White Practical Theology. Unsurprisingly, one of the defining characteristics of this analysis is MacIntyre's virtue ethics, which they argue reinscribes colonial frameworks by suggesting a "tight connection between belief and practice."[55] However, they also point to the way white scholars cite one another, fail to appreciate context, and situate the white experience as universal. In many ways the essay is gestural, naming realities, and situating whiteness within the field while challenging its universality and dominance, but it is also aspirational, with Beaudoin and Turpin hoping it will "lead to theories of whiteness in practical theology richer and broader than what we have proposed in this chapter."[56] This chapter takes up just such a challenge, arguing for whiteness as a central category of analysis—not just for the Sanctuary Movement, but practical theology more broadly—and also putting forth a subjectivity model for analyzing whiteness within the field, a theoretical contribution which enables more thoroughgoing analysis of whiteness than other frameworks currently in use in practical theology. In doing so, I join other practical

[54]Woolf, "Holy Risk: Old Cambridge Baptist Church and the Sanctuary Movement."
[55]Tom Beaudoin and Katherine Turpin, "White Practical Theology," in *Opening the Field of Practical Theology: An Introduction*, ed. Kathleen A. Cahalan and Gordon S. Mikoski (Lanham, MD: Rowman & Littlefield, 2014), 263.
[56]Ibid., 268.

theologians who are doing rich work on whiteness like Todd Whitmore, who demonstrates a willingness to "tarry," as Yancy puts it, with his own whiteness and how it constructs, enables, and restrains his scholarship.

Within the broader field of religious studies and theology, this chapter centers whiteness in the study of a progressive, humanitarian, and political movement at a time in which that project seems increasingly urgent.[57] Although he is widely read, James Cone's 1970 definition of "white theology"[58] and haunting question, "Why do White theologians ignore racism?"[59] continue to challenge whiteness and point at the need for an account of it in scholarship.[60] While white supremacy is widely regarded as playing a foundational role in American society, analyses of whiteness within religious studies have remained "limited," according to Rachel Schneider and Sophie Bjork-James, "due to fears that it will serve to reinforce the cultural power and discursive authority of whiteness."[61] Citing the consequences of such thinking, Schneider and Bjork-James argue that there is "a need to interrogate how racial privilege—including 'unstated norms, invisibility, fragility' (Corbin 2016)—is both protected and expressed through religious practice and theology."[62] It is my hope that this book contributes to the growing engagement with whiteness in religion in precisely the way that Schneider and Bjork-James name. While whiteness and white supremacy deserve scholarly attention in a variety of locations, scholars have been somewhat quicker to apply these lenses to self-avowedly racist, white supremacist, and conservative religious movements. In offering the Sanctuary Movement up as a touchstone for whiteness in the study of religion, I argue that whiteness ought to be the salient category of analysis for a wide variety of movements, including those that achieve measurable good, generate solidarity, and are even beloved by the researcher, as is the case with this project. In short, whiteness as a category should not be reserved for people, movements, or theologies with which we do not share an affinity. James Cone's "white theology" is more nefarious and pervasive than many give it credit for, and it resides in progressive institutions as well as conservative ones.

---

[57]Aisha M. Beliso-De Jesús, "Confounded Identities: A Meditation on Race, Feminism, and Religious Studies in Times of White Supremacy," *Journal of the American Academy of Religion* 86, no. 2 (2018): 308, https://doi.org/10.1093/jaarel/lfx085.

[58]James H. Cone, *A Black Theology of Liberation*, 1st ed. (Philadelphia, PA: Lippincott, 1970), 25.

[59]James H. Cone, "Theology's Great Sin: Silence in the Face of White Supremacy," *Black Theology: An International Journal* 2, no. 2 (2004): 142, https://doi.org/10.1558/blth.2.2.139.36027.

[60]Karen Teel, "Can We Hear Him Now? James Cone's Enduring Challenge to White Theologians," *Theological Studies (Baltimore)* 81, no. 3 (2020), https://doi.org/10.1177/0040563920960034.

[61]Rachel C. Schneider and Sophie Bjork-James, "Whither Whiteness and Religion?: Implications for Theology and the Study of Religion," *Journal of the American Academy of Religion* 88, no. 1 (2020): 177, https://doi.org/10.1093/jaarel/lfaa002.

[62]Ibid., 191.

Conclusion

In this chapter, I have tried to come to terms with instances in my research where activists used trauma in *testimonios* to fuel their own self-actualization or uncritically suggested that recipients were empowered by the movement. Was I seeing a regrettable personal decision or viewpoint? A lack of reflection on the part of the activist? Over time, I came to see the issue at hand as only truly explainable by whiteness. Sentimental reportativity, with regards to the Sanctuary Movement, also played a role in this analysis, and I argue that the politics of sentimentality emerges within the movement as a technology of whiteness—white activists seeking "feeling right" centered their own affective desires and needs within the movement. As a researcher, I struggle with this conclusion because I doubt that many of my subjects would recognize themselves in such claims, which would typically cause me to reexamine my perspectives, but is that not exactly how whiteness functions? Its simultaneous visibility and invisibility is precisely the point, and paying attention to whiteness' function in the Sanctuary Movement is vital. Otherwise, one risks missing how the Sanctuary Movement functioned as a site of white subject formation, a mistake that would only serve to reify and make more concrete the power of whiteness as it would render such questions absent from any theological reflection and critical reflection on practice. With this understanding firmly in hand, we turn to that project in the next chapter, but not before considering hope.

At first glance, such an account of whiteness, white subjectivity, and the Sanctuary Movement may seem to foreclose the possibility of ethical action, rendering it hopeless. Put another way, if the Sanctuary Movement is a site of white subject formation and the opacity of the self renders whiteness dangerous even its acknowledgment, are there ethical ways forward? I would like to believe so. Perhaps the best place to answer that question is, again, in Butler's work, where she asks a similar question: "But can we say that the experience of being imposed upon from the start, and against one's will, heightens a sense of responsibility? Have we perhaps unwittingly destroyed the possibility for agency with all this talk about being given over, being structured, being addressed?"[63] In the end, Butler's concept of subjection and opacity of the self grounds an ethic of responsibility, as these concepts "can provide a way to understand the way in which all of us are already not precisely bounded, not precisely separate, but in our skins, given over, in each other's hands, at each other's mercy. This is a situation we do not choose; it forms the horizon of choice, and it is that which grounds our responsibility. In this sense, we are not responsible for it, but it is that

---

[63]Judith Butler, "Giving an Account of Oneself," *Diacritics* 31, no. 4 (2001): 39, https://doi.org /10.1353/dia.2004.0002.

for which we are nevertheless responsible."[64] Butler's account of the self does not render ethical action impossible; it becomes the new grounding of ethical action based on relationality and vulnerability on the "horizon of choice." This conviction—the possibility of ethical action—undergirds this project, and it is not only to the theological that we turn in the next chapter but to the practical.

Theological *Excursus*: Trauma, Suffering, and Redemption

In Chapter 2, I argued that a practice framework remains useful for practical theological analysis of the Sanctuary Movement, but that it falls short due to a lack of sufficient analysis of power, which is critical for any engagement with the movement. In particular, one of the strengths of considering sanctuary as a practice is the assiduous attention that it gives to activists and their "feeling right," one of the components of which was using recipient experiences of trauma and victimhood as material from which to base theological reflection. For Christian activists, the suffering and trauma of recipients were mapped onto the crucifixion, with recipients' trauma affecting salvation for white activists and the United States, whose failures to live up to its ethical commitments were deeply troubling. Among the Jewish activists that I interviewed, one of the consistent connections was between the suffering of Central Americans and Holocaust, which produced what Rachel called a "powerful" experience of "connection" and "understanding," words which resemble the affective qualities of "feeling right" that Stuelke highlights. Another connection made by Noam recounts that "helping" through the Sanctuary Movement was connected to tzedakah, the Jewish notion of charity, as well as the mandate to "not stand idly by." That imperative to not stand idly by was connected with the sorts of political activism that one might expect, but it was also a profound spiritual insight that changed how Noam thought about daily life: "You know, when people say don't sweat the details—it's all details. You know, it's all in the little things that you do."

Among Christians, theological reflection was mainly focused on suffering, the cross, and necessity for moral action. As Joan recounts, participation in the Sanctuary Movement was about producing a "global perspective" grounded in the siblingship of citizenship of the United States and Central Americans: "Our ultimate goal was to help build a global perspective in our congregation and in our faith community here in Milwaukee to see that we are connected with our siblings in other countries and that we

---

[64]Ibid.

need to respond with action when they are being repressed." Through the experiences of recipients, one activist remarked, "I see Jesus, the crucified one, not just the resurrected one."[65] Dorothee Sölle, an ally of the movement and participant in solidarity practices, argued that in the torture and death of Central Americans, we are invited to witness the cross of the present in a way that American Christianity has not paid attention to: "This kind of religion knows the cross only as a magical symbol of what he has done for us, not as the sign of the poor man who was tortured to death as a political criminal, like thousands today who stand up for his truth in El Salvador."[66] Theological connections to the resurrection were far less common, finding only one mention in Eileen Purcell's oral history of sanctuary activists. Importantly, it is focused on the movement and individual participants' ability to "change things": "The faith of the gospel is that we can change things. That there is resurrection. And I guess we just have to keep living like that. We have to keep living as if that were true."[67] The Sanctuary Movement did change things through landmark victories like ABC v. Thornburgh, a court case that changed US asylum law, and these changes led to further senses of "feeling right" among activists, who took pride in, in the words of Jim, "defeat[ing] Reagan," and felt part of the movement that challenged authority and won.

One of the key ways that white activists theologically reflected on the movement was by connecting recipient experiences to the crucifixion, mapping the suffering of recipients onto the suffering of Christ. In this chapter, I have shown how the politics of sentimentality, and indeed solidarity activism in general, takes trauma that is not its own and uses it to produce affective responses that move hearers to change their politics and actions. I have also connected this same practice with the way that the movement centered whiteness. Taken together, these arguments form the foundation for the following theological reflection about trauma, the limits of the crucifixion, and the persistence of recipient bodies, narratives, and activism. Such persistence interrupts the theological lens that white activists used to make sense of recipient experiences, an observation that leads to an account of remaining, if not resurrection, that draws on the work of Shelley Rambo and joins other voices that question the ability for Christ's suffering to be redemptive.

Calling it a "founding disappearance," de Certeau argues that "Christianity is founded *upon the loss of a body*—the loss of the body of Jesus Christ."[68] It is this lack of the body that enables the Christian story,

---

[65]Bob McKenzie, "Interview with Rev. Bob McKenzie" interview by Eileen Purcell, *The Public Sanctuary Movement: An Historical Basis of Hope*, 1998.
[66]Dorothee Sölle, *The Window of Vulnerability: A Political Spirituality*, 1st English-language ed. (Minneapolis, MN: Fortress Press, 1990), 140.
[67]Chilcote, interview.
[68]Michel de Certeau, *The Mystic Fable: The Sixteenth and Seventeenth Centuries* (Chicago, IL: University of Chicago Press, 1992), 81.

whereby Jesus' disciples take up his story as their own, since Jesus' "body is structured by dissemination, like a text."[69] Christ's missing body becomes the foundation for the institutions of the church as well, "producing institutions and discourses that are the effects of and substitutions for that absence," as the believers "'invent' a mystic body—missing and sought after—that would also be their own."[70] The disappearance of Jesus' body is generative, allowing the question of where Jesus' body is to generate new practices, hermeneutics, as well as "structure[ing] the apostolic discourse."[71] Graham Ward, in his essay, "the Displaced Body of Jesus Christ," which draws on Certeau's work, is quick to point out that these practices should not be read as "endless simulacra for fulfillment," but rather as the "Logos creating a space within himself, a womb, within which (*en Christoi*) the Church will expand and creation be recreated."[72] For Ward, Jesus' body is not *lost* at all—his absenting and withdrawal is "not a decisive break," but through its permeability, transcorporeality, and transpositionality "all other bodies are situated and given their significance," an insight which, for Ward, grounds the possibility of the omniprescence and ubiquity of God.[73]

Whether Jesus' body is lost, displaced, withdrawn, or obscured, its inaccessibility makes possible the church. In a very real way, the community of faith takes on Jesus' story, complete with wounds, and makes its own through practices like the Eucharist, which reenacts that wounding through sacrificial language, perhaps reaching its apogee in Paul's mystical naming of the church as the body of Christ. Moreover, the displacement of Jesus' body allows for the possibility of communication that grounds "the poetics of the New Testament itself": "the absenting body of Christ gives place to (is supplemented by) a body of confessional and doxological discourse in which the Church announces, in a past tense which can never make its presence felt immediately, 'We have seen him. He is risen.'"[74] Drawing on Maryra Rivera's work on the poetics of the Gospel of John, we can see how those textual disseminations and *Logos* are related to flesh, which "is distributed, transformed as it is given, and transforms those who receive it."[75] Christ's displaced body grounds not only the church's practices, but the very telling of his story "like a text," mediated by the disciples themselves, as well as the poetics of flesh that Rivera so artfully explicates.[76]

But the bodies of sanctuary recipients persist—they are not absent. They testify in ways that are recognized and affirmed by the Sanctuary Movement,

---

[69]Ibid., 82.
[70]Ibid.
[71]Ibid.
[72]Graham Ward, *Cities of God* (New York: Routledge, 2000), 113.
[73]Ibid., 112, 13.
[74]Ibid., 111.
[75]Mayra Rivera, *Poetics of the Flesh* (Durham, NC: Duke University Press, 2015), 101.
[76]Certeau, *The Mystic Fable: The Sixteenth and Seventeenth Centuries*, 82.

and they also exceed those same limitations, grasping for and at times seizing agency that exceeds the confines of white activists' criteria for sympathy, compassion, or intelligibility. The bodies of recipients, their struggles for agency must also be accounted for. Their bodies are not absent in the same way that Christ's was, enabling de Certeau's generative vision of the loss of the body. And yet, in the Sanctuary Movement, stories, practices, and hermeneutics were used to interpret suffering and trauma; their story was often told for them. This presents several problems that are probably best ascertained when discussing the foundational theological lens that white activists used to interpret recipient experiences—the cross.

Over the last several decades, feminist and womanist scholars have critiqued the redemptive suffering of the cross.[77] Calling the cross "divine child abuse," Joanne Carlson Brown and Rebecca Parker note that such child abuse is citational—"The Christian is to 'be like Jesus'—ad imitation of Christ is first and foremost obedient willingness to endure pain."[78] As such, the cross must be imagined solely as a "travesty," in order to begin to renounce the "abusive theology that glorifies suffering."[79] Likewise, for Dolores Williams, the cross is not a symbol of redemption.[80] Linking the cross to Black women's experiences of surrogacy, Williams argues that the cross is a "reminder of how humans have tried throughout history to destroy visions of righting relationships that involve transformation of tradition and transformation of social relations and arrangements sanctioned by the status quo," a response to Jesus' "ministerial vision," which offers salvation.[81] Feminist and womanist theologians question whether the event of the cross has saving power in any real sense both because of what it says about God and the value of suffering. Rejecting accounts that see Jesus as a singular figure to whom rules about suffering do not apply,[82] they problematize a narrative about Jesus that instructs his followers to do likewise, suffering without complaint.

However, this account is by no means undisputed, particularly in womanist scholarship, where many propose a nuanced view of Jesus'

---

[77]The project is deeper than just an interrogation of the cross, with Rosemary Radford Ruether asking the question, "Can a Male Savior Save Women?" The question of redemptive suffering is a subset of feminist and womanist critiques and, importantly, constructive proposals, and it takes place within a broader project. See: Rosemary Radford Ruether, *To Change the World: Christology and Cultural Criticism*, Kuyper Lectures (New York: Crossroad, 1981), 45–56.

[78]Joanne Carlson Brown and Rebecca Parker, "For God So Loved the World?," in *Christianity, Patriarchy, and Abuse: A Feminist Critique*, ed. Joanne Carlson Brown and Carole R. Bohn (New York, NY: Pilgrim Press, 1989).

[79]Ibid., 27, 26.

[80]"There is nothing divine in the blood of the cross." Delores S. Williams, *Sisters in the Wilderness: The Challenge of Womanist God-Talk* (Maryknoll: Orbis Books, 1993), 167.

[81]Williams, *Sisters in the Wilderness: The Challenge of Womanist God-Talk*, 167.

[82]See: Mary VandenBerg, "Redemptive Suffering: Christ's Alone," *Scottish Journal of Theology* 60, no. 4 (2007), https://doi.org/10.1017/S0036930607003717.

suffering that makes place for it within the Black Church experience. Womanist theologian JoAnne Marie Terrell, although acknowledging critiques of redemptive suffering, focuses her account on the "once for all" nature of his sacrifice to argue for the cross as a symbol of "God's with-us-ness" that uncouples questions of merit and salvation: "suffering and merit are unrelated, just as love and merit are, and that we who suffer can be redeemed."[83] Feminist theologian Deanne Thompson likewise imagines the continued power of the cross in feminist theological reflection. She expresses a hope that conversation between Martin Luther's "happy exchange" model of atonement and feminist critiques of the cross can be accomplished "in ways that preserve the integrity of both sides" through a model of soteriological friendship.[84] These are just two examples that wrestle with questions of redemptive suffering and the cross and emerge with accounts that still retain the cross as valid site of theological reflection that can be understood in a nuanced manner. However, the brief sketch presented here moves us to the question of whether a valid theological account of suffering in the Sanctuary Movement might be developed.

My research has demonstrated the dangers of crucifixion as a theological lens, leading to my sense that the most stringent critiques of it are correct. In white activists' reflections on the suffering of recipients, recipients were placed on the cross as suffering bearers of trauma. This suffering led to conversion experiences and spiritual advance for white activists, who used such images to move hearers to compassion through the politics of sentimentality. Put another way, they substituted the suffering of Central American recipients for the suffering of Christ. In the same way that traditional accounts of atonement state that Christ's suffering is for the redemption of the world, recipient suffering led to redemption for white activists, helping them make spiritual advance and feel as if they were practicing the right kind of politics that went against Regan's policies, and for the idealized United States, which could then live up to its ethical commitments in the Refugee Act of 1980. Such suffering only served to reinscribe suffering as redemptive, even as it attempted to use it to upend political frameworks that led to that same suffering. The interpolation and substitution that I have documented only serve to underline the most stringent critiques of the crucifixion that I have presented here. Nuanced reflections on the cross *may* be possible, but we must approach such reflections carefully, taking note of the ways that the cross is citational and, perhaps, if done well, liberative. Those possibilities seem most firmly grounded when they arise from those who make meaning

---

[83]JoAnne Marie Terrell, *Power in the Blood: The Cross in the African American Experience* (Maryknoll, NY: Orbis Books, 1998), 125.
[84]Deanna A. Thompson, *Crossing the Divide: Luther, Feminism, and the Cross* (Minneapolis, MN: Fortress Press, 2004), xi, 136.

of their own suffering through the lens of the cross.[85] Theological reflection that maps the cross onto others' suffering forecloses the possibility of liberative understandings of suffering and runs the very real risk, as with the Sanctuary Movement, of reducing them to their suffering.

It is important to note that those who defend the role of the cross do so, not because of what the cross signifies in and of itself, but also because of what follows—resurrection or redemption. We have already seen how Terrell sees the cross and redemption as linked, and Kathryn Tanner also gives some tools for imagining this by centering "the whole of Jesus' life" and not just the cross as redemptive.[86] The key here is that, just as the bodies of recipients persist, trauma is not the endpoint of theological reflection. Put another way, while the movement could make sense of recipient experiences through the lens of crucifixion, there must also be an account of what comes after the cross. In centering the entirety of recipient experience—their activism in their home countries and the United States, migration narratives, and struggles for agency—a fuller theological account might be developed.

While it would be theologically irresponsible to jump directly to the resurrection, simultaneously we must recognize that Jesus' story did not end at the cross. This tension, wherein resurrection is both an important theological concept but also carries with it the danger of elision of suffering, defines post-cross accounts. Mayra Rivera clearly articulates the danger of resurrection talk while also gesturing toward the possibilities of "relational transcendence" in an interview where she states, "A danger of 'resurrection' talk is that it is often either-or: so if you have resurrection it is the end of trauma, oppression, and suffering. And I want to resist that dichotomy, if only because in the midst of the worst of suffering, there are experiences of what I would call relational transcendence."[87] Shelly Rambo joins her in articulating the dangers of the resurrection[88], but she also notes the importance of developing a theology of "life resurrecting amid the ongoingness of death."[89] These two concepts—relational transcendence and Rambo's concept of "remaining"—help to give an account of what

---

[85]Indeed, Terrell makes this point clear as she notes how meaningful the suffering of Christ is for oppressed communities. See: Terrell, *Power in the Blood: The Cross in the African American Experience*, 123–6.

[86]Kathryn Tanner, "Incarnation, Cross, and Sacrifice: A Feminist-Inspired Reappraisal," *Anglican Theological Review* 86, no. 1 (2004): 56.

[87]Mayra Rivera, "'Theologians Engaging Trauma' Transcript," *Theology Today (Ephrata, Pa.)* 68, no. 3 (2011), https://doi.org/10.1177/0040573611416539.

[88]And indeed, Rambo also articulates the dangers of removing the cross entirely from redemptive narratives: "There is a danger in not theologizing suffering at all." She also speaks of her moves to reimagine resurrection as being in conversation with those reimaginings of the cross: "While keen attention was paid to rethinking the suffering *on the cross*, it is critical to think *after the cross*." Shelly Rambo, *Resurrecting Wounds: Living in the Afterlife of Trauma* (Waco, TX: Baylor University Press, 2017), 6.

[89]Rambo, *Resurrecting Wounds: Living in the Afterlife of Trauma*, 7.

comes after suffering and trauma. [return to Rambo] "a much more tenuous beginning in which the divine breath is handed over into the space where life is not evidenced as such."[90] It is an account of the "power of remaining, a spirit of persisting," which yields an account that is not centered on the "rising out of the depths, but a transformation of the depths themselves."[91] Remaining is not resurrection, and neither is relational transcendence, but it provides tools for naming what happens after suffering. The recipients of the Sanctuary Movement experienced great trauma, but they were not reducible to it.

In a curious way, Jesus' body too persists for a brief time after his resurrection but before his ascension, but it is changed. Shelly Rambo's *Resurrecting Wounds* centers on an account from this time—Thomas' encounter with Christ in the upper room, wherein Thomas places his fingers in Christ's wounds, leading to the exclamation, "my Lord and my God!"[92] In this brief anecdote from the time between Jesus' resurrection and ascension, Jesus' body is both absent and remaining, appearing as changed and, critically for Rambo, "marked by wounds."[93] But these wounds and the discourse about them are very rarely about the wounds themselves; they are either erased, skipped over, elided, or used as a causeway to belief. Rambo proposes a vision of "touching" wounds that can be a way of envisioning the theological project more generally and dealing with the realities of trauma more specifically. The Sanctuary Movement's reduction of recipients to their trauma also replays this pivotal Johannine account, with activists gazing at or, indeed, plunging their fingers into wounds. Frozen in this frame, there exists very little way for accounts of grace or "new creation" to take place. Indeed, in replaying recipient woundedness again and again for an audience, plunging their fingers into wounds, the wounds themselves counterintuitively can be missed. They again serve as a "performance of faith over doubt, of belief over unbelief" for the worthiness of recipients as refugees and the outcomes of Reagan's Central America policy, but the wounds themselves are missed in the jump to conversion.[94] Such accounts again privilege the epistemic agency of white activists, who take center stage in the movement through their conversion narratives.

Building on her foundational image of the upper room, Rambo speaks of "misrecognition" as being a foundational part of the post-crucifixion Jesus narrative as the Gospel of John "highlights the problem of seeing"

---

[90]Shelly Rambo, *Spirit and Trauma: A Theology of Remaining*, 1st ed. (Louisville, KY: Westminster John Knox Press, 2010), 137.
[91]Ibid., 136, 72.
[92]Rambo's analysis of the narrative occurs throughout her work, but for her most important analysis and reworking, see: Rambo, *Resurrecting Wounds: Living in the Afterlife of Trauma*, 8–11, 17–21, 89–103, 39–42.
[93]Rambo, *Resurrecting Wounds: Living in the Afterlife of Trauma*, 7.
[94]Ibid., 10.

and "places a wedge between seeing and recognition."[95] Rambo links this problem with Melissa Harris-Perry's notion of the crooked room to read the narrative's many failures of vision onto racism—"in the room, rooms cannot surface, truths cannot be told."[96] It is not that these wounds are hidden so much as the disciples cannot see them; their preconceptions and fear prevent them from seeing what is right in front of them. In this chapter, I have drawn extensively on George Yancy's account of whiteness, specifically its capacity to ambush well-meaning whites, as a way of analyzing the Sanctuary Movement. I wonder if the disciples clearly understood their inability to see Jesus? Certainly, there are moments of recognition, but for the most part they seem to be unaware of their own failure of sight. Yancy's notion of ambush might be helpful in this case as we try to make sense of the ways that vision fails intermittently. It is not as if the disciples are incapable of seeing completely, but they are not capable of seeing with total fidelity. In the same way, the whiteness of those who undertake a project like the Sanctuary Movement and who see themselves as practicing reparative politics prevents the reflection necessary to see with fidelity. In some ways, the Sanctuary Movement flips the scene from the upper room on its head—white activists saw only the wounds of recipients. In others, it maps on perfectly with Rambo's account—those same activists could not "see" the recipients or the ways the movement was structured to attend to white activist agency.

However, that is not the end of the story. The disciples do eventually see, and Rambo claims that a community is formed through Jesus' confrontation of the disciples, inviting them to "feel their way into the world again."[97] Redemption remains open as a possibility, even as I, as a white scholar of the Sanctuary Movement, am suspicious of these words as I write them—such a redemption arc to the story feels like an easy out, one that again privileges the one in need of redemption. And yet, Lucy is able to see; separated by decades from her experience, she sees anew the movement's paternalism and white supremacy. If there is a possibility of such redemption, it comes through being challenged to see anew, to feel wounds, and to center voices that have been placed at the margins. I imagine this chapter as being a part of George Yancy's idea of white antiracist racists wrestling with the tension of their accounts of self and their movements. He writes, "white antiracist racists must begin to attempt to give an account of themselves, critique themselves, and continue to reimagine themselves even as these processes will inevitably encounter limitations and failures."[98] This chapter is at least in part an attempt to do precisely that, even as it doubtlessly has limitations and failures.

---

[95]Ibid., 80.
[96]Ibid., 86.
[97]Ibid., 107.
[98]Yancy, *Look, A White! Philosophical Essays on Whiteness*, 175.

The disciples' eventual correction of sight and subsequent redemption is the foundation of the Gospel's claim to authoritative relevance, even as it too is an encounter with limitations and failures. One of the difficulties with the model I have proposed is that, in mapping the disciples' misrecognition of Jesus onto my own account of whiteness in the Sanctuary Movement, the Gospel account itself becomes suspect. In effect, this is no different than other critiques that question whether or not the accounts of disciples preserved by subsequent Christian communities and distilled into texts are reliable accounts of Jesus. What makes the Gospels ultimately intelligible to me is the exceptional absence of Jesus' body. Even accounts of the resurrection are grounded in absence: "*He is not here. He is risen.*" That singular, all-pervading absence allows Jesus' story to be told and the church to form, but the presence of the bodies and experiences of recipients means that such authoritative retellings of their trauma constitute erasure, not the generative moments of revelation the Gospels promise. Perhaps that is the most important part of this analysis—people of faith must be careful not to put others in the role of Jesus, and they must not think of themselves as disciples. The authority of the Gospels is one thing, but the use of them and how they can enable white subjectivity is another. In telling the story of Jesus' trauma, the church can believe that it can appropriate others' trauma as well and tell their story. In seeing Jesus' crucifixion, believers must be careful not to map that crucifixion onto the suffering of others.

Rambo's account assumes that Thomas touches the wounds of Jesus, but that moment is not actually captured in the text. Jesus instructs Thomas to "put your finger here" and "see my hands," and the Gospel of John records Thomas' proclamation immediately after Jesus' invitation: "My Lord and my God!" Instead of assuming that Thomas has felt Jesus' wounds, the lack of his touch may provide a way forward for thinking about trauma that is based on listening and seeing. The capacity for sight and listening is inexorably linked to whiteness; the possibility only exists through a deep commitment to both relationality and, to use Yancy's term, embeddedness. In deep listening to trauma in context and attention to the "horizon of choice" Butler explicates, one can come to see the work of God without replicating the problems that I have explicated in the Sanctuary Movement.

In conclusion, remaining and relational transcendence provide an account of the "afterliving" and "ongoingness" of trauma that does not make the cross the end of the story. These theological innovations serve as a counterweight to reflections that solely focus on recipient suffering. Indeed, they embrace the ways that trauma produces nonlinear narratives, where those who have suffered trauma also create a new community, surface other wounds, or exist in ways that are marked by but not determined by woundedness. In short, they are theological accounts that center on the agency of recipients as opposed to white activists, challenging the dominant narrative of the Sanctuary Movement. It is important to note that life amid death continued even within the constraints of the movement, as recipients struggled for agency. However, the theological underpinnings of the Sanctuary Movement, particularly its concept of suffering as qualifying one for refugee status and its mapping of the crucifixion onto the experience of recipients, made that struggle necessary. They are, as Mayra Rivera points out in her account of flesh, "creative renderings with material effects."[99] Or perhaps, with the trauma theology that has been presented here, it is better to say that they have an afterlife beyond their stated doctrinal concerns. They also demonstrate the dangers of using others' suffering in theological reflection, an act which in this case performs a double move of looking at suffering without actually seeing it fully or in context. Such observations demand constructive theological proposals that center on recipient agency, a task that I will turn to in the next chapter.

---

[99]Rivera, *Poetics of the Flesh*, 157.

5

The Insurgent Collaborative Church

Ecclesiologies beyond Sanctuary

"I believe in the Gospel—in the action of the Gospel. So, my spirituality has to do with how we see Christ in one another. Christ is being disappeared., massacred, abused. It's my responsibility as a follower of Christ to do something." These words, spoken by Marisol, challenged me to think harder about the theologizing done by recipients. Sanctuary activists have always drawn theological connections to their actions, but I found recipients engaged in more nuanced theological reflection about the movement, including how the Gospel moved *them* to act. Formed by her participation in Christian Base Communities, Marisol saw receiving sanctuary as a way to follow the Gospel. This was especially true in her commitment to asking the question, "¿*Y hora que?*(and now what?)" of the community that offered her sanctuary, challenging them to wrestle with the question, "what is God telling me right now?" and overcome *their* fear. Crucially, that question refuses to be reduced to a simple, concrete answer about what action to take. It is instead a hermeneutic that opens the door to a process of listening, understanding, and acting. Marisol's ministry upturns an ecclesiology of sanctuary that is grounded in the triptych of the church's action, recipients' receipt of benevolence, and the fear of recipients. Although still grounded in practice, Marisol's refusal to be identified by her fear moved me to consider an ecclesiological vision that could account for her agency and theological reflection—something beyond sanctuary.

The previous four chapters have argued that sanctuary as a movement and concept relies on the limiting of the agency of recipients. In this chapter, I more fully articulate the genealogy of such limitation, arguing that the concept of sanctuary is dependent on these limitations as well as a blending of civil and religious authority. In particular, I argue that the performance of embodied fear qualifies recipients of sanctuary from Biblical and medieval sources, a principle that the movement extended in its practice of sanctuary. This is especially important because white activists routinely cited the Biblical and medieval concepts of sanctuary in order to buttress their arguments, arguing that the Sanctuary Movement did not invent the concept of sanctuary and was only implementing a Biblical mandate. The performance of fear, in addition to limiting recipient agency, also places recipients outside of the Christian community, or at least on the border of it. In drawing on sanctuary frameworks to develop ecclesiologies, the movement often grounds its account in God's sovereignty over and against the state. However, white activists' willingness to imagine themselves as enforcing the Refugee Act of 1980 led to a reinforcement of the state's sovereignty, a conundrum that I utilize Giorgio Agamben's deployment of the idea of inoperativity to unpack. In response to the surfacing of those limits, I propose an ecclesiological framework based on Linda E. Sánchez and Susan Bibler Coutin's concepts of "insurgent collaboration" and an "ethic of fugitivity, " which in turn leads to a consideration of subjectivity and agency at the border. In doing so, I highlight some of the problems of virtue ethics frameworks in practical theology, arguing that practice and its focus on excellence fails to account for the totality of the sanctuary experience and that a fugitivity framework would be better suited for this work. In important ways, the movement practiced fugitivity, but that fugitivity was often utilized to buttress white becoming and actualization. Building on this claim, I then highlight some of the ways sanctuary became something more in its attendance to fugitivity and posit a reimagining of a key ecclesial practice—Eucharist or Communion. In doing so, I propose a model for church that is grounded in fugitivity and inoperativity.

Sanctuary as an Ecclesiology

Sanctuary activists carefully cultivated a movement that was connected to a tradition of refuge in the Hebrew Bible. Specifically, they argued that sanctuary was rooted in Exodus 23:9, Exodus 21:14, and Numbers 35:6-28. These three sets of verses comprise different definitions of sanctuary, but all are important for considering how activists sought to apply the Hebrew Bible's mandates to a present crisis, thereby creating an ecclesiology. Exodus 23:9 is by far the most expansive view of sanctuary, with a simple injunction to the fair treatment of migrants:

"You shall not oppress a resident alien; you know the heart of an alien, for you were aliens in the land of Egypt." Sometimes this verse was paired with Leviticus 19:33-34, which carries the commandment further than non-oppression, commanding the Israelites to "love" those that reside in their land: "The alien who resides with you shall be to you as the citizen among you; you shall love the alien as yourself, for you were aliens in the land of Egypt: I am the LORD your God." Activists deployed these citations from the Hebrew Bible to develop an ecclesiology that focused on the "love" of migrants from Central America through the practice of sanctuary, which challenged Regan officials' insistence that they were economic migrants in America for a "Cadillac and a color TV."[1] Indeed, sanctuary activists made sure to point out that Central Americans were only seeking asylum in the United States because of the Reagan administration's foreign policy, making the need to practice love even more important due to the responsibility activists felt.[2] While these verses are indeed important and seem to provide more room for the agency of recipients, they are not the primary Biblical groundings for sanctuary as a practice, instead comprising a broader set of Biblically informed, ethical commitments that the movement espoused.

While Exodus 23:9 and Leviticus 19:33-34 present commandments about the treatment of immigrants, Exodus 21:14 and Numbers 35:6-28 form a firmer basis for the movement's practice of sanctuary through the outlining of two different models of refuge—cities of refuge, a concept in Mosaic law that provides a safe haven for those accused of accidental homicide, and altar sanctuary, a more amorphous guarantee of safety for those accused of the same crime if they make their way to a cultic center and receive clemency from the monarch.[3] Exodus 21:14 establishes the safety of the altar by referencing that willful, premeditated murder places the killer outside of the protections of the altar: "But if someone willfully attacks and kills another by treachery, you shall take the killer from my altar for execution." The inference is that for lesser crimes and incidents that might be deemed "accidental homicide," the altar would serve as a safe haven.[4] However, altar sanctuary is not merely a theoretical practice, and 1 Kings 1:50-53 and 2:28-34 demonstrate two accounts of the limits of the practice. In the first, Adonijah, having failed to acquire the throne, pleads with Solomon while grasping "the horns of the altar" and receives clemency. In the second, Joab,

---

[1] CARECEN, *Central American Refugee Fact Sheet* (1985), 29.

[2] For example, a Quaker community linked the declaration of sanctuary and Regan's Central America policy in this way: "We take this stand . . . as our response to the continuing violation of human rights in Central America and as an expression of our concern for our government's share in the responsibility for that violence." Chestnut Hill Friends Meeting, "Declaration of Sanctuary" (February 10, 1985).

[3] See: Ignatius Bau, *This Ground Is Holy: Church Sanctuary and Central American Refugees* (New York: Paulist Press, 1985), 124–9. Bau calls these two "communitarian sanctuary" and "altar sanctuary," and also discusses Greco-Roman traditions of sanctuary in 129–30, as well as sanctuary in Christian churches and the Theodosian Code of 392 on 130–3.

[4] Pamela Begaj, "An Analysis of Historical and Legal Sanctuary and a Cohesive Approach to the Current Movement," *The John Marshall Law Review* 42, no. 1 (2008): 138. Begaj makes the argument that "accidental homicide," her category for sanctuary-eligible killing, was eligible for sanctuary, while premediated murder was not had to do with the conditions of settlement with the victim's family.

because of his treachery and murder is deemed ineligible for sanctuary, even though he entered the tabernacle and grasped the "horns of the altar" in the same manner as Adonijah. In both cases, the altar was seen as a sacred place to which the accused could flee, but the altar only protects those who are innocent of premeditative murder. However, it is important to note that despite references to murder, one need not be accused of murder to take advantage of altar sanctuary, as Adonijah was only accused of treason, not murder. Thus, it was only necessary that the refugee be "sufficiently similar to the narrative paradigm of Exodus 21:13," a judgment that was applied on a case-by-case basis by a monarch or other accuser.[5]

This altar sanctuary would also come to be embodied in the Christian tradition through the establishment of churches, abbeys, and monasteries as sanctuaries in the Middle Ages,[6] but again, not everyone was able to avail themselves of sanctuary. "Public debtors, . . . Jews, heretics and apostates,"[7] as well as "sorcerers [and] those already convicted of an offense and suspected or indicted traitors"[8] were barred from sanctuary. Having sought refuge, the refugee could not remain in a sanctuary for a lengthy period of time. The bishop, priest, or abbot would seek to mediate the conflict, usually seeking a resolution within forty days, after which time the refugee had a choice between exile and surrender to authorities.[9] However, there were some rare places set up as permanent refuge, and if a tradesman with skills a religious community could use were to seek sanctuary, that person might be elevated to become a lay brother or oblate, thereby gaining permanent protection.[10] Additional restrictions were placed on the seeker of refuge, but interestingly enough they could not reside in the church itself, demonstrating some of the tensions in medieval sanctuary between a sacred space and "secular desecration personified by the fugitive criminal."[11] Over time, various monarchs sought, sometimes successfully and sometimes not, to curtail the rights and privileges of sanctuary in European religious communities, with the end result being that the tradition had largely fallen into disuse, although southern and eastern Europe still maintained some form of highly restricted sanctuary into the nineteenth century.[12]

[5]Jonathan Burnside, "Flight of the Fugitives: Rethinking the Relationship between Biblical Law (Exodus 21:12-14) and the Davidic Succession Narrative (1 Kings 1–2)," *Journal of Biblical Literature* 129, no. 3 (2010): 425, https://doi.org/10.2307/25765941.

[6]See: Karl Shoemaker, *Sanctuary and Crime in the Middle Ages, 400–1500*, 1st ed. (New York: Fordham University Press, 2011).

[7]Bau, *This Ground Is Holy: Church Sanctuary and Central American Refugees*, 131.

[8]H. Feen Richard, "Church Sanctuary: Historical Roots and Contemporary Practice," *In defense of the Alien* 7 (1984): 133.

[9]Ibid., 134.

[10]Linda Rabben, *Sanctuary and Asylum: A Social and Political History* (Seattle: University of Washington Press, 2016), 51.

[11]Bau, *This Ground Is Holy: Church Sanctuary and Central American Refugees*, 131.

[12]Rabben, *Sanctuary and Asylum: A Social and Political History*, 53.

Historically, cities of refuge as defined in Numbers 35:6-28, as well as Deuteronomy 19:1-13, emerged as a development of altar sanctuary, having a "genetic dependence" on Exodus 21:14.[13] Instead of being located an altar, entire cities could be designated as refuges for those accused of accidental homicide, but the perpetrator was limited to the city itself and any venture outside of the walls would remove the protection of the city. Again, one guilty of premeditated murder is not eligible for sanctuary in a city of refuge, and murderers are to be killed by the family of the slain, the "avenger of the blood" of Numbers 35:19. Importantly, Numbers 35 and Deuteronomy 19:1-13 disagree about the penalty for accidental homicide:

> Accordingly, in Numbers the "unintentional" manslayer is liable to death and his blood is permitted, but his flight to the city of refuge prevents implementation of the sentence, whereas the "unwitting" manslayer in Deuteronomy is not liable to death and his flight to the city of refuge is intended to ensure the implementation of this ruling. Indeed, Deuteronomy specifies that killing the manslayer is not a service of justice, conducted with due consideration, but rather a consequence of the "hot anger" of the blood-avenger, who is unable to distinguish between the unintentional and the intentional.[14]

Thus, cities of refuge represent safety for those accused of accidental homicide, but in one case they represent a forestallment of the correct sentence and in the other they exist to ensure an unjust sentence is not carried out. This is for theological as well as legal reasons since unjustly spilled blood was seen to have a polluting effect on the land, which was God's dwelling place.[15] Importantly, these cities of refuge served both resident aliens and citizens of Israel (Numbers 25:15).

Sanctuary activists intentionally connected its practice of sanctuary with its antecedents in the Hebrew Bible, and citations of the aforementioned scriptures abound in sanctuary documents, interviews, and official declarations of support from mainline Protestant denominations. Indeed, this strategy of connecting the practice of sanctuary in the 1980s to cities of refuge came about at the very beginning of the movement, during a Tucson Ecumenical Council meeting in which "the ancient Hebrews, Fife remembered, declared entire cities sanctuaries of refuge for accused

---

[13]Jeffery Stackert, "Why Does Deuteronomy Legislate Cities of Refuge? Asylum in the Covenant Collection (Exodus 21:12-14) and Deuteronomy (19:1-13)," *Journal of Biblical Literature* 125, no. 1 (2006): 38, https://doi.org/10.2307/27638345.
[14]Eliezer Hadad, "'Unintentionally' (Numbers 35:11) and 'Unwittingly' (Deuteronomy 19:4): Two Aspects of the Cities of Refuge," *AJS Review* 41, no. 1 (2017): 157, https://doi.org/10.1017/S0364009417000071.
[15]Ibid., 165–6.

criminals."[16] Jim Corbett also, when asked how the movement began, does not answer with a story from the border, but with a citation of Exodus, presumably altar sanctuary: "How did it get started? You'll have to consult Exodus on that. It's very important to realize that the sanctuary movement is not something that someone, somewhere, suddenly invented. It has been around better than 3,000 years."[17]

Doing so was doubtlessly a strategic decision,[18] but this citation is not a mere rhetorical flourish. Indeed, in making a sanctuary explicitly a citational practice, white activists carried over some of the same restrictions on agency that made the Biblical and medieval sanctuary tradition possible. Just as the development of cities of refuge had a "genetic dependence" on altar sanctuary, the Sanctuary Movement has a genetic link to these previous sanctuary traditions. First, there are the spatial restrictions of sanctuary. Simply put, altar sanctuary seems to apply to direct presence at the altar, literally "grasping the horns" of the altar in order for a claim of sanctuary to be made. The altar is a sacred place in which blood may not be unjustly spilled, but the seeker of sanctuary must place themselves so close as to literally touch the altar. Similarly, with the cities of refuge, those accused of accidental murder must not leave the city proper or risk retaliatory murder. In medieval tradition, the recipient of sanctuary must stay within the lands of the religious community itself. Sanctuary is a spatial practice that inherently restricts the recipient of sanctuary to predefined safe zones, where murderous power can be temporarily held at bay, and white activists practiced this same spatial organization of recipient bodies, restricting them to certain safe locations more broadly understood as the religious community's sphere. As one contemporaneous article puts it, "sanctuary focuses not so much upon a supposedly inviolable building as upon a community of refuge for the fleeing and oppressed."[19] Thus, a recipient may live in a church, but they were also encouraged to leave that church building to give *testimonios*, to work, often in community members' homes, or to participate in broader community life under the protection of a sanctuary faith community.

More than this somewhat self-evident observation, the Biblical and medieval traditions of sanctuary restrict agency in other ways. Jonathan Burnside notes that the central qualifier for seekers of altar sanctuary was fear for one's life, not accidental homicide. "From a narrative perspective, [Joab's fear] is absolutely vital. Being in mortal fear is central to the image of

---

[16]Smith, *Resisting Reagan: The U.S. Central America Peace Movement*, 67.

[17]"Conspiracy of Compassion: Four Indicted Leaders Discuss the Sanctuary Movement."

[18]Indeed, grounding in scripture allowed for a readymade sermon and script, examples of which were used in sanctuary literature in order to demonstrate the power of grounding in the Biblical tradition. See: Committee, *Sanctuary for Refugees from El Salvador and Guatemala—A Resource Guide for Friends*.

[19]Betty R. Nute, "Sanctuary: New Challenge to the Conscience," *Friends' Journal* 29, no. 11 (1983): 5.

the refugee . . . mortal fear can establish a claim to asylum, notwithstanding the absence of a killing."[20] However, the "further one move away from the paradigm [of fear for one's life], the less likely it is that asylum will be available."[21] Recipients of sanctuary are fearful, and the recitation of that fear is their qualification for sanctuary. As Chapter 3 demonstrates in detail, white activists cultivated a refugee identity that prized traumatic narratives that emphasized the legitimate fear of recipients. In doing so, recipients were qualified as worthy of sanctuary by their mortal fear, an important grounding for refugee status under UN documents. Through the recitation of fear and trauma in the *testimonio*, recipient subjectivity was limited to that of the refugee, a consistent aspect of the Biblical, medieval, and modern practice of sanctuary. Recipients in sanctuary models across time and space were limited to a few set ideas and tropes, perhaps the most common of which in the Sanctuary Movement is the idea that Central American recipients "running for their lives," as opposed to the more complicated view that I present in Chapter 2 of recipients who might be fleeing persecution but often come from activist backgrounds, saw the movement as a site for continuing that activism, and successfully led activist efforts in the United States during their time in sanctuary.

Finally, sanctuary in the medieval tradition also presents certain proscriptions on dress for self-imposed exile or abjuration of the realm, one of the choices available to a recipient of sanctuary who had not resolved the central issue that caused their seeking of sanctuary. Abjurers of the realm dressed in sackcloth, carried a cross, and were expected to go without shoes and hat as a sign of their humility.[22] Those who were granted sanctuary were also often expected to don "religious garb and take part in daily activities such as the ringing of bells and the attending of Mass."[23] Sanctuary is not only a spatial practice but a practice that enforces bodily comportment and presentation; the recipient is marked as either being separate from a community by distinctive dress or by dressing in the same manner as the religious community that provides sanctuary. Either way, sanctuary necessitates and demands a change in dress to signify the unique status as a recipient. The Sanctuary Movement also included such changes in dress. Coutin notes the ways that activists put on clothing that marked them as Mexican, Central American, pilgrims, tourists, or shoppers, for border crossings, enabling them to temporarily inhabit a different identity from their own.[24] For recipients, a uniform began to take shape early on, consisting of a

---

[20]Burnside, "Flight of the Fugitives: Rethinking the Relationship between Biblical Law (Exodus 21:12-14) and the Davidic Succession Narrative (1 Kings 1–2)," 428, 29–30.
[21]Ibid., 423.
[22]Rabben, *Sanctuary and Asylum: A Social and Political History*, 47.
[23]Richard, "Church Sanctuary: Historical Roots and Contemporary Practice," 134.
[24]Coutin, *The Culture of Protest: Religious Activism and the U.S. Sanctuary Movement*, 59.

bandana tied around the face in order to conceal one's identity from INS or retaliatory forces in one's own country. Providing an evocative visual, news articles and books placed the images of bandanaed recipients prominently in their coverage of the movement.[25] The principal effect of the bandana was to render the recipient as someone who had something to fear in having their identity known—the restriction of agency that is the foundation of sanctuary practice across time and space.

Fear marks recipients of sanctuary as other to the communities they inhabit. Many recipients were the ostensible focus of worship services or worshipped during the week with communities that offered them sanctuary. Some of them even experienced profound feelings of connection to faiths other than their own, such as Quaker meetings and Shabbat services at synagogues. It is not my desire to undercut such connections, but fear, especially in the Christian tradition, marks one as separate from the gathered community. Consider the Biblical injunctions against fear, as well as the Gospel of John's statement, "perfect love casts out all fear," each mark the lack of fear as being a core part of Christian identity. In their distinctive clothing and status on the edges of community, they have much in common with those making public penance and catechumens, who are preparing to be received into Baptism and community and may hear proclamations of the word for forty days to three years in preparation for the sacrament. In fact, the two communities overlap frequently, such as when Tertullian writes, "Those about to enter on Baptism should supplicate with frequent prayers, fastings, genuflexions and vigils, and with confession of all their past sins, that they set forth the baptism of John . . . We must be congratulated if we now in the presence of the congregation confess our iniquities or meanness."[26] Indeed, they often were admitted and readmitted at the same times in the liturgical calendar and followed one another in a procession.[27] Being admitted and readmitted to community demonstrates the precarious position of penitents and catechumens in a way that might touch upon the status of recipients of sanctuary, who were expected to embody fear as a prerequisite for their status as recipients and refugees. In the end, those who grasp the horns of the altar, flee to sanctuary cities, or receive sanctuary are at the edges of the community where they seek sanctuary, always dependent on those with legal and moral power to legitimate their presence.

While the Biblical basis for the practice of sanctuary is found in Exodus 21:14 and Leviticus 19:33-34, I also want to revisit the injunctions for the treatment of immigrants in Exodus 23:9, Exodus 21:14, and Numbers 35:6-

---

[25]See: cover art for Golden, *Sanctuary: The New Underground Railroad.*
[26]Tertullian, *Tertullian's Treatises: Concerning Prayer, Concerning Baptism*, trans. Alexander Souter (England: Society for Promoting Christian Knowledge Macmillan, 1919).
[27]E. Johnson Maxwell, *Baptismal Spirituality in the Early Church and Its Implications for the Church Today* (Minneapolis, MN: Augsburg Fortress Publishers, 2015), 5.

28. On the surface, they form a firmer basis for an ecclesiology based on full inclusion to the community of faith, but that inclusion is based on the ability of the church to truly wrestle with its own experience of exile. Without that identity, then the inclusion and justice it promises fail to manifest. The idea that the immigrant "shall be to you as the citizen among you," similarly requires the community of faith to think of immigrants as citizens, but that condition has always been dependent on the community of faith to extend that citizenship, entangling it in a web of sovereignties that I will explore later. What is clear with regard to the Sanctuary Movement is that the promises of these verses depend on white activists to tarry with their own exile in a way that they sometimes accomplished and often did not. Certainly, centering the experiences of fear and trauma of recipients excluded them from claims of citizenship, as they inhabited a space simultaneously at the center and edge of sanctuary communities.

Questions of Sovereignty—Sanctuary Ecclesiologies

Sanctuary as a practice is built on the restriction of agency of recipients, but this caused little reflection from activists.[28] Perhaps this was because sanctuary as a practice *enhanced* the power and agency of those who gave it, thereby obscuring the agential effects of sanctuary. Moreover, as I have argued in Chapter 3, power-obliviousness is one of the defining characteristics of whiteness, which is essential for developing any account of the movement. In this chapter, I will analyze sanctuary as an ecclesiology, a practice that enacts the church. I contend that in deploying the concepts of sanctuary, activists were developing an ecclesiology, a normative vision of faith in community. Obviously, the term has been applied to the church and churches, but I also understand ecclesiology as applying to movements like sanctuary. Despite its inclusion of Jewish communities, the Sanctuary Movement remained largely Christian, and while my arguments about ecclesiology are expansive, they will also be directed largely to Christian communities of faith.

Substantial scholarly and popular attention has been paid to sanctuary as an ecclesiology, even if it is not always named as such. Ignatius Bau's *This Ground Is Holy*, Renny Golden's *Sanctuary: The New Underground Railroad*,

---

[28]Though it comes from the New Sanctuary Movement, one source does wrestle with the fact that the Hebrew Bible tradition of cities of refuge and altar sanctuary presupposes the criminality of recipients of sanctuary, a problematic assumption. See: Lev Meirowitz Nelson and Salem Pearce, *Mikdash: A Jewish Guide to the New Sanctuary Movement* (2019), 22. https://www.truah.org/wp-content/uploads/2019/03/Mikdash-Handbook-Expanded-FINAL.pdf.

and Jim Corbett's *Goatwalking* can all be understood as constructive, monograph-length developments of sanctuary as an ecclesiology, even if the authors themselves might not have categorized their own works as ecclesiology. While they are substantial works, one problem is glaring: they all develop their ecclesiologies from the perspective of activists, the ones who are giving refuge. Recipients appear, of course, as the experiencers of trauma, victims of state-sponsored violence, and the end results of a failed Central American foreign policy, but the basic ecclesiology of sanctuary is buttressed by their presence as refugees, the role that is carved out for them. Two important aspects of sanctuary ecclesiologies will receive the most attention in the paragraphs that follow: the ways they restrict the agency of recipients and the ecclesiologies' citations of sovereignty. This is not to say the ecclesiologies presented are crude, unnuanced, or unsubstantive. Rather, they center the acts of white activists, their trials, conversions, and acts of defiance without grappling with the full scope of recipient subjectivity and agency. They also claim that sanctuary threatens or interrupts the sovereignty of the state, but those claims are undercut by notions of the idealized United States and its asylum laws.

For instance, in Jim Corbett's *Goatwalking*, while the focus is on personal transformation, the church receives considerable attention. Sanctuary is developed by focusing on the church's call to oppose Regan's foreign policy, which is compared to Vichy France.[29] For Corbett and the Tucson camp of the Sanctuary Movement, "there is no sanctuary movement apart from what the Christians among us customarily call 'the church.'"[30] This church is a covenant community that sees sanctuary "prophetic" and "integral to the practice of . . . faith."[31] In Corbett's account, the church has a responsibility to safeguard asylum seekers, who appear as "torture scarred" and "peoples of the cross."[32] Much attention is paid to the precise relationship between church and state. Sanctuary invites the church into an "unsubordinated" relationship with the state, while at the same time imagining itself as practicing "community practice of the law" in collaborations that will be detailed later in the chapter.[33] The sanctuary community is one that "decisively rejects the nation-state" in favor of the "sole sovereignty" of God's kingdom.[34] Much of Corbett's ecclesiology is laudable,[35] but the

---

[29]Corbett, *Goatwalking*, 115.
[30]Ibid., 161.
[31]Ibid., 176.
[32]Ibid., 182, 19.
[33]Ibid., 102.
[34]Ibid., 114, 206.
[35]In should be noted that Corbett goes further than any other ecclesiology in extending the church's call to sanctuary beyond the movement. Through connections to the seventeenth century Diggers movements in England, Corbett makes the case that the same principles of sanctuary ought to extend to the "land," developing an ecological focus that demonstrates a creative

tension between upholding the law and his contention that sanctuary makes the church "unsubordinated" to the state is irreconcilable.

In *This Ground Is Holy*, Ignatius Bau states that his account of the Sanctuary Movement tells the "story" of "hundreds of churchpeople across the United States" who "face risk of criminal prosecution" due to their activism.[36] Bau heavily focuses on those prosecutions and the people who face them for their faith, arguing that sanctuary makes a new community out of the old: "there is a new urgency about being a genuine community; the person in the next pew is no longer a stranger but a potential co-felon."[37] For Bau, the movement of sanctuary from "the building" to its present manifestation in "the people," is the key, and the power of sanctuary to enable authentic community and therefore authentic church through the solidarity and "conversion" is a primary focus of the work.[38] This community is made possible by the urgent need of refugees crossing the border, who experience horrific pain and suffering, including torture, sexual violence, and traumatization. Bau does not spare readers the details, and even appears to linger over them, possibly as means of forcing readers to wrestle with the pain and trauma of those crossing the border.[39] Although Bau cites a warning against objectifying refugees, that objectification is nonetheless reified in his ecclesiology. Recipients of sanctuary carry tales of "despair and desperation," while white activists represent "the future of sanctuary."[40] Recipient suffering becomes the precondition for individual and communal regeneration.

A product of the Chicago camp of the movement, *Sanctuary: The New Underground Railroad* weaves in recipient accounts to its ecclesiology. Even so, the ecclesiology that develops is said to be "the story of North Americans who . . . chose to stand with the dispossessed."[41] Each section of the book starts with a story from a refugee that is presented as "festering sores," which if readers are "courageous and honest enough" can clearly show the root causes of refugee suffering and lead to a movement that can "make history."[42] Crucially, the monograph acknowledges the realities of paternalism and racism that caused "Anglos" to "liste[n] politely" but

---

imaging of the sanctuary ecclesiological project. In addition, Corbett goes much further than many of his fellow activists in linking I-9 Employment Eligibility Verification to the Sanctuary Movement, calling coordination with such verification "the definitive act of apostasy" for the sanctuary church. See: Corbett, *Goatwalking*, 184, 90–4, 211–16.

[36]Bau, *This Ground Is Holy: Church Sanctuary and Central American Refugees*, 8.

[37]Ibid., 15.

[38]Ibid., 174, 76.

[39]I am uncomfortable quoting from Bau here, but depictions of sexual violence and graphic depictions of murder can be found here: Bau, *This Ground Is Holy: Church Sanctuary and Central American Refugees*, 76–80.

[40]Bau, *This Ground Is Holy: Church Sanctuary and Central American Refugees*, 183.

[41]Golden, *Sanctuary: The New Underground Railroad*, 1.

[42]Ibid., 4, 4–5, 5.

ultimately ignore recipients.[43] At the same time, the ecclesiology presented is focused on building a movement of those same white people to respond to Central America through a humanitarian and political lens that "obey[s] God's law" not the state's, and ultimately places recipients in the same role as the previous ecclesiologies.[44] Recipients bear wounds, but resurrection is possible, but that resurrection too often takes place in white lives and congregations.

Other options for ecclesiological investigation of sanctuary abound. For instance, Eric Jorstad wrote one of the most cited theological visions of sanctuary, which he says places the church in an adversarial relationship with the state. Sanctuary means that the church is "obedien[t] to God alone . . . relativiz[ing] the claims of any particular nation-state" and "transcend[s] all their boundaries."[45] As opposed to the particularity of any nation-state's claims, Jorstad articulates a sanctuary ecclesiology that emphasizes "the universality of the church," prompting resistance to the state in its moments of injustice.[46] This understanding of the sanctuary is not contained to activists themselves. Book titles like Hillary Cunningham's *God and Caesar at the Rio Grande* presented the movement as a contest between two sovereignties, and Lane Van Ham interprets the movement as moving "away from uncritical deference to nation-state standards of sovereignty, and herald[ing] a willingness to create spheres of action autonomous from state supervision."[47]

As I will argue further, the Sanctuary Movement did accomplish some of these aims, but in many ways it also collaborated in complex ways with US immigration enforcement through its vision of ideal border enforcement and the use of civil initiative. That being said, one of the key marker of sanctuary ecclesiologies is wrestling with sovereignty—whose is sovereign? Whose law is sovereign? Sanctuary ecclesiologies have a strong sense of commandment and God and the church's universality and sovereignty, and that sense of God's sovereignty drives activists to action. The questions about what God's sovereignty means for recipients of sanctuary go unexplored, a task that I will turn to in these pages.

This book's central contribution to the analysis of the Sanctuary Movement has been the centering of recipient experiences, and those experiences illustrate the slippages of sanctuary as a citational practice and ecclesiology. In Chapter 3 of this book, I develop a detailed account of

[43]Ibid., 5.
[44]Ibid., 6.
[45]Eric Jorstad, "A Theological Reflection on Sanctuary: Politics, Social Ministry, or Basic Mission?," *Christianity & Crisis* 43, no. 17 (1983): 405.
[46]Ibid.
[47]Lane Van Ham, "Sanctuary Revisited: Central American Refugee Assistance in the History of Church-based Immigrant Advocacy," *Political Theology: The Journal of Christian Socialism* 10, no. 4 (2009): 624, https://doi.org/10.1558/poth.v10i4.621.

the agency, subjectivity, and melancholia of recipients using Judith Butler's theoretical contributions. That account reveals the struggles for subjectivity of recipients in an ecclesiology that had no space for them to exceed the power that instantiated their victimhood, but I argue for an ecclesiology that stretches beyond sanctuary's structures to something new, a view that is directly informed by the centering of voices that the Sanctuary Movement used but struggled to hear.

An Ecclesiology of Insurgent Collaboration and Fugitivity

In their recent article, "Insurgent Collaboration: Sanctuary as Research Practice," Linda E. Sánchez and Susan Bibler Coutin offer an anthropological guide to doing research in ways that fight against dehumanization and illegalization.[48] While Sánchez and Coutin would probably not have anticipated their relevance to ecclesiology, their formulations offer an intriguing starting point for considering an ecclesiology that is rooted and in and reaches beyond sanctuary. Grounded in the Sanctuary Movement, a movement of which Coutin is the most eminent scholar, they offer up an "insurgent model of collaboration" as the guiding principle of research on immigration. For Sánchez and Coutin, this model has four components: accompaniment, the rejection of "essentializing terminology," an ethic of "fugitivity," and a collaboration with and documentation of the already present sanctuary models devised by immigrant communities. Each of these contributions shapes my argument for an insurgent collaborative ecclesiology, and I will spend the next several pages discussing each in turn.

First, Sánchez and Coutin argue for a model that "practices accompaniment by entering spaces of risk and working alongside those who are in these spaces to transform unjust social conditions." Crucially, this is a collaborative enterprise with those experiencing the dehumanizing effects of American immigration policy, ensuring that research "is by, with, and for, not merely about, people who have been 'illegalized.'" I find it surprising that the Sanctuary Movement is cited as the foundational experience for this model since the mutual aid and political organizations organized by Central Americans themselves seem like a better source material for such claims. Perhaps this is because the theoretical frameworks proposed by Sánchez and Coutin are aimed at scholars, who possess privilege in their engagement with these movements. Nevertheless, Sánchez and Coutin cite sanctuary as a

---

[48]Unless otherwise noted, all citations in the following paragraphs come from Linda E. Sánchez and Susan Bibler Coutin, "Insurgent Collaboration," *Departures in Critical Qualitative Research* 9, no. 1 (2020), https://doi.org/10.1525/dcqr.2020.9.1.106.

movement where "participants understood such actions as accompaniment, that is, as sharing the journey—and risks—of oppressed groups." Of course, part of the point of my argument has been to illustrate the ways that this self-understanding reinforced whiteness (Chapter 4) and enhanced the agency of activists[s] while diminishing that of recipients (Chapter 3). However, Sánchez and Coutin's point still offers an important model for ecclesiology. Simply put, an insurgent collaborative ecclesiology moves beyond the politics of sentimentality deployed by the movement, embracing a vision of a church that is constructed "by, with, and for, not merely about, people who have been 'illegalized.'" An insurgent collaborative ecclesiology exceeds one based on sanctuary, which see themselves as "for" recipients but never affords them the agency to challenge, create, lead, or inhabit identities other than a refugee. The striving for such agency nonetheless occurs, but recipients did so against the theological weight of sanctuary ecclesiology. In some sense, an insurgent collaborative church is one where that weight is lifted and true accompaniment can occur, but that process will not be led by white clergy, who will not have their agency enhanced by such an ecclesiology.

Second, Sánchez and Coutin point out the importance of challenging terminology, since how people are spoken or written about can reify damaging, "illegalizing" ideologies. They argue, "one way to find new alternatives for talking about individuals who have been labeled as 'undocumented' is by listening to their narratives" and using their terms as the organizing framework for accompaniment. The use of terms favored by those facing dehumanization is important to counteract the work of the state: "State apparatuses that strip people of their humanity often begin to do so through ideology, and therefore should also be contested through ideology." But what about the instrumentalizing terminologies of non-state actors, like the Sanctuary Movement? I have striven to avoid describing recipients as refugees, even though some recipients use the term, precisely because that identity is not neutral. Indeed, it reifies power dynamics between the activists who offer refuge and those who seek it. Moreover, it is a term derived from the state, with its insistence on creating subjects worth and unworthy of compassion. Similarly, insurgent collaborative communities understand the power of identities and terminologies, striving when possible to acknowledge the diversity of identities that each individual has. As we have seen, refugees are often also activists. Where sanctuary ecclesiologies have clearly defined roles and terms for actors, communities practicing insurgent collaboration strive to challenge harmful terminology, even when it emerges from movements like sanctuary.

Third, Sánchez and Coutin draw on "histories and theories of black resistance," particularly the notion of fugitivitiy to argue for research that "enact[s] new forms of sociality" that resist characterizations by the state and challenge hierarchies. Tina Campt in her *Listening to Images* develops an account of fugitivity that "not an act of flight or escape or a strategy of resistance." Instead, she argues, "it is defined first and foremost as a practice of refusing the terms of negation and dispossession."[49] It is "a refusal of the very premises that have reduced the lived experience of blackness to pathology and irreconcilability in the logic of white supremacy."[50] Fugitivity is useful for Campt because it "tensions between the acts or flights of escape and creative practices of refusal—nimble and strategic practices that undermine the category of the dominant."[51] For Campt, this fugitivity is evident in the "quotidian," as she analyzes the control mechanisms of imperial domination like passport photographs that, on their own, lack these qualities, but when "listened" to rather than viewed contain a fugitivity that outstrips their function.[52] Similarly, scholars such as Damien Sojoyner analyze Black fugitivity as "generative" refusal within the education system, documenting how Black fugitive practices oppose, are illegible within, and expose the "liberal project."[53] For the purposes of this project, three aspects of fugitivity are most important—its basis in the quotidian, its capacity for refusal that challenges systems of domination and illegalization, and its capacity to hold within it tension, even at times possessing contradictory meanings.

In some sense, the Sanctuary Movement was clear about its commitment to fugitivity, with activists coordinating with recipients still in Mexico to cross the US border. However, the movement was also inordinately focused on presenting itself as legal. Sanctuary activists cast themselves as participating in a "citizen's initiative" that sought to enforce the Refugee Act of 1980. Likewise, the movement argued that recipients were lawful refugees, fleeing trauma inflicted by the Reagan administration, which they argued bore a responsibility for giving them asylum. In doing so, they participated in a citational practice of sanctuary that only allowed recipients to be seen in certain roles, spatializations, and identities. In contrast, insurgent collaborative ecclesiologies move beyond a practice that is itself a powerful system of ordering and "enclosing," as Sojoyner puts it, the bodies of Central American recipients.[54] In drawing on the lessons of Sánchez and Coutin's article as well as Campt and Sojoyner, fugitive, insurgent collaborative ecclesiologies eschew the protection of law, instead opting to criticize the laws that uphold systems of racialized violence as unjust. As I documented in Chapter 4, white activists presented themselves as sharing in the risk of recipients, while also benefiting from the privilege of whiteness. That whiteness reveals itself in the desire to risk while also simultaneously being within the contructs of the law. Can such a formulation ever truly

[49]Tina Campt, *Listening to Images* (Durham, NC: Duke University Press, 2017), 96.
[50]Ibid., 32.
[51]Ibid.
[52]Ibid., 32, 33.
[53]Damien M. Sojoyner, "Another Life Is Possible: Black Fugitivity and Enclosed Places," *Cultural Anthropology* 32, no. 4 (2017): 533, 34, https://doi.org/10.14506/ca32.4.04.
[54]Ibid., 516.

challenge state power in any meaningful way, or does it merely reinscribe and buttress that same power? The ecclesiological futures that I argue for move beyond the safety of such configurations. While risk will always be disproportionately borne by those without the privilege of whiteness and citizenship, fugitivity opens a pathway to the sharing, even if partially of those risks. It is to that ecclesiological vision that I now turn.

Toward an Insurgent Collaborative Ecclesiology—Borders, Borderscapes, Bordering

Sánchez and Coutin's article presents a powerful framework for considering what an ecclesiology based on insurgent collaboration might look like. Indeed, they might be argued to add to what has been thought of as the traditional "marks of the church" that signify the body of Christ.[55] In the following pages, I develop an account of the border that incorporates the significant theoretical contributions of critical border studies. In linking borderscapes to citations of sovereignty and seeing borders as a set of performances that do not only take place at border checkpoints between nation-states, sovereignty again comes to the fore. This is especially important because sanctuary ecclesiologies saw themselves as disrupting the sovereignty of the border through appeals to God's sovereignty and compassionate action. However, such an account relies on an overly simplistic view of borders. In the pages that follow, sanctuary activists are argued to have actually reinforced the sovereignty of the United States, an argument that has profound theological import.

Sanctuary as an ecclesiology paid much attention to borders, their crossing, and bordering as a grounding for its ecclesiology. Activists used border crossings to achieve self-actualization and a feeling of shared identity with refugees,[56] with the experiences attending borders producing conversion experiences for white activists—John Fife reflected after one such experience, "This may come as some shock to you, but I have been converted to the Christian faith since I was last with you."[57] Activists also saw the fact they were bordering Central American nations as a spatial relationship that demanded and enabled action in a way that other conflicts, like the Vietnam War, did not. In the spatial construction of bordering, white activists experienced a twin call to compassion and responsibility.

---

[55]The four marks are—one, holy, catholic, and apostolic. Contemporary ecclesiologies have not been content to merely leave these four untouched, however, and have added their own. See: Letty M. Russell, *Church in the Round: Feminist Interpretation of the Church*, 1st ed. (Louisville, KY: Westminster/J. Knox Press, 1993).
[56]Coutin, *The Culture of Protest: Religious Activism and the U.S. Sanctuary Movement*, 56–62.
[57]"Conspiracy of Compassion: Four Indicted Leaders Discuss the Sanctuary Movement."

Borders were also sites of violence and death for activists, who cited as their founding narrative the deaths of several Salvadoran migrants who were abandoned by their coyote while attempting to cross the border.[58] As such, they were a unique space in which activists cultivate compassionate action through detention visits, the offering of medical care, the transport to alternative locations of refuge, and sanctuary. Activists conceived of the crossing of the border from Mexico to the United States as a crossing from violence, persecution, and repression to safety, refuge, and freedom on the other—Central Americans were "fleeing for their lives" across a border to a flawed, even critiqued as imperialist, America, but to a better and freer space.[59] As such, the movement and its attending ecclesiology viewed borders as fixed sites of violence, white activist becoming, and crisis, but also as a place where activist actions could alleviate suffering through acts of compassion.

Sanctuary ecclesiologies have a more complex identification with the border than I have previously detailed. As I have noted in this chapter, the Biblical and medieval concept of sanctuary that undergirds the movement carries with it a conception of a certain dichotomy between those who offer sanctuary and those who receive. Within that framework, the civil authorities are also the ones who grant sanctuary—that is the monarch and high priest grant clemency to those accused of certain crimes. Thus, the sanctuary's power, even when it is an exception to the usual application of law, is derived through its association with the authorities. Of course, the Sanctuary Movement's situation is more complicated, with activists antagonizing and baiting *La Migra*/INS in ways that reveal an inherent antagonism between the two groups, and ecclesiologies emphasize the dichotomy between God's sovereignty and the nation-state. Yet, this antagonism is not the entire story. Activists, especially those associated with Tucson, saw themselves as undertaking a "civil initiative," whereby they could uphold the obligations of the United States to asylum seekers through what Corbett calls "community practice of the law," which he defines as "acting within the legal system while remaining unsubordinated to the state."[60] In doing so, they also engaged in (b)ordering practices that explicitly rejected "economic migrants" from those who could receive sanctuary or indeed, any help at all.[61] In decrying the Regan administration's categorization of Central Americans as economic

---

[58]Ibid.

[59]In some ways, Canada occupied an even more privileged position than America in the Sanctuary Movement's imagination. See: Randy Lippert, "Wither Sanctuary?," *Refuge (Toronto. English edition)* 26, no. 1 (2010), https://doi.org/10.25071/1920-7336.30606. And Randy Lippert, "Rethinking Sanctuary: The Canadian Context, 1983-2003," *The International Migration Review* 39, no. 2 (2005), https://doi.org/10.1111/j.1747-7379.2005.tb00271.x.

[60]Corbett, *Goatwalking*, 102.

[61]Coutin, *The Culture of Protest: Religious Activism and the U.S. Sanctuary Movement*, 113–16.

migrants, they chose to not render aid to those whom they thought the label aptly applied. Thus, while activists opposed the state in creative ways, they ultimately adopted the logics of the Reagan administration and applied them, assessing the worthiness of asylum cases as experts. As one activist put it, "I knew they were refugees because I had heard so many of their stories."[62] In hearing those stories, not only was a spiritual and political consciousness raised, but activists positioned themselves as experts on migrant deservingness and legitimacy. Thus, in a real sense, they shared in the power of the civil authorities, a gordian knot at the heart of sanctuary as concept and ecclesiology. Far from remaining "unsubordinated" to the state, sanctuary activists were often collaborators with it, though in different ways than *La Migra*/INS.

Having theorized the movement's relationship to the border, I would like to now turn to a body of scholarship that offers a more complex account of the border as a site of subjectivity and agency, as well as misery, violence, and crisis. Critical border studies are quick to point out that much of the movement's account of borders is accurate, since borders are sites of violence, where states "assert sovereignty, broker deals, neglect bodies, kill those designated as Other, build empires, craft racist narratives, whip-up nationalism, and ultimately, 'claim the center.'"[63] But borders have theoretical importance that exceeds their violence, playing the tripartite role of "bordering, ordering, and othering," whereby borders are spatial, organizational principles that relies on the creation and presence of others in order to "maintain the cohesion in the formatted order of a territorially demarcated society."[64] Borders are not simply lines on a map, they are a part of a broader imaginary in which societies reproduce others as a project of identity formation and cohesion, with much of the regulatory activity of borders taking place away from what is typically thought of as a border. As such, they are less fixed than they might first appear, introducing the question of whether the border can even be discussed in any meaningful way, or, as one scholar put it, "where is the border in border studies?"[65] This has led to a view of the border less as a space or even spatial organizational tool, but as "dynamic functional processes," giving rise to "bordering" as a preferred term in literature.[66]

---

[62]Ibid., 116.

[63]Levi Gahman, "Border Imperialism, Racial Capitalism, and Geographies of Deracination," *ACME: An International Journal for Critical Geographies* 18, no. 1 (2019): 109.

[64]H. J. van Houtum and A. L. van Naerssen, "Bordering, Ordering and Othering," *Tijdschrift voor economische en sociale geografie* 93, no. 2 (2002): 134, https://doi.org/10.1111/1467 -9663.00189.

[65]Corey Johnson et al., "Interventions on Rethinking 'the border' in Border Studies," *Political Geography* 30, no. 2 (2011), https://doi.org/10.1016/j.polgeo.2011.01.002.

[66]Vladimir Kolossov and James Scott, "Selected Conceptual Issues in Border Studies," *BELGEO (Leuven)* 1, no. 1 (2013): 7, https://doi.org/10.4000/belgeo.10532.

Conceiving of the border as a fluid place where "alternative political subjectivities and agencies" are contested and developed, allows subjectivation, citationality, and performativity to rise to the fore.[67] Mark Salter in particular utilizes Judith Butler's theoretical framework to argue for a conceptualization of the border based on citationality:

> Sovereignty, like gender, has no essence, and must continually be articulated and rearticulated in terms of "stylized repetition of acts" of sovereignty. The state, through its policies, actions, and customs, thus performs itself as sovereign and this is particularly visible at borders when the self-evidence of the state's control over populations, territory, political economy, belonging, and culture is so clearly in question.[68]

(B)orders are sites of subjectivation, where subjects are produced through the effects of power and citationality, but they also open up space for consideration of how those subjects experience and create themselves. Filled with tensions, borders are not only sites of imperial domination and control, they are also "a site of generative struggles where alternative subjectivities and agencies could be shaped."[69]

Perhaps the most striking way that agency can be thought of is through the lens of fugitivity discussed earlier. Interestingly enough, Reece Jones gives an account of fugitivity without utilizing the term in his work, which focuses on "spaces of refusal":

> A space of refusal is a zone of contact where sovereign state practices interact with alternative ways of seeing, knowing, and being. In those spaces, people adopt various means for avoiding the sovereignty regime of the state, even when the traditional response of flight is not available (Agnew 2005; Scott 2009). . . . Spaces of refusal are not zones where there is a revolution against the state, nor are they spaces of romanticized resistance. Instead, they are characterized by a simple dismissal of the state's claim to define subjects and activities in those spaces.

Just as fugitivity concerns creative practices of refusal that are not reducible to resistance, Jones highlights how subjects in borderscapes reject the logics and systems of ordering and othering that characterize borders as

---

[67]Chiara Brambilla, "Revisiting 'Bordering, Ordering and Othering': An Invitation to 'Migrate' Towards A Politics of Hope," *Tijdschrift voor economische en sociale geografie* 112, no. 1 (2021): 15–16, 15, https://doi.org/10.1111/tesg.12424.

[68]Johnson et al., "Interventions on Rethinking 'the border' in Border Studies."

[69]Chiara Brambilla and Reece Jones, "Rethinking Borders, Violence, and Conflict: From Sovereign Power to Borderscapes as Sites of Struggles," *Environment and Planning D: Society and Space* 38, no. 2 (2020; 2019), https://doi.org/10.1177/0263775819856352, https://journals.sagepub.com/doi/abs/10.1177/0263775819856352.

citational practices of sovereignty. People do not merely submit to border regimes, they evade them, refuse them, or employ other such means of rejecting dehumanization and illegalization. I would add to these accounts that, while borders are sites of subjectivation and alternative agencies, the capacity for those inhabiting borderscapes to exhibit subjectivities is not limitless. I would argue that Butler's melancholia is an important way to conceive of the limits on subjectivities created by the subject formation of borderscapes. Put another way, fugitivity is a particular kind of agency, and in all the afore-mentioned works on fugitivity there is ample attention paid to melancholia—the frustrated desire for different ways of being a subject. That is certainly true of borders, as well as the subjects that are formed by and inhabit them, who produce agency through creative practices of refusal.

But disrupting the sovereignty of nation-states and borders is more complex than it first appears. Certainly, sanctuary activists became border crossers in their work, and they practiced other forms of fugitivity, too. In forming transnational networks that transported and housed those they considered refugees but were not recognized by the Reagan administration, they did in some ways subvert the notion of borders. But in other ways, they strongly reinforced borders through their citations of the Refugee Act of 1980 and their ideal imagining of what border enforcement and asylum seeking would look like. Perhaps they most clearly reinforce nation-state sovereignty in their rejection of economic migrants and their status as the upholders of immigration law. This ought to give us some pause since it means that churches and individuals can also be places where borders come into being—that is certainly the case with the Sanctuary Movement.

Ecclesiology and Inoperativity

In placing the Sanctuary Movement's view of the border in conversation with critical border studies, my hope is to illustrate some of the limitations of the movement and indeed sanctuary ecclesiologies more generally. In coming to view the border as a citational practice that is not constrained to one particular location, the border becomes more amorphous and yet more visible as the site of subject formation. The common thread that runs through both sanctuary ecclesiologies and critical border studies is the question of sovereignty. As we have seen, sanctuary ecclesiologies emphasize the sovereignty of God and God's law in opposition to that of the nation-state, viewing the church and God as universal realities that supersede the particularity of the state. In the following pages, I will use Giorgio Agamben's understanding of sovereignty, *oikonomia*, and glory to explicate this theology, while underlining the ways in which the state and God's power are linked. Then, I will use fugitivity in conversation with Agamben's articulation of the notion of inoperativity as a concept to lay out a future vision of an insurgent collaborative ecclesiology that takes seriously the ways that movement has practiced fugitivity while underscoring how that same fugitivity, if not dealt with explicitly, can be utilized by white activists to enhance their agency in ways that undercut the notion of fugitivity I have outlined.

While it seems difficult to do so due to his many interlocutors and varied sources, I would like to constrain my engagement with Agamben to only a few pages. In utilizing Agamben I want to accomplish two tasks: to complicate ideas of sovereignty through his emphasis on *oikonomia* and glory in *The Kingdom and the* Glory and to place his idea of inoperativity in conversation with fugitivity. As such, my engagement with Agamben will be tightly focused on these aspects.

Agamben develops his notion of the sovereign in relation to Carl Schmitt's famous thesis that the "sovereign is he who decides on the exception."[70] The sovereign is thus the one who can act outside the law, deciding that a state of exception exists. This understanding originally belonged to theology— "all significant concepts of the modern theory of the state are secularized theological concepts"—but now grounds the state, with the state of exception being analogous to the "miracle."[71] Agamben develops this thesis further, demonstrating that the exemption grounds the law itself or "juridical order,"[72] which "encompasses living beings."[73] Perhaps his most enduring contribution to sovereignty is his elucidation of the concept of *homo sacer*, who "has been excluded from the religious community and from all political life . . . his entire existence is reduced to a bare life stripped of every right by virtue of the fact that anyone can kill him without committing homicide; he can save himself only in perpetual flight or a foreign land."[74] Far from being an exception, the state of exception is the norm of human life, giving all laws their meaning.[75] Agamben's contributions to sovereignty do not end here, but in this short summary, one can already see that citations of God's sovereignty over and against the state's sovereignty are more complex than they first appear. If the state's sovereignty and God's sovereignty, as well as God's law and the state's law, are inextricably linked in such a way, then citations of sovereignty may do more harm than good. Doubtlessly, appeals to God's sovereignty are well-intended, and sanctuary ecclesiologies join a rich tradition of appeals to God's law over and against the state. However, those same appeals to sovereignty risk the potential of reinscribing the state's sovereignty. This is most clearly seen in sanctuary activists' pursuit of God's law through an ideal enactment of the state's law. God's law is

---

[70]Carl Schmitt, *Political Theology: Four Chapters on the Concept of Sovereignty* (Cambridge, MA: MIT Press, 1985), 5.
[71]Ibid., 36.
[72]Giorgio Agamben, *Homo Sacer: Sovereign Power and Bare Life* (Stanford, CA: Stanford University Press, 1998), 18.
[73]Giorgio Agamben, *State of Exception* (Chicago, IL: University of Chicago Press, 2005), 3.
[74]Agamben, *Homo Sacer: Sovereign Power and Bare Life*, 183.
[75]Ibid., 19–22.

imagined as a perfect application of asylum and refugee protections and the cessation of Reagan's Central America policy. This is perhaps the most important illustration of how the two sovereignties can become hopelessly entangled in sanctuary ecclesiology.

However, in *The Kingdom and Glory* Agamben turns his attention to *oikonomia* as a foundational aspect of theology and politics—it is not merely the kingdom, but the government that is important as they "constitute the two elements or faces of the same machine of power."[76] Agamben is clear that *oikonomia* has its beginnings in Aristotelian thought.[77] However, it quickly assumes a very important role in theology: "from the beginning theology conceives divine life and the history of humanity as an *oikonomia*."[78] For Agamben, oikonomia reveals, "the real problem, the central mystery of politics, is not sovereignty, but government; it is not God but the angel; it is not the king, but the ministry; it is not the law, but the police."[79] Bureaucracies and collaborations are the way that the state functions, just as in the heavenly order God makes Godself known through angels, a necessity because God constitutes pure being and cannot in any real sense act.[80] The sanctuary ecclesiologies in a very real way think of activists as carrying out the divine will—God acts through human hands. In becoming part of the divine bureaucracy, activists also became part of the state through their ideal application of asylum laws. The entanglement of state and God's kingdom gives way to the entanglement of their government. This analysis is also useful in thinking about the subjection of the border. While Reagan and his policies were identified by the Sanctuary Movement as a primary opponent, the border patrol agents, regional administrative officials, and courts were how the government's sovereignty was enacted. Placing concepts from critical border studies, particularly how borders come to play a major role in nation-state identity through exclusion, into dialogue with Agamben focus on the administration of the state, we can come to understand the memoranda within INS that see sanctuary activists as subversives and communists that threaten the sovereignty of America.[81]

Here, Agamben picks up the notion of the "empty throne," a continuation of Schmitt's king who rules but does not govern. Attempting to answer the

---

[76]Giorgio Agamben, *The Kingdom and the Glory: For a Theological Genealogy of Economy and Government (Homo Sacer II, 2)*, ed. Lorenzo Chiesa and Matteo Mandarini (Stanford, CA: Stanford University Press, 2011), 230.
[77]Ibid., 17.
[78]Ibid., 3.
[79]Ibid., 276.
[80]Giorgio Agamben, *Potentialities: Collected Essays in Philosophy*, ed. Daniel Heller-Roazen (Stanford, CA: Stanford University Press, 1999), 253.
[81]See: Campbell, "Operation Sojourner: The Government Infiltration of the Sanctuary Movement in the 1980s and Its Legacy on the Modern Central American Refugee Crisis," 480, n. 37. And Smith, *Resisting Reagan: The U.S. Central America Peace Movement*, 297.

question, "why does power need glory?" Agamben states, "the center of the machine is empty, and glory is nothing but the splendor that emanates from this emptiness, the inexhaustible *kabhod* that at once reveals and veils the central vacuity of the machine."[82] Glory is the "perfect cypher of the majesty of the empty throne . . . captur[ing] within the governmental machine that unthinkable inoperativity —making it is internal motor—that constitutes the ultimate mystery of divinity."[83] For Agamben, glory is not just a question for God, but also grounds "contemporary democracy," which is "entirely founded on glory."[84]

But if God's throne is empty, and glory accumulates and emanates from the inoperativity at the center of the machine, it may seem like there is precious little to ground faith-based action Certainly sovereignty seems like an unsure foundation for such praxis, but inoperativity provides a fundamental ground for thinking about the basis and future of sanctuary. Thinking in terms of the sabbath[85] and messianic time, inoperativity can "be found in the abyss of potentiality. To be free is not simply to have the power to do this or other thing, nor is it simply to have the power to refuse to do this or other thing. To be free is to be capable of one's own impotentiality, to be in relation to one's own privation."[86] Inoperativity fundamentally grounds the possibility of human life for Agamben,[87] and it grounds the "new use of the body" that he speaks of in *Nudities*.[88] For Agamben, "properly human praxis is sabbatism that, by rendering the specific functions of the living inoperative, opens them to possibility."[89] Inoperativity has much in common with the fugitivity that I have outlined earlier, forming a more robust framework for thinking about the religious and political project of sanctuary than sovereignty. In inoperativity and fugitivity, the potential for creative practices of refusal and the simultaneous refusal of the binaries of legality and illegality begin to emerge. If thinking in terms of sovereignty leads to collaborations with the state in ways difficult to entangle, inoperativity and fugitivity question the very foundations of the state's power through a "potentiality that is

---

[82]Agamben, *The Kingdom and the Glory: For a Theological Genealogy of Economy and Government (Homo Sacer II, 2)*, 211.

[83]Ibid., 245.

[84]Ibid., 255.

[85]Giorgio Agamben, *Nudities*, ed. David Kishik and Stefan Pedatella (Stanford, CA: Stanford University Press, 2010), 211.

[86]Agamben, *Potentialities: Collected Essays in Philosophy*, 183.

[87]"Human life is inoperative and without purpose, but precisely this argia and this absence of aim make the incomparable operativity of the human species possible." Agamben, *The Kingdom and the Glory: For a Theological Genealogy of Economy and Government (Homo Sacer II, 2)*, 245–6.

[88]Agamben, *Nudities*, 102.

[89]Agamben, *The Kingdom and the Glory: For a Theological Genealogy of Economy and Government (Homo Sacer II, 2)*, 251.

not exhausted" that results in an innovative account of subjectivity.[90] In many ways this account of subjectivity shifts the focus from traditional accounts of agency that I have often used in the preceding pages. However, I would maintain that agency is not entirely out of place within this paradigm because inoperativity is not passivity. The embrace of the messianic and the practices of refusal that constitute inoperativity, all require action and will.[91]

This account of inoperativity, closely linked as it is to the messianic, has much import for the church. In *The Church and the Kingdom*, Agamben's homily roots the church in sojourning or exile. In making the sojourning church in some sense inoperative, cut off from the legitimation of power, the possibility for community exists.[92] One should not be quick to find in Agamben a hopeful politics that valorizes resistance, much in the same way that fugitivity eschews the same. For Agamben, the potentiality of inoperativity is also bound up in what might fail to come to pass. In writing about Tiananmen Square, his example par excellence of community, the tanks are always on the horizon.[93] Melancholia about the church and its failure to sojourn is also a part of this ecclesiological vision. In this sense, we might look to Jean-Luc Nancy and *The Inoperative Community* for some sense of what an inoperative or fugitive ecclesiology might look like. Here, Nancy puts forth the idea of community which is formed "by the subtraction of . . . work."[94] For Nancy, "community is presuppositionless," and in becoming a "single thing," it "loses the *in* of being-*in*-common."[95] Community is formed by the work that is not taken up. This helps to explain why community is "haunted" by "ambiguous" notions like "foundation and sovereignty," which as we have seen provide foundations for community that are strong, but potentially reproduce that which they seek to counter.[96] Such communities comprise the church of Agamben's critique, while the potentiality of the messianic, existing within and outside time, comprises the inoperative church.

The foundations of such an ecclesiology seem anything but firm. In this way Agamben's stubborn refusal to translate his analysis of the political economy to a concrete path to action makes him a strange conversation

---

[90]Agamben, *Homo Sacer: Sovereign Power and Bare Life*, 62.

[91]For a well-developed account of agency and will in Agamben, or as well-developed as one can find with his work, see: Gavin Rae, "Agency and will in Agamben's Coming Politics," *Philosophy & Social Criticism* 44, no. 9 (2018), https://doi.org/10.1177/0191453718771115.

[92]For a helpful explication of some of the practical uses of Agamben for thinking about the church, see: Charles M. Stang, "Giorgio Agamben, the Church, and Me," *Harvard Divinity Bulletin* (Spring/Summer 2020). https://bulletin.hds.harvard.edu/giorgio-agamben-the-church-and-me/.

[93]Giorgio Agamben, *The Coming Community* (Minneapolis, MN: University of Minnesota Press, 1993), 86–7.

[94]Jean-Luc Nancy, *The Inoperative Community* (Minneapolis, MN: University of Minnesota Press, 1991), xxxiv.

[95]Ibid.

[96]Ibid.

partner for a movement that prided itself on resistance and action. As I have heretofore demonstrated, those foundations are just as slippery and entangled as Agamben's, but in a different direction. Where the Sanctuary Movement excels and errs, as the next section will explicate, is in the concepts of resistance as connoted in idealized action. In that way, the movement mirrors the practical theological conversation with Aristotelian virtue ethics. But there is more than just practice and virtue in the Sanctuary Movement and theology more generally. What does ecclesiology and practical theology have to say about inoperativity and fugitivity? Here Agamben's thesis about the church might yield some insights: "The only way that a community can form and last is if these poles [Kingdom and Church] are present and a dialectical tension between them prevails."[97] In order to understand the whole of the movement, the two poles of practice and inoperativity/fugitivity must both be analyzed. Otherwise, one is left with a semi-analysis, which has always excelled at telling the story of white activists.

Fugitivity and Inoperativity—Sanctuary Failures and Futures

In many ways, the Sanctuary Movement embraces the ethic of fugitivity. On the one hand, it warned its participants about the risks inherent in the activity, creating elaborate covenant agreements between participants should they be detained,[98] while on the other they ceaselessly stated that sanctuary was legal. In some instances, they baited immigration officials or openly mocked their infiltrations of their movement.[99] Immigration officials would accuse them of "taunt[ing]" them through their actions, which were simultaneously said to be open, but comprised networks of clandestine activity.[100] Sanctuary was not a secret—news coverage abounded, especially of the trials of sanctuary activists—but within church basements and offices there were files that Operation Sojourner agents were willing to break into to seize.[101] The simultaneous within and outside the law of sanctuary is inherently fugitive, eschewing boundaries and dichotomies, while opening space for action at the borders of sovereignty.

---

[97]Giorgio Agamben, *The Church and the Kingdom*, ed. Leland De la Durantaye and Alice Attie (New York: Seagull Books, 2012), 35.

[98]For an example of one such covenant, see: Corbett, *Goatwalking*, 170–1.

[99]See: Cox, "The Spy in the Pew." And Crittenden, *Sanctuary: A Story of American Conscience and the Law in Collision*, 72.

[100]Official Trail Transcripts quoted in: Coutin, "Smugglers or Samaritans in Tucson, Arizona: Producing and Contesting Legal Truth," 533.

[101]See: John-Manuel Andriote, "Charges of Break-Ins and Infiltration: Did the FBI Use Illegal means to Gather Evidence against the Sanctuary Movement?," *Christianity Today (Washington)* 31 (1987): 44.

White activists were simultaneously a moral movement of people of faith and willing to use less-than-sincere methods in order to protect those in prison. Corbett is perhaps the best storyteller in this vein. He tells of pretending to be a judge with the same name as him in order to get information about a detained refugee, and reflects on his willingness to don the garb of a priest in Mexico to advance the cause of the movement.[102] Other activists too speak frequently about the fabrications they used at the border, the innocent and quotidian explanations they were prepared to give and often did give when confronted by administrative officials.[103] When infiltrated, agents gave this description of those who gathered for a meeting: "Aside from the old people, most of them looked like the anti-Vietnam war protestors of the early 70s. In other words, political misfits."[104] They were a "trivial novelty," and most of their activities seemed to be centered around singing hymns.[105] Their quotidian front, with a willingness to use less-than-moral means, strikes me as a creative practice of refusal that flowed from compassion and a sense of purpose that according to one INS official in an internal memoranda "threatened U.S. sovereignty."[106]

At their trials, the Tucson activists and their lawyers mocked the government's attempt to strike their moral and religious convictions from discussion.[107] The indicted received lax sentences, but as a condition of their probation, were asked to give up their sanctuary work. Defiant, they refused, saying that it was a part of their faith; they promised to immediately return to sanctuary work if given probation.[108] They presented themselves as lambs led to the slaughter at the hands of the criminal justice system, but they were anything but meek and mild, using defiance to turn that same criminal justice system against itself, successfully using "spectacle" and religious ritual to shape the narrative of the trail and the movement.[109] They refused to be any one thing. Idealist at one turn, courageous at another, "good citizen[s]" and true Americans at another.[110] These slippages from one identity to another confounded a criminal justice system that was afraid of making martyrs out of the movement.

In many ways, the Sanctuary Movement embraced fugitivity, but the concept of inoperativity can shed light on some of the dangers of fugitivity

[102]Corbett, *Goatwalking*, 132, 39–40.
[103]Coutin, *The Culture of Protest: Religious Activism and the U.S. Sanctuary Movement.*
[104]Quoted in Smith, *Resisting Reagan: The U.S. Central America Peace Movement*, 88.
[105]Smith, *Resisting Reagan: The U.S. Central America Peace Movement*, 84.
[106]Campbell, "Operation Sojourner: The Government Infiltration of the Sanctuary Movement in the 1980s and Its Legacy on the Modern Central American Refugee Crisis," 404.
[107]Michael L. Altman, "The Arizona Sanctuary Case," *Litigation* 16, no. 4 (1990): 24.
[108]Coutin, "Smugglers or Samaritans in Tucson, Arizona: Producing and Contesting Legal Truth," 562.
[109]Ibid., 559–62.
[110]Rabben, *Sanctuary and Asylum: A Social and Political History*, 144.

when adopted by white activists in a movement that failed to embrace that same fugitivity in recipients. The movement—particularly those affiliated with Tucson—imagined themselves as enacting a civil initiative, a topic I covered more extensively earlier. In becoming the arbiters of those to whom the Refugee Act of 1980 applied and those to whom it did not—particularly those deemed economic migrants—sanctuary activists far from creatively refusing the binaries of an immigration system, became instead border enforcement officials of a different sort. They became entangled in the questions of sovereignty and administration of the State, rendering it glory through the reinscribing of worth and unworthy receipt of asylum. They too partake in the othering and citations of sovereignty at the border, which as critical border studies has pointed out, does not have to take place at the physical border, but can be located far from it—in churches and synagogues, even. They took up the "work" that Nancy speaks of in *The Inoperative Community*, that necessarily forms a being together based around an organizing concept that creates dichotomies between activist and recipient. In doing so, they were less of a threat to the sovereignty of the United States than the INS feared.

That same work meant that recipients became refugees with little opportunity to become anything else. Still, recipients practiced fugitivity by assuming activist roles, leading solidarity and mutual aid organizations, changing their sanctuary hosts, and creating community together. The blending of those identities in a quotidian way, as well as the ability to exceed the subjection of the border, was fugitivity in its highest form. Take for example Marisol, whose words began this chapter. In her ministry, she centered the fear of white activists in her Gospel-informed action, flipping the ecclesiology of sanctuary on its head. Her question "¿Y hora que (And now what?)" is firmly grounded in the quotidian, even as it refuses to be reduced to an easy or singular answer for those to whom she ministers. An insurgent collaborative ecclesiology is one that embraces fugitivity not just for white activists, who find spiritual actualization and enhancement of agency from their practices of fugitivity, but for recipients as well. In grounding an ecclesiological vision in fugitivity and inoperativity, such possibilities emerge but only through conscious self-reflection and a commitment to accountability and relationship. Grounding an ecclesiological vision in sovereignty cannot produce such an ecclesiology.

Instead of weeding out "economic migrants" from so-called legitimate refugees, an insurgent collaborative church would listen to the critiques of those impacted by American imperialism. In doing so, the church would be able to see that American military intervention, colonialism, and capitalism are linked, and that the neoliberal order is economic violence. Can economics truly be so casually decoupled from violence and fear? Many of the recipients that I interviewed described labor organizing as their primary form of activism in their country of origin, and this organizing work led to torture, kill lists, and the death of family members. For them, economic and state violence were inextricably linked, and the economic conditions were the result of the United States and its enforcement of neoliberal order through military, economic, and other means. Instead of deciding who is worthy of help, insurgent collaborative churches work alongside those whose creative practices of refusal challenge a regulatory system that refuses to see their humanity and the violence of American empire. Such a church does not argue for its own legality, legitimacy, or legibility to the state, but instead refuses the very frameworks that delineate which types of subjectivities and agencies are recognized and which are illegalized. As Sonia Shah forcefully argues in *The Next Great Migration*, the idea of immigration as a crisis is grounded in racial fear and anxiety, obscuring the fact that immigration is part of what it means to be human, "an unexceptional ongoing reality."[111] The insurgent collaborative church embraces immigration as one of the few experiences that might have a claim to being universal, celebrating it as critical to human flourishing. It is a quotidian practice that eschews questions of borders, but, more than that it sees borderscapes and their crossing and recrossing as generative. Here queer Chicana theorist Gloria Anzaldúa might be helpful in articulating the Mexican-American borderscape as the site of a "mestiza consciousness" that "break[s] down the subject/object duality" and demonstrates how duality might be "transcended."[112]

As I have reflected elsewhere, I found myself drawn to the movement because of its vision, but my affinity for sanctuary ecclesiologies was also bound up with my own whiteness. It is hard to imagine any social movement that does not see itself as oriented around some work. And yet, in reaching toward fugitivity and inoperativity, an ecclesial vision comes about that exceeds sanctuary as a concept and builds on the insights of Sánchez and Coutin's insurgent collaboration. Far from being completely different from sanctuary, sanctuary has the potential to even grow into and strive for that vision of community. Those same strivings and yearnings can be seen within the movement itself, and there are two examples that came to the fore in my research.

Of central import here is the question of those who are enclosed by the American Empire but not Central American, the identity that the movement focused on. In particular, the economic and military violence perpetrated by the United States on Mexico makes the refusal of frameworks of immigration as a crisis to be managed of vital importance. The nineteenth-century military mission to seize Mexican territory and the twentieth-century economic mission to make it subservient to American interests are surely violence. Of course, the New Sanctuary Movement acts on precisely this premise, but

---

[111]Sonia Shah, *The Next Great Migration: The Beauty and Terror of Life on the Move* (New York: Bloomsbury Publishing, 2020), 28.
[112]Gloria Anzaldúa, *Borderlands/La frontera*, 2nd ed. (San Francisco, CA: Aunt Lute Books, 1999), 102.

one community in Los Angeles, La Placita also took sanctuary further to apply to Mexican undocumented immigrants, one of the only communities that has been shown to do so.[113] Led by a Mexican-American priest, Fr. Luis Olivares, the community hired undocumented workers in violation of the law, encouraging other institutions to do so as an act of faith, and declared themselves a sanctuary for the undocumented.[114] While La Placita was still rooted in the sanctuary paradigm, its actions gesture toward the insurgent collaborative ecclesiology that I argue for here, and its example fleshes out that argument in two key ways. First, Fr. Olivares was different from the vast majority of clergy that participated in the movement—he was Mexican-American, and his identity and previous participation in the Farmworkers movement led him much further toward the embrace of fugitivity than his white counterparts. Second, La Placita's actions placed it outside of the traditional hierarchy of the Roman Catholic Church. Fr. Olivares operated against the wishes of his bishop, lost power within his religious order, and was under constant pressure from both the diocese and his own parishioners to not extend sanctuary to undocumented workers.[115] The most commonly cited reason for disavowing Fr. Olivares' offering of sanctuary to the undocumented was the fear of losing tax-exempt status, demonstrating the ways that entanglements with the state muzzle dissent.

One monastery in the Northeast gestured toward the possibilities of insurgent collaboration by connecting an indigenous recipient to Native American communities in the United States, a transformative experience for the recipient that grounds their current activism. Indeed, while the Sanctuary Movement sometimes struggled with how to make sense of indigenous identity, the monks in question responded to Rosalina's desire to speak of Western imperialism, indigenous issues, and the need for action with collaboration and capacity building:

> We received a lot of support from the monastery, because the monastery knew all about the discrimination and deaths that we had come from and they were very motivated to help them. They introduced us to various indigenous groups—the Blackhawks—in the US, and building this kind of relationship helped us learn more about basic human rights and the things we could expect as an indigenous group, and without that, we wouldn't have known what we deserved. The monks took us on trips to

---

[113]A closely affiliated parish also joined them, Dolores Mission. Garcia, *Father Luis Olivares, a Biography: Faith Politics and the Origins of the Sanctuary Movement in Los Angeles*, 355.

[114]Garcia, *Father Luis Olivares, a Biography: Faith Politics and the Origins of the Sanctuary Movement in Los Angeles*, 348–9.

[115]Some of the most virulent opposition came from those who supported Central American sanctuary, but did not agree with Fr. Olivares' extension of it to the undocumented. Garcia, *Father Luis Olivares, a Biography: Faith Politics and the Origins of the Sanctuary Movement in Los Angeles*, 357.

see communities—the Cherokee, the Mohawks, the Maki, and without
that we wouldn't have known that those people and those communities
exist. A lot of people came to see us, to hear our testimony and to explain
that they had the ability to be proud of our identity and have flourishing
communities as well. That was how we got along with the monks. That's
our relationship.

This collaboration led to a more robust articulation of the connection
between various struggles within indigenous communities in North and
South America and critiques of US imperialism that pushed the limits of
sanctuary's capacity. The pushing of those limits is the condition of an
insurgent collaborative ecclesiology.

Resourcing an Insurgent Collaborative Ecclesiology—Jesus and Eucharist

While an ecclesial vision of insurgent collaboration has taken some shape,
the questions of Jesus' identity and significance for such a community remain
open. At its heart, an insurgent collaborative church takes seriously Jesus'
fugitivity. This fugitivity is more complex than what some have offered,
such as Miguel De La Torre's vision of Jesus as an anticolonial "border
crosser," but it also builds on those representations of Jesus.[116] Born in a
place where rulers attempted to trade among themselves but no one wanted
(1 Kings 9:11b-14)[117] in a region that was dominated by the Roman Empire,
Jesus' subjectivity was profoundly shaped by borders and yet not defined
by it. Indeed, the Roman Empire's citations of sovereignty were on display
constantly to him,[118] playing a large part in his ministry, especially his final
week.[119] Questions of agency and melancholia within such a borderscape
mark his parables, as he places vineyard owners, their workers, and Roman
soldiers center stage in stories that force profound questions of what

---

[116]Miguel A. De La Torre, "A Colonized Christmas Story," *Interpretation* 71, no. 4 (2017), https://doi.org/10.1177/0020964317716131, https://doi.org/10.1177/0020964317716131.
[117]"King Solomon gave to Hiram twenty cities in the land of Galilee. But when Hiram came from Tyre to see the cities that Solomon had given him, they did not please him. Therefore he said, 'What kind of cities are these that you have given me, my brother?' So they are called the land of Cabul[ᵇ] to this day. But Hiram had sent to the king one hundred twenty talents of gold." Cabul means literally, "good for nothing."
[118]Indeed, they were on display and opposed by Jewish rebels who resisted those citations of sovereignty. See: Flavius Josephus, *The Wars of the Jews, by Flavius Josephus*, trans. by William Whiston (England: J.M. Dent & Sons, Ltd. E. P. Dutton & Co., 1915), Chapter 33.
[119]See: Allan T. Georgia, "Translating the Triumph: Reading Mark's Crucifixion Narrative against a Roman Ritual of Power," *Journal for the Study of the New Testament* 36, no. 1 (2013), https://doi.org/10.1177/0142064X13495132.

constitutes ethical action on the border.[120] His ministry is marked by creative practices of refusal and fugitivity, seemingly pleasing neither imperial forces nor his coreligionists.

Consider this well-known narrative, in which Jesus is given a choice between pleasing the crowd or the state through his response about taxation in Luke 20:20-26:

> So they watched him and sent spies who pretended to be honest, in order to trap him by what he said, so as to hand him over to the jurisdiction and authority of the governor. So they asked him, "Teacher, we know that you are right in what you say and teach, and you show deference to no one, but teach the way of God in accordance with truth. Is it lawful for us to pay taxes to the emperor, or not?" But he perceived their craftiness and said to them, "Show me a denarius. Whose head and whose title does it bear?" They said, "The emperor's." He said to them, "Then give to the emperor the things that are the emperor's, and to God the things that are God's." And they were not able in the presence of the people to trap him by what he said; and being amazed by his answer, they became silent.

Aware of the entrapment that his coreligionists imagined for him, Jesus deftly refuses the very foundation of the question. Instead, he offers his own set of implied questions about what belongs to God, what belongs to the emperor, and the navigation between the two. Crucially, the answers to those questions remain open, and readers of this narrative have offered dichotomous interpretations of Jesus' answer. Some have read it as an instruction to pay taxes in obedience to the state, others have claimed Jesus is arguing that everything belongs to God and therefore resistance to Caesar is demanded. These opposing interpretations and several more moderate positions all remain possible. But Jesus' answer refused to be converted into work, just as it denies the "enclosure" of picking between which law and sovereignty—God or Caesar's—to pledge fealty to.

The refusal of binaries and the passage's openness to interpretation invite consideration of fugitivity in Jesus' life. Certainly another such passage centers on his trial before Pilate. When asked whether he is the king of the Jews, Jesus responds, "you have said it," instead of claiming for himself such a role. Confronted with the charges against him, Jesus is "silent," making "no response to the charges." Such responses should not be read as passivity, but as fugitivity and inoperativity. If the reader expects a cosmic standoff between earthly and heavenly kingdoms, as might be imagined

---

[120]For analysis of the way imperial borderscapes form the parables of Jesus, see: William R. Herzog, *Parables as Subversive Speech: Jesus as Pedagogue of the Oppressed*, 1st ed. (Louisville, KY: Westminster/John Knox Press, 1994).

when theological analysis is centered on sovereignty, the result is far less conclusive. Agamben picks up the lack of conclusion in his *Jesus and Pilate*:

> Here two judgments and two kingdoms truly stand before one another without managing to come to a conclusion. It is not at all clear who judges whom, whether it is the judge legally invested with earthly power or the one who is made a judge through scorn, who represents the kingdom that is not from this world. It is possible, in fact, that neither of the two truly pronounces a judgment.[121]

In Jesus' lack of response, the two kingdoms theory that has dominated Western thought come under scrutiny. In refusing such a binary through a very quotidian practice of silence and deflection, we can come to see Jesus as practicing fugitivity and as grounding an insurgent collaborative ecclesiology in his life.

The question of whether there is any "saving power" in the practices of refusal that constitute Jesus' fugitivity is an open one. Certainly, fugitivity does not equal success or eventual victory, as it stands against such ideas. But drawing on Nancy's *Inoperative Community*, we might think about salvation as the being-*in*-common that he speaks of. Shared experiences of fugitivity, to the extent that they might be shared, enable the forming of community *qua* church and community with God. That theological vision was forcefully articulated by Marisol: "Christ is real, and is not up in the air, but is in every one of us in every place we see. In every set of eyes we see, we see Christ. And when we do that, I think we even lose a fear of being careful, or of being arrested or whatever has to happen." That loss of fear is in sharp contrast to a sanctuary model that has fear as its central qualifying attribute. Crucially, that lack of fear is constituted by a community based on Christ's presence in human community—not in the sovereignty of one kingdom over another. Eduardo offers another vision—that, in Jesus' life and ministry we see "the theological component of running the risk." One of the ways that we can name that theological component is through thinking about fugitivity in Jesus' life as a central component of what it means to be the church.

In keeping with practical theology's focus on the practices of the church, I would like to offer an imagining of the role of Eucharist in the insurgent, collaborative church. In Chapter 3, I took up the problem of Jesus' suffering as redemptive as well as the Sanctuary Movement's use of recipient suffering to ground theological reflection. While de Certeau and Ward posited that it is the displacement of Jesus' body that creates the possibilities for the church's existence, recipient bodies are still present in ways that underline

---

[121]Giorgio Agamben, *Pilate and Jesus* (Stanford, CA: Stanford University Press, 2015), 37.

the difficulty of utilizing suffering as a foundation of the church. Indeed, building on that critique, I would argue for a practice of communion that is not grounded in sacrifice and suffering but in collaboration and in-gathering. These principles are placed at the forefront in the *Didache*, a first-century CE church manual that contains one of, if not the, oldest eucharistic prayers recorded:

> As for thanksgiving, give thanks this way.
> First, with regard to the cup:
> "We thank you, our Father,
> For the holy vine of David your servant,
>   which you made known to us
>   through Jesus your servant.
> To you be glory forever."
> And with regard to the *Bread:
> "We thank you, our Father,
> For the life and knowledge
>   which you made known to us
>   through Jesus your servant.
> To you be glory forever.
> As this < . . . > lay scattered upon the
> mountains
> and became one when it had been gathered,
> So may your church be gathered into your
>   kingdom from the ends of the earth.
> For glory and power are yours, through Jesus Christ, forever.[122]

The rich image of disparate grains being gathered into one bread is about the present and eschatological promise and possibility of community and collaboration. Kurt Niederwimmer describes it like this, "As the bread has come into being through the gathering of grains once scattered on the surrounding hills, so may God gather the diaspora of the church from the ends of the earth into God's reign."[123] For the insurgent collaborative church, the *Didache*'s liturgy offers a moment of slippage in the citations of sovereignty that form borderscapes and therefore an opportunity for resignification. The body of Christ is dispersed, "lay[ing] scattered upon the mountains," but it can be gathered, a gathering which reveals and "enacts

---

[122]Niederwimmer Kurt, *The Didache: A Commentary* (Minneapolis, MN: Fortress Press, 2016), 144. The questions of interpretation of the elided and asterisked portions of the prayer do not mean that the words are unknown. There is a question of whether it should be rendered grain, particle of the host, or some other formulation. It is clear that the words in question refer to bread, but the exact rendering is questionable.
[123]Kurt, *The Didache: A Commentary*, 152.

new forms of sociality."[124] The liturgy imagines and enacts a time when "all dispersion will be at an end," in much the same way that the church must oppose those same technologies and citations of dispersion even as it imagines the being-*in*-common of Nancy.[125] The conditions of the scattering, the technologies, and the power that prevents it are refused categorically in a eucharistic vision that connects Jesus' body to fugitivity.

But what the text does not say is equally important. Specifically, Jesus' servantship, as opposed to his lordship is emphasized, and Jesus' death is not rendered salvific. Indeed, Christ is only used once in the entire *Didache*. In delineating the difference between Paul's eucharistic renderings in Corinthians and the *Didache* Dietrich-Alex Koch sums up the incongruence between the two this way: "Here we can recognize a fundamental difference: In the prayers of the Didache the designation 'Lord' is totally absent, Jesus is constantly called 'your servant,' and there is neither the slightest reference to the death of the Lord nor to the salvation granted to the participants of the meal by his death."[126] Indeed, for Koch, the differences between the two indicate potentially "important differences in the understanding of the ritual meal."[127] This does not mean that the prayers completely eschew questions of atonement. So much of the Christian tradition has focused on Jesus' death and suffering as in some way salvific, but in the absence of such declarations, new visions of salvation come into focus. Instead of Jesus' death, it is his fugitivity, his refusal of the technologies of empire, and his in-gathering promise that take center stage.

Even so, the text contains a reference to kingdom that should create pause. Crucially, the kingdom is that into which the community is gathered, even as the liturgy practices glory. Perhaps this points to a possibility of rethinking the reign of God. In Jesus' words, that reign is not an imperium, but is instead located in each person: "the kingdom of God is within you." (Luke 17:21b) It is never quite present, instead "drawing near" and can be glimpsed, not through signs of kingly rule, but in the quotidian—nets, fish, yeast, salt, seeds, and people (Matthew 13:47; Matthew 13:33; Matthew 5:13-16; Mark 4:30-32; Mark 4:26). It can never be truly found or definitively located— "nor will they say, 'Look, here it is!' or 'There it is!'" (Luke 17:21a)—and it refuses to be reduced to any political movement. Jesus crucially refuses to place that kingdom in contest with Pilate's manifestation of empire—he is silent; he evades. If Jesus' ministry is bound up with fugitivity, then the reign of God can be, too. The reign of God shows itself, not in the contest of dueling sovereignties between God and the state, but in the everyday

---

[124]Sánchez and Coutin, "Insurgent Collaboration."
[125]Kurt, *The Didache: A Commentary*, 152.
[126]Dietrich-Alex Koch, "Eucharistic Meal and Eucharistic Prayers in Didache 9 and 10," *Studia Theologica* 64, no. 2 (2010): 209, https://doi.org/10.1080/0039338X.2010.517382.
[127]Ibid., 213.

practices of those Jesus preached to, who lived in an imperial borderscape par excellence. Being grounded in fugitivity, the reign of God resists being reduced to the types of sovereignty critiqued by Agamben.

While the ancientness of the *Didache* presents an enticing option for the insurgent collaborative church, it should not be bound to such a document. Indeed, in arguing for the *Didache*'s vision of communion, I am not suggesting that it be authoritative. Rather, in articulating a new vision grounded in the ancient, I am both connecting the insurgent collaborative ecclesiology to the church's earliest moments and inviting it to challenge long-held beliefs and practices. Indeed, for all its radical de-centering of suffering, the *Didache* still offers a model that might not make sense for certain communities and contexts. For instance, bread is central to its eucharistic vision, but bread's importance is not universal, being itself part of a particular context that happens to resonate with Western readers.[128] An insurgent collaborative church must ask whether this too is part of a "power(oblivious) Eurocentrism"[129] that I noted forms a key part of whiteness in Chapter 3. The insurgent collaborative church does not only oppose othering from the state but within its own tradition, being willing to shift its practices and interrogate its own frameworks are part of its commitment to fugitivity. That is most especially true of its most foundational ideas and concepts. In doing so, the possibility for agency, for a subjectivity that exceeds the power that grounded it, emerges in the decentering of Christ's suffering and trauma. Something new is articulated, and that new vision of church remains grounded in Christ. Similarly, this insurgent collaborative ecclesiology builds on the idea of sanctuary, but exceeds it, articulating new futures shaped by the border.

Conclusion: Can Practical Theology See Fugitivity?

The preceding argument has been rooted firmly within practical theology, while also stretching its boundaries. For instance, practical theology has been focused in many ways on lived experiences of Christians through a practice lens. Such a focus has naturally led to analysis of ecclesial practice. The Sanctuary Movement is not a church, but a practical theological study

---

[128]The work of Kwok Pui-lan points is particularly adept at pointing out the way that the Bible's renderings of bread are alienating to Asian Christians, as well as Asian women's capacity for creative reimagining of eucharistic practice. Pui-lan Kwok, *Discovering the Bible in the Non-biblical World* (Maryknoll, NY: Orbis Books, 1995). Pui-lan Kwok, *Introducing Asian Feminist Theology* (Cleveland, OH: Pilgrim Press, 2000); Pui-lan Kwok, *Postcolonial Imagination and Feminist Theology*, 1st ed. (Louisville, KY: Westminster John Knox Press, 2005).
[129]Teel, "Whiteness in Catholic Theological Method," 411.

of the movement that can yield valuable ecclesiological insight. But practical theology's use of MacIntyrian practice as an organizing category hamstrings its capacity for a full account of subject formation that is central to understanding not only social movements like sanctuary, but also Christian practice more generally. Utilizing practice as an organizing framework yields valuable insight into the Sanctuary Movement, but that insight is focused on the white activists, not the recipients. Here I want to focus on two aspects of MacIntyre's theory of practice that obscure a fuller account of sanctuary—excellence and power.

As I have stated earlier, the Sanctuary Movement engaged in "work" as Nancy understood it, but there is an additional layer at play here for scholarship about the movement: that work—its effects of self-actualization, the doing of crossing borders, the defiance at trials—is what is most easily discerned and captured by the scholar's attention. Practical theology, with its focus on practice, is exceedingly qualified to describe and develop theological reflection from this work. One of the reasons for this is the focus on excellence that comprises an essential part of MacIntyre's thesis and make their way into many of the foundational texts of practical theology. In virtue ethics, the virtue of a practice is only achieved "in the course of trying to achieve those standards of excellence" associated with the practice, and one becomes bound with those whose "achievements" constitute the excellence of practice. One can easily see how practitioners of sanctuary drew on past "achievements" in the Middle Ages and Vietnam War to achieve excellence. Such connections are rendered clear by a practice framework, and I myself have traced the connection between the Sanctuary Movement and Vietnam War resister sanctuary in an article.[130] Those same ideas about excellence in the practice of sanctuary were also used to spark debates between Chicago and Tucson over what the strategy and organizing principles of the movement should be.

But sanctuary also involves other components on which excellence and achievement do not have any bearing. Consider the Biblical example cited in the first part of this chapter. Is there a way to more excellently hold onto the horns of an altar and claim for oneself sanctuary? Such an example demonstrates that there are limits to what a practice framework can see. In the Biblical model ideas of excellence and achievement are irrelevant, as is MacIntyre's explication of internal goods and virtue. Grasping the horns of the altar, fleeing to a sanctuary city, and crossing borders are not analogous to the examples of architecture or farming that MacIntyre cites. In a similar way, it seems difficult to think about fugitivity as a practice that is oriented around excellence and virtue. Indeed, fugitivity as a concept undermines those concepts through its refusal of enclosement. Both practice

---

[130]Woolf, "Holy Risk: Old Cambridge Baptist Church and the Sanctuary Movement."

and fugitivity are grounded in the quotidian, but they speak to different subjectivities and communities. Indeed, given MacIntyre's understanding of practice, they would not qualify. But that should not mean they are outside the scope of practical theological reflection. It simply means that the discipline needs more theoretical frameworks.

In addition to its focus on excellence, MacIntyre's work is essentially power-oblivious. While it does imagine tradition and the ways that practitioners can amend that tradition through their own practices, MacIntyre's work presupposes choice and effective agency through the pursuit of virtue. In Aristotelian ethics, as MacIntyre understands it, one can pursue *eaudamoia*, but only through willing subjection to tradition and the practice of virtue. In doing so, one joins a community of practice, and that community, oriented as it is toward excellence and virtue, can only be for the good. Such an account may be worthwhile for some communities and individuals, but thinking about power is essential for understanding the movement. While imagining unrestricted moral agents may actually be useful for analyzing the actions of activists, my work has shown the ways that the movement constrained the agency of recipients, often through the operationalization of ideas about excellence and practice. The tensions between white activists and recipients over the correct subject material for *testimonios* and how to best portray fear indicate that the movement itself carried with it notions of excellence that in turn restricted the agency of recipients. But those bodily comportments and citations of trauma were oriented to the work of the movement, which pursued excellence in persuading white Americans through the politics of sentimentality discussed in Chapter 4. That is not to say that recipients remained entirely enclosed by the movement's instantiating power; recipients strove for, achieved, and pushed against the edges of agency. What practical theology struggles to see is that recipients did not only practice fugitivity at the border but also within the Sanctuary Movement through creative practices of refusal directed at the unrestricted moral agents and practitioners that MacIntyre imagines.

This does not mean that practical theology must discard MacIntyre's theoretical contributions entirely, which might be impossible given his stature as "extraordinarily generative" in practical theology.[131] Indeed, MacIntyre's theory of practice opened up the theoretical space for me to consider the Sanctuary Movement as a valid site for practical theological reflection. Upon my first reading of MacIntyre I was struck by one key facet of his theory—practices are not inherently religious, and therefore practical theology need not be confined to the walls of the church.[132] That opening at

---

[131]Ted A. Smith, "Theories of Practice," in *The Wiley-Blackwell Companion to Practical Theology*, ed. Bonnie J. Miller-McLemore (New York: Wiley-Blackwell, 2011), 248.

[132]This conviction was strengthened through reading practical theological reflection on faith-based community organizing. See: Altagracia Pérez, "Latina/o Practical Theology: Reflections

the edges of MacIntyre has made possible my project, but now I am thankful for MacIntyre's precise definition of practice. Not everything is a practice, but that does not mean that the discipline of practical theology must cease to operate where MacIntyre ends. Instead, his sudden curtailment invites analysis other subjectivities and experiences that exist outside of the practice framework he proposes. I have proposed fugitivity as a starting point for that analysis, but perhaps Nancy and Agamben's inoperativity is also useful. Grounded as it is in Aristotle, it represents an alternative use of the same philosophical tradition that problematizes the very idea of practices. MacIntyre argues that institutions are necessary for the continuation, cultivation, and perfection of practices, and Agamben would certainly agree. But where one sees a helpful manifestation of tradition, the other sees something far more sinister. Practical theology needs both perspectives in order to create a robust analysis of the Sanctuary Movement and, indeed, of human life.

This chapter began with an analysis of the concept of sanctuary in the Hebrew Bible and the Middle Ages, which activists readily cited as the grounding sources for its practice of sanctuary in the 1980s. I argue that sanctuary as a concept carries with it three foundational assumptions—the need for demonstrable fear for recipients, the restriction of their agency, and sanctuary's use as technology of state. Each of these distinctive marks of sanctuary was extended to the Sanctuary Movement. Acknowledging sanctuary's limitations, I argue that Linda E. Sánchez and Susan Bibler Coutin's concepts of "insurgent collaboration" and an "ethic of fugitivity" yield a more fruitful, liberative ecclesiological model than sanctuary, even as the possibility of its emergence from sanctuary frameworks remains. In articulating an insurgent collaborative ecclesiology, I draw on the work of scholars of borders, bordering, and borderscapes to argue for a church that is formed by its engagement with the border and recognizes the complex subjectivities and agencies that are formed there, even as I situate the Sanctuary Movement as playing a complex role in the maintenance and reification of those borders. Seeking to explicate this gordian knot, I problematize sovereignty through engagement with Agamben and Nancy, which help ground an ecclesiological vision that moves beyond sovereignty as a ground, slippery as it is. Finally, I articulate a vision of that church, arguing for an insurgent collaborative perspective on Jesus' ministry and offering the *Didache*'s eucharistic prayer as a way that Jesus might ritually ground such a church.

This chapter covers much ground, but at the heart of it is one commitment—the church and practical theology are better when they keep power, subjectivity, and agency at the center of what they do. Otherwise,

---

on Faith-Based Organizing as a Religious Practice," in *The Wiley-Blackwell Companion to Latino/a Theology*, ed. Orlando O. Espín (Malden, MA: John Wiley and Sons, Inc., 2015).

it seems far too easy to engage in collaborations with state power that betray its stated purpose, becoming part of the enclosing of agency that it attempts to curtail. In learning from Sánchez and Coutin, as well as scholars of Black fugitivity and borders, the church can be forthright about power, while attempting to collaborate with those whose subjectivities have been shaped by the technologies of the state. Of course, such a church will also continually be reflecting on itself and the collaborations it forms, leading to a sort of parallax problem whereby a change in the subject also produces a change in the object. Yet, embracing this instability and reflexivity form the conditions for the possibility of faith, perhaps even resurrection.

Conclusion

The Sanctuary Movement was a successful social movement that created networks of religious white liberals who gathered to hear the *testimonios* of Central American recipients. These networks cultivated a sense of affective connection with recipients and the "crucified peoples" of Central America that produced demands for real change—in asylum protections and United States' foreign policy, especially. But those networks were built on the bedrock of sanctuary and refugee status in international law—recitations of fear and victimhood. That same foundation often undercut the work of genuine accompaniment and collaboration that many white activists desperately wanted to undertake. In many cases, that desire was more developed than the systems that were put in place to ensure that desire could come to fruition, with the result that many recipients that I interviewed felt that their full stories could not be told and that their leadership, activism, and power were obscured by a movement that offered to support them. Those tensions—between desire and reality, support and effacement—form the bedrock of this book.

In highlighting those tensions, I am not primarily a critic of the Sanctuary Movement. Rather, I have been in love with this movement, its history, and its activism ever since I first encountered it as an MDiv student. But that love is connected to my own whiteness, my own searching for ways that white religious liberals have been a force for good—my own desires. Previously, the desire that I have had to write about the Sanctuary Movement in a liberative way has been at odds with my inability to see the tensions at the heart of this movement. In paying attention to the tensions at the heart of the movement, I am also marking the tensions in my own work as a white researcher, who pastors a church in the New Sanctuary Movement. The critical lens that I turn on the Sanctuary Movement is also a critical lens on myself and my own work. My hope is that something constructive might come out of naming those tensions, and the arguments herein have been in many ways an attempt to work out my own salvation, even as I remain skeptical as to whether writing can ever produce such an effect and whether redemption for white religious liberals like myself ought to be a goal. In doing so, my utmost desire has been to be a constructive analyst of a movement that I love, even as I note slippages, failures, and difficulties.

Many of the lessons that I highlight here have been taken up by the New Sanctuary Movement, which offers sanctuary to those threatened with deportation and attempts to humanize immigration debates by hearing the testimonies of recipients, who often use their real names and appear in news media with pictures of their unobscured faces. Organized around 2005,[1] most of those currently in sanctuary with the movement are undocumented Mexican Americans, but there exists some Central American presence in the movement as well. Instead of presenting recipients as refugees fleeing exceptional circumstances, Houston and Morse note that the primary strategy of the NSM is to present recipients as ordinary proto-neighbors: "Not just any unauthorized migrant would do. Anyone entering into sanctuary should be ordinary enough (i.e., married, heterosexual, parent, and employed as indicated in the description earlier) to be familiar as a proto-neighbor or community member for the US-born activists."[2] In trying to make undocumented immigrants relatable to activists, a familiar trope appears from the Sanctuary Movement, even if the framing is different. In many ways, recipients have more autonomy over their stories in the New Sanctuary Movement, but those who receive sanctuary are expected to perform neighborliness in a way that constrains their agency[3] and appeals to the sensibilities of white religious liberals, who, like in the original movement, claim to not be the leaders of the New Sanctuary Movement.[4]

Moreover, both sanctuary movements center fear in recipients. In the case of the New Sanctuary Movement, the fear of deportation, the severing of family and community ties, and the movement highlights qualify an individual or family for sanctuary. Another area where connections between the two movements are apparent is their shared strategies of affective appeals to white activists and restrictions of agency on recipients. Grace Yukich has demonstrated that in many ways the New Sanctuary Movement is a movement without much immigrant involvement, which lends credence to an understanding of sanctuary as a practice that privileges white activists, who can seek further spiritual actualization with or without immigrant participation.[5] Such similarities lend credence to the idea that movements rooted in the Biblical and medieval tradition of sanctuary are not merely genealogically linked but consist of the same practice enacted in different places and applied to specific contexts. Building on this claim, it is my hope that, in writing a practical theological analysis of sanctuary, a similar project might be undertaken by undocumented scholars better positioned

---

[1]The movement has multiple origin stories.
[2]Houston and Morse, "The Ordinary and Extraordinary: Producing Migrant Inclusion and Exclusion in US Sanctuary Movements," 39.
[3]Ibid., 42.
[4]Ibid., 43.
[5]See: Grace Yukich, *One Family under God: Immigration Politics and Progressive Religion in America* (New York: Oxford University Press, 2013). Especially chapter 4: "An Immigrant Rights Organization Without Immigrants?"

to see facets of the movements that I may miss. Rich analysis of the New Sanctuary Movement from a variety of disciplines has contributed much to the task of understanding the movement,[6] and a practical theological investigation might yield additional insights about the nature of solidarity, accompaniment, and agency in sanctuary movements.

Directions in Practical Theology

In taking on the challenge of subjectivity, practical theological inquiry might be rendered inoperative—that is, focused less on the work of practice— but that inoperativity builds on and enhances current trends in scholarship. Take for instance, Marianne Garden's recent monograph, *The Third Room of Preaching*, which utilizes interviews with sermon listeners to move homiletics beyond knowledge transfer, wherein a preacher transfers knowledge to listeners, to conceiving of the sermon as "an interactive event, generating meaning in the consciousness of the listener in the dynamic interplay between preacher and listener."[7] Utilizing the image of the third room—a space that is neither the preacher's or the listener's—Gaarden forcefully argues for a model of homiletics wherein "listeners in an internal dialogue create a surplus of meaning that was previously not present in either the preacher's intent or the listener's frame of reference."[8] If a subjectivity model that is power sensitive were adopted in Gaarden's analysis, it would be strengthened by paying attention to the ways that a sermon forecloses certain interpretations, powerfully shaping a third room in which one's sexuality, racial identity, or other markers of difference can either be obscured or empowered. Shifting the focus from preacher to listener is an important step in homiletics, but Gaarden articulates a vision in which the preacher is a "tool" in the hand of "the real carpenter" (God) and they only "participate" in the creation of the room.[9] Such an account begins to gesture toward the way that the preacher is not autonomous, allowing God agency

---

[6]See: A. Naomi Paik, "Abolitionist Futures and the US Sanctuary Movement," *Race & Class* 59, no. 2 (2017), https://doi.org/10.1177/0306396817717858; Grace Yukich, "Constructing the Model Immigrant: Movement Strategy and Immigrant Deservingness in the New Sanctuary Movement," *Social Problems (Berkeley, Calif.)* 60, no. 3 (2013), https://doi.org/10.1525 sp.2013.60.3.302; Vargas, "Ghostly Others: Limiting Constructions of Deserving Subjects in Asylum Claims and Sanctuary Protection"; Caminero-Santangelo, "The Voice of the Voiceless: Religious Rhetoric, Undocumented Immigrants, and the New Sanctuary Movement in the United States"; Kara L. Wild, "The New Sanctuary Movement: When Moral Mission Means Breaking the Law, and the Consequences for Churches and Illegal Immigrants," *Santa Clara Law Review* 50, no. 3 (2010): 981–1015.
[7]Marianne Gaarden, *The Third Room of Preaching: The Sermon, the Listener, and the Creation of Meaning* (Louisville, KY: Westminster John Knox, 2017), 47.
[8]Ibid., 107.
[9]Ibid., 114–15.

in the outcome of the sermon, but it also obscures the power of the preacher. A subjectivity model means taking seriously the way that words often serve as a subjecting power that listeners either assent to or pursue objectives unintended by that same power. If a shift from speaker to hearer is done without accounting for power, the power of words and symbols spoken by the preacher can be occluded. The third room is not outside the power of discourse, and meaning is not freely pursued.

A turn to subjectivity and performance can also help the discipline wrestle with the fundamental question of normativity in the discipline—does the discipline presuppose that some forms of practice are better than others, or at least more in keeping with the Christian tradition? How does whiteness construct or enable normativity? Many of the twenty-first century's most celebrated practical theologians have argued that the normative is an important category in practical theology. For instance, Richard Osmer locates the normative as the third of four tasks for practical theology, where the practical theologian asks "what ought to be going on?"[10] Likewise, Bonnie Miller-McLemore argues, "As theology, practical theology is normative. It makes demands on those who practice it to live by the sacred and transcendent convictions it professes."[11] I am not advocating for the complete abandonment of normativity. Indeed, my practical theological account of the Sanctuary Movement has ethical commitments about the ways sanctuary ought to be practiced. However, my understanding of practical theology is shaped by Courtney Goto's insightful argument that, despite appeals to context, normativity has been racialized within the discipline and privilege's white perspectives and accounts.[12] One's ideas about God's desire for faithful living are always mediated by one's social location, and those normative prescriptions for practice often reflect one's own biases more than God's will. Taking her work to heart, we might instead look for slippages, elisions, and silences in practices that constitute the grounds for agency that this book pays attention to. When recipients of sanctuary fail to properly cite the refugee identity that constitutes the normative practice of sanctuary, that is not a failure of practice but an indication that the normative constructs of the practice itself ought to be questioned. Slippages are not indications of failure in a particular practice but become indications that the practical theologian ought to slow down, question assumptions, and build theologically from the data the researcher has gathered.

---

[10]Richard Robert Osmer, *Practical Theology: An Introduction* (Grand Rapids, MI: William B. Eerdmans Pub. Co., 2008).
[11]Bonnie J. Miller-McLemore, "Five Misunderstandings about Practical Theology," *International Journal of Practical Theology* 16, no. 1 (2012): 25, https://doi.org/10.1515/ijpt-2012-0002.
[12]Goto, *Taking on Practical Theology*.

Building on Goto's assertion, normativity's usefulness as an organizing principle in practical theology depends on its ability to contend with race. In failing to account for refusal, contradiction, and power, practical theology only analyzes part of any given practice, and that part has consistently been the experiences of white practitioners. Normativity in practical theology has thus far been grounded in excellence in practice, but making fugitivity a criterion as important as excellence offers a rich grounding for the discipline's path forward. In paying attention to those instances of refusal of the normative grounds of excellence, practical theology presents a more robust analysis of Christian subject formation. The shared view of both liberation theology and practical theology has been that theology must be conceived of from the ground up, rather than top down. In making subject formation just as, if not more, important than practice, the discipline can fulfill that commitment.

The promise of such an approach is not only scholarly; it is also grounded in faith. I began this book by noting the ways that memory is integral to the project and how remembrance of the movement is linked to remembrance in the Eucharist. Here, a further opportunity for memory appears. In paying attention to the fugitive church, practical theologians can give voice to a church that is not only practicing ministry to those formed by borderscapes but also tarries in and remembers its own experience of exile. Put another way, the church is not only about doing things excellently but also about refusals of excellence and other subjectivities, including those of Exodus 21:14 and Numbers 35:6-28, which emphasize compassionate action borne out of deep engagement with the church's exile identity. The story of the Sanctuary Movement reveals how acting out of compassion can be powerful, but it also demonstrates the dangers of making church about the work of Nancy or the practice of MacIntyre, which only reinscribes white supremacy. In seeing fugitivity, the church can find itself. When it does, it will be the voices of those like the recipients documented here that lead the way.

In Chapter 1, I wrestled with the idea brought up by a congregant in my church that there is a real danger of feeling like, as white sanctuary workers who are white saviors, we can or should do nothing. This book is an attempt to think outside of such a dichotomy, toward the sort of activism that, while it might never escape white saviorism and white supremacy, might embrace true collaboration and accountability to those ostensibly at the center of the movement. Doing so will be costly—it will demand structural changes. Charles Mills argues, "whiteness is not really a color at all, but a set of power relations," and it will feel as if white activists are losing power, because they are—that power will have to be redistributed.[13] Such changes in power

---

[13]Charles W. Mills, *The Racial Contract* (Ithaca, NY: Cornell University Press, 1997), 127.

relationships are necessary for salvation, but as Christ's question in John 5:6 so artfully puts on display, we are always offered a choice of whether to participate in that saving power. As Dietrich Bonhoeffer taught us, it is not cheap grace that saves, but costly grace. I pray that white activists—myself included—will take up the costly grace of analyzing and repenting of liberal, religious white supremacy, even if it demands that everything must change.

BIBLIOGRAPHY

Abrell, Elan Louis. "Saving Animals: Everyday Practices of Care and Rescue in the US Animal Sanctuary Movement." ProQuest Dissertations Publishing, New York, 2016.

Agamben, Giorgio. *The Church and the Kingdom*. Edited by Leland De la Durantaye and Alice Attie. New York: Seagull Books, 2012.

Agamben, Giorgio. *The Coming Community*. Minneapolis, MN: University of Minnesota Press, 1993.

Agamben, Giorgio. *Homo Sacer: Sovereign Power and Bare Life*. Stanford, CA: Stanford University Press, 1998.

Agamben, Giorgio. *The Kingdom and the Glory: For a Theological Genealogy of Economy and Government (Homo Sacer Ii, 2)*. Edited by Lorenzo Chiesa and Matteo Mandarini. Stanford, CA: Stanford University Press, 2011.

Agamben, Giorgio. *Nudities*. Edited by David Kishik and Stefan Pedatella. Stanford, CA: Stanford University Press, 2010.

Agamben, Giorgio. *Pilate and Jesus*. Stanford, CA: Stanford University Press, 2015.

Agamben, Giorgio. *Potentialities: Collected Essays in Philosophy*. Edited by Daniel Heller-Roazen. Stanford, CA: Stanford University Press, 1999.

Agamben, Giorgio. *State of Exception*. Chicago, IL: University of Chicago Press, 2005.

Ahmed, Sara. "A Phenomenology of Whiteness." *Feminist Theory* 8, no. 2 (2007): 149–68. https://doi.org/10.1177/1464700107078139.

Altman, Michael L. "The Arizona Sanctuary Case." *Litigation* 16, no. 4 (1990): 23–54.

Anderson, Leon. "Analytic Autoethnography." *Journal of Contemporary Ethnography* 35, no. 4 (2010): 373–95. https://doi.org/10.1177/0891241605280449.

Andriote, John-Manuel. "Charges of Break-Ins and Infiltration: Did the FBI Use Illegal Means to Gather Evidence against the Sanctuary Movement?" *Christianity Today (Washington)* 31 (1987): 44.

Anzaldúa, Gloria. *Borderlands/La Frontera*. 2nd ed. San Francisco, CA: Aunt Lute Books, 1999.

Ayres, Jennifer R. *Good Food: Grounded Practical Theology*. Waco, TX: Baylor University Press, 2013.

Banchoff, Thomas, and Robert Wuthnow. *Religion and the Global Politics of Human Rights*. Cary: Oxford University Press, 2011. doi:10.1093/acprof:oso/9780195343397.001.0001.

Barba, Lloyd D., and Tatyana Castillo-Ramos. "Latinx Leadership and Legacies in the US Sanctuary Movement, 1980–2020." *American Religion* 3, no. 1 (2021): 1–24. https://doi.org/10.2979/amerreli.3.1.01.

Bau, Ignatius. *This Ground Is Holy: Church Sanctuary and Central American Refugees*. New York: Paulist Press, 1985.

Beaudoin, Tom, and Katherine Turpin. "White Practical Theology." In *Opening the Field of Practical Theology: An Introduction*, edited by Kathleen A. Cahalan and Gordon S. Mikoski, 251–68. Lanham, MD: Rowman & Littlefield, 2014.

Beeman, Angie. *Liberal White Supremacy: How Progressives Silence Racial and Class Oppression*. Athens: The University of Georgia Press, 2022.

Begaj, Pamela. "An Analysis of Historical and Legal Sanctuary and a Cohesive Approach to the Current Movement." *The John Marshall Law Review* 42, no. 1 (2008): 135.

Behrman, Simon. "Accidents, Agency and Asylum: Constructing the Refugee Subject." *Law and Critique* 25, no. 3 (2014): 249–70. https://doi.org/10.1007/s10978-014-9140-x.

Beliso-De Jesús, Aisha M. "Confounded Identities: A Meditation on Race, Feminism, and Religious Studies in Times of White Supremacy." *Journal of the American Academy of Religion* 86, no. 2 (2018): 307–40. https://doi.org/10.1093/jaarel/lfx085.

Bell, V., and J. Butler. "On Speech, Race and Melancholia. An Interview with Judith Butler: Performativity and Belonging." *Theory, Culture & Society* 16, no. 2 (1999): 163–74.

Bennett, Nolan. "To Narrate and Denounce: Frederick Douglass and the Politics of Personal Narrative." *Political Theory* 44, no. 2 (2016): 240–64. https://doi.org/10.1177/0090591714549075.

Berlant, Lauren Gail. *The Female Complaint: The Unfinished Business of Sentimentality in American Culture*. Durham, NC: Duke University Press, 2008.

Bielo, James S. "An Anthropologist Is Listening: A Reply to Ethnographic Theology." In *Theologically Engaged Anthropology*, edited by J. Derrick Lemons, 140–55. Oxford: Oxford University Press, 2018.

Bonilla-Silva, Eduardo. "Feeling Race: Theorizing the Racial Economy of Emotions." *American Sociological Review* 84, no. 1 (February 01, 2019): 1–25. https://doi.org/10.1177/0003122418816958. https://doi.org/10.1177/0003122418816958.

Bonner, Ali. *The Myth of Pelagianism*. 1st ed. Oxford: Oxford University Press, 2018.

Bourdieu, Pierre. *Outline of a Theory of Practice*. New York: Cambridge University Press, 1977.

Brambilla, Chiara. "Exploring the Critical Potential of the Borderscapes Concept." *Geopolitics* 20, no. 1 (2015): 14–34. https://doi.org/10.1080/14650045.2014.884561.

Brambilla, Chiara. "Revisiting 'Bordering, Ordering and Othering': An Invitation to 'Migrate' Towards a Politics of Hope." *Tijdschrift voor economische en sociale geografie* 112, no. 1 (2021): 11–17. https://doi.org/10.1111/tesg.12424.

Brambilla, Chiara, and Reece Jones. "Rethinking Borders, Violence, and Conflict: From Sovereign Power to Borderscapes as Sites of Struggles." *Environment and Planning D: Society and Space* 38, no. 2 (2019; 2020): 287–305. https://doi.org/10.1177/0263775819856352. https://doi.org/10.1177/0263775819856352.

Bretherton, Luke. *Christ and the Common Life: Political Theology and the Case for Democracy*. Grand Rapids, MI: William B. Eerdmans Publishing Company, 2019.

Brook, Freeda, Dave Ellenwood, and Althea Eannace Lazzaro. "In Pursuit of Antiracist Social Justice: Denaturalizing Whiteness in the Academic Library." *Library Trends* 64, no. 2 (2015): 246–84. https://doi.org/10.1353/lib.2015.0048.

Brown, David. *God and Grace of Body: Sacrament in Ordinary*. New York: Oxford University Press, 2007.

Brown, Joanne Carlson, and Rebecca Parker. "For God So Loved the World?." In *Christianity, Patriarchy, and Abuse: A Feminist Critique*, edited by Joanne Carlson Brown and Carole R. Bohn. New York: Pilgrim Press, 1989.

Burnside, Jonathan. "Flight of the Fugitives: Rethinking the Relationship between Biblical Law (Exodus 21:12-14) and the Davidic Succession Narrative (1 Kings 1–2)." *Journal of Biblical Literature* 129, no. 3 (2010): 418–31. https://doi.org/10.2307/25765941.

Bush, Melanie E. L. *Breaking the Code of Good Intentions: Everyday Forms of Whiteness*. Lanham, MD: Rowman & Littlefield, 2004.

Bussey, Marcus, and Camila Mozzini-Alister. *Phenomenologies of Grace: The Body, Embodiment, and Transformative Futures*. Cham: Springer International Publishing AG, 2020.

Butcher, Charity, and Maia Hallward. "Religious Vs. Secular Human Rights Organizations: Discourse, Framing, and Action." *Journal of Human Rights* 17, no. 4 (2018): 502–23. https://doi.org/10.1080/14754835.2018.1486701.

Butler, James. "The 'Long and Winding Road' of Faith: Learning About the Christian Life and Discipleship from Two Methodist Congregations." *Practical Theology* 13, no. 3 (May 03, 2020): 277–89. https://doi.org/10.1080/1756073X.2019.1678859. https://doi.org/10.1080/1756073X.2019.1678859.

Butler, Judith. *Bodies That Matter: On the Discursive Limits of "Sex."* New York: Routledge, 1993.

Butler, Judith. *Excitable Speech: A Politics of the Performative*. New York: Routledge, 1997.

Butler, Judith. *Gender Trouble: Feminism and the Subversion of Identity*. New York: Routledge, 1990.

Butler, Judith. "Giving an Account of Oneself." *Diacritics* 31, no. 4 (2001): 22–40. https://doi.org/10.1353/dia.2004.0002.

Butler, Judith. *Giving an Account of Oneself*. New York: Fordham University Press, 2005.

Butler, Judith. *The Psychic Life of Power: Theories in Subjection*. Stanford, CA: Stanford University Press, 1997.

Caminero-Santangelo, Marta. "The Voice of the Voiceless: Religious Rhetoric, Undocumented Immigrants, and the New Sanctuary Movement in the United States." In *Sanctuary Practices in International Perspectives: Migration, Citizenship and Social Movements*, edited by Randy Lippert and Sean Rehaag, Chap. 6, 110–23. New York: Routledge, 2013.

Campbell, Kristina M. "Operation Sojourner: The Government Infiltration of the Sanctuary Movement in the 1980s and Its Legacy on the Modern Central American Refugee Crisis." *University of St. Thomas Law Journal* 13, no. 2 (2017): 474–507.

Campt, Tina. *Listening to Images*. Durham, NC: Duke University Press, 2017.

CARECEN. *Central American Refugee Fact Sheet*, 1985. https://afsc.org/sites/
    default/files/documents/1985%20Sanctuary-%20for%20refugees%20from%20
    El%20Salvador%20and%20Guatemala%20-%20A%20resource%20guide
    %20for%20Friends.pdf.
Carter, J. Kameron. *Race: A Theological Account*. New York: Oxford University
    Press, 2008. doi:10.1093/acprof:oso/9780195152791.001.0001.
Caton, Steven Charles. *Yemen Chronicle: An Anthropology of War and Mediation*.
    New York: Hill and Wang, 2005.
Certeau, Michel de. *The Mystic Fable: The Sixteenth and Seventeenth Centuries*.
    Chicago, IL: University of Chicago Press, 1992.
Chilcote, Marilyn. "Interview with Reverend Marilyn Chilcote." By Eileen Purcell.
    The Public Sanctuary Movement: An Historical Basis of Hope. Berkley, CA:
    Graduate Theological Union, 1998.
Chinchilla, Norma Stoltz, Nora Hamilton, and James Loucky. "The Sanctuary
    Movement and Central American Activism in Los Angeles." *Latin
    American Perspectives* 36, no. 6 (2009): 101–26. https://doi.org/10.1177
    /0094582X09350766.
Cone, James H. *A Black Theology of Liberation*. 1st ed. Philadelphia, PA:
    Lippincott, 1970.
Cone, James H. "Theology's Great Sin: Silence in the Face of White Supremacy."
    Black Theology: An International Journal 2, no. 2 (2004): 139–52. https://doi
    .org/10.1558/blth.2.2.139.36027.
"Conspiracy of Compassion: Four Indicted Leaders Discuss the Sanctuary
    Movement." By Jim Wallis and Joyce Hollyday. *Sojourners*, March 14–18,
    1985.
Corbett, Jim. *Goatwalking*. New York: Viking, 1991.
Coutin, Susan Bibler. *The Culture of Protest: Religious Activism and the U.S.
    Sanctuary Movement*. Boulder: Westview Press, 1993.
Coutin, Susan Bibler. "Enacting Law through Social Practice: Sanctuary as a Form
    of Resistance." In *Contested States: Law, Hegemony, and Resistance*, edited by
    Susan F. Hirsch and Mindie Lazarus-Black. New York: Routledge, 1994.
Coutin, Susan Bibler. *Legalizing Moves: Salvadoran Immigrants' Struggle for U.S.
    Residency*. Ann Arbor, MI: University of Michigan Press, 2000.
Coutin, Susan Bibler. "Smugglers or Samaritans in Tucson, Arizona: Producing
    and Contesting Legal Truth." *American Ethnologist* 22, no. 3 (1995): 549–71.
    https://doi.org/10.1525/ae.1995.22.3.02a00050.
Cox, Harvey. "The Spy in the Pew." *New York Times*, Monday, March 3, 1986.
Crittenden, Ann. *Sanctuary: A Story of American Conscience and the Law in
    Collision*. 1st ed. New York: Weidenfeld & Nicolson, 1988.
CRTFCA. *Basta: Newsletter of the Chicago Religious Task Force on Central
    America*. Chicago, IL, 1983.
Cunningham, Hilary. *God and Caesar at the Rio Grande: Sanctuary and the
    Politics of Religion*. Minneapolis, MN: University of Minnesota Press, 1995.
Dale, Mariana. "Church Sanctuary Movement of 1980s Revived in Tucson." *The
    Republic*, 2014. https://www.azcentral.com/story/news/local/arizona/2014/08/22
    /church-sanctuary-movement-s-revived-tucson/14471415/.
Davidson, Miriam. *Convictions of the Heart: Jim Corbett and the Sanctuary
    Movement*. Tucson: University of Arizona Press, 1988.

De La Torre, Miguel A. "A Colonized Christmas Story." *Interpretation* 71, no. 4 (2017): 408–17. https://doi.org/10.1177/0020964317716131. https://doi.org/10.1177/0020964317716131.

Delgado Bernal, Dolores, Rebeca Burciaga, and Judith Flores Carmona. *Chicana/Latina Testimonios as Pedagogical, Methodological, and Activist Approaches to Social Justice.* New York: Routledge, 2016.

DiAngelo, Robin. "White Fragility." *International Journal of Critical Pedagogy* 3 (2011): 3.

"Diversity Examen." Mindfulness BU, accessed August 20, 2022, https://blogs.baylor.edu/mindfulnessbu/simple-practice/examen/diversity-examen/.

Dold, R. Bruce. "Fearful Sanctuary Fugitive Flees Child-Molesting Trial." *Chicago Tribune*, 1985. https://www.chicagotribune.com/news/ct-xpm-1985-02-26-8501110586-story.html.

Dorrien, Gary J. *The Obama Question: A Progressive Perspective.* Lanham, MD: Rowman & Littlefield Publishers, 2012.

Douglass, Frederick. *Autobiographies.* Edited by Henry Louis Gates. New York: Library of America: Distributed to the trade in the United States by Penguin Books USA, 1994.

Dyer, Richard. *White.* New York: Routledge, 1997.

Ellis, Carolyn. *The Ethnographic I: A Methodological Novel About Autoethnography.* Walnut Creek, CA: AltaMira Press, 2004.

Ellis, Carolyn, Christine E. Kiesinger, and Lisa M. Tillmann-Healy. "Interactive Interviewing: Talking About Emotional Experience." In *Reflexivity and Voice*, edited by Rosanna Hertz. Thousand Oaks, CA: Sage Publications, 1997.

Faimau, Gabriel. "Religious Testimonial Narratives and Social Construction of Identity: Insights from Prophetic Ministries in Botswana." *Cogent Social Sciences* 3, no. 1 (2017): 1356620. https://doi.org/10.1080/23311886.2017.1356620.

Fife, John. "From the Sanctuary Movement to No More Deaths: The Challenge to Communities of Faith." In *Religious and Ethical Perspectives on Global Migration*, edited by Elizabeth W. Collier and Charles R. Strain. Lanham, MD: Lexington Books, 2014.

Firestone, William A. "Alternative Arguments for Generalizing from Data as Applied to Qualitative Research." *Educational Researcher* 22, no. 4 (1993): 16–23. https://doi.org/10.3102/0013189x022004016.

Fitch, Bob. "Interview with Bob Fitch." *The Public Sanctuary Movement: An Historical Basis of Hope.* By Eileen Purcell. Berkley, CA: Graduate Theological Union, 1998.

Foley, Michael S. *Confronting the War Machine: Draft Resistance during the Vietnam War.* Chapel Hill, NC: The University of North Carolina Press, 2003.

Francis, Megan Ming. "The Price of Civil Rights: Black Lives, White Funding, and Movement Capture." *Law & Society Review* 53, no. 1 (2019): 275–309. https://doi.org/10.1111/lasr.12384.

Friends Peace Committee. *Sanctuary for Refugees from El Salvador and Guatemala—A Resource Guide for Friends.* Philadelphia, PA: Philadelphia Yearly Meeting, 1985.

Fuentes, Emma Haydée, and Manuel Alejandro Pérez. "Our Stories Are Our Sanctuary: Testimony as a Sacred of Belonging." *Association of Mexican American Educators Journal* 10, no. 2 (2016): 1–15.

Fulkerson, Mary McClintock. *Places of Redemption: Theology for a Worldly Church*. Oxford, New York: Oxford University Press, 2007.

Gaarden, Marianne. *The Third Room of Preaching: The Sermon, the Listener, and the Creation of Meaning*. Louisville, KY: Westminster John Knox, 2017.

Gahman, Levi. "Border Imperialism, Racial Capitalism, and Geographies of Deracination." *ACME: An International Journal for Critical Geographies* 18, no. 1 (2019): 107–29.

Garcia, Maria Cristina. *Refugees or Economic Migrants? The Debate over Accountability in the United States*, 84–118. Berkeley, CA: University of California Press, 2019.

Garcia, Mario T. *Father Luis Olivares, a Biography: Faith Politics and the Origins of the Sanctuary Movement in Los Angeles*. Chapel Hill, NC: The University of North Carolina Press, 2018. doi:10.5149/9781469643335_garcia.

Garza, Amy Villareal. "Places of Sanctuary: Religious Revivalism and the Politics of Immigration in New Mexico." PhD, University of California—Santa Cruz, 2014.

Georgia, Allan T. "Translating the Triumph: Reading Mark's Crucifixion Narrative against a Roman Ritual of Power." *Journal for the Study of the New Testament* 36, no. 1 (2013): 17–38. https://doi.org/10.1177/0142064X13495132.

Giovanni, Batz. "Maya Cultural Resistance in Los Angeles: The Recovery of Identity and Culture among Maya Youth." *Latin American Perspectives* 41, no. 3 (2014): 194–207. https://doi.org/10.1177/0094582X14531727.

Golden, Renny. *Sanctuary: The New Underground Railroad*. Edited by Michael McConnell. Maryknoll, NY: Orbis Books, 1986.

Golden, Renny. "The White Way, the Native Way." In *Dangerous Memories: Invasion and Resistance since 1492*. Chicago, IL: Chicago Religious Task Force on Central America, 1991.

Goodfriend, Hilary "What Immigrant Rights Activists Can Learn from the Original Sanctuary Movement." *In These Times*, 2017. https://inthesetimes.com/article/a-demand-for-sanctuary-el-salvador-central-america-solidarity-trump.

Goto, Courtney T. *Taking on Practical Theology: The Idolization of Context and the Hope of Community*. Leiden, Boston, MA: Brill, 2018.

Goto, Courtney T. "Writing in Compliance with the Racialized 'Zoo' of Practical Theology." In *Conundrums in Practical Theology*, edited by Joyce Ann Mercer and Bonnie Miller-McLemore, 110–33. Boston, MA: Brill, 2016.

Green, Adam. "Omnisubjectivity and Incarnation." *Topoi* 36, no. 4 (2017): 693–701. https://doi.org/10.1007/s11245-016-9391-2.

Hadad, Eliezer. "'Unintentionally' (Numbers 35:11) and 'Unwittingly' (Deuteronomy 19:4): Two Aspects of the Cities of Refuge." *AJS Review* 41, no. 1 (2017): 155–73. https://doi.org/10.1017/S0364009417000071.

Hallie, Philip P. *Lest Innocent Blood Be Shed: The Story of the Village of Le Chambon, and How Goodness Happened There*. 1st ed. New York: Harper & Row, 1979.

Harding, Susan F. "Convicted by the Holy Spirit: The Rhetoric of Fundamental Baptist Conversion." *American Ethnologist* 14, no. 1 (1987): 167–81. https://doi.org/10.1525/ae.1987.14.1.02a00100.

Hearlson, Adam. "The Promise of Pierre Bourdieu's Social Theories of Practice for the Field of Homiletics." *Practical Matters*, no. 6 (2014): 9–26.

Hector, Perla, and Coutin Susan Bibler. "Legacies and Origins of the 1980s US—Central American Sanctuary Movement." *Refuge: Canada's Journal on Refugees*

26, no. 1 (October 10, 2010). https://doi.org/10.25071/1920-7336.30602. https://refuge.journals.yorku.ca/index.php/refuge/article/view/30602.

Herzog, William R. *Parables as Subversive Speech: Jesus as Pedagogue of the Oppressed*. 1st ed. Louisville, KY: Westminster/John Knox Press, 1994.

Hobson, Emily K. "Central American Solidarity Movement." In *Global Encyclopedia of Lesbian, Gay, Bisexual, Transgender, and Queer (Lgbtq) History*, edited by Howard Chiang, Anjali Arondekar, Marc Epprecht, Jennifer Evans, Ross G. Forman, Hanadi Al-Samman, Emily Skidmore, and Zeb Tortorici, 310–15. Farmington Hills, MI: Charles Scribner's Sons, 2019.

Hollywood, Amy. *Acute Melancholia and Other Essays: Mysticism, History, and the Study of Religion*. New York: Columbia University Press, 2016.

Hollywood, Amy. "Performativity, Citationality, Ritualization." *History of Religions* 42, no. 2 (2002): 93–115. https://doi.org/10.1086/463699.

Horning, Payne. "Armed at Church: Why This Congregation Is 'Not a Gun-Free Zone.'" *NPR* (2018). https://www.npr.org/2018/04/08/599772810/armed-at -church-why-this-congregation-is-not-a-gun-free-zone.

Houston, Serin D., and Charlotte Morse. "The Ordinary and Extraordinary: Producing Migrant Inclusion and Exclusion in US Sanctuary Movements." *Studies in Social Justice* 11, no. 1 (2017): 27–47. https://doi.org/10.26522/ssj.v11i1.1081.

Houtum, H. J. van, and A. L. van Naerssen. "Bordering, Ordering and Othering." *Tijdschrift voor economische en sociale geografie* 93, no. 2 (2002): 125–36. https://doi.org/10.1111/1467-9663.00189.

Johnson, Corey, Reece Jones, Anssi Paasi, Louise Amoore, Alison Mountz, Mark Salter, and Chris Rumford. "Interventions on Rethinking 'the Border' in Border Studies." *Political Geography* 30, no. 2 (2011): 61–9. https://doi.org/10.1016/j .polgeo.2011.01.002.

Jones, Reece. "Spaces of Refusal: Rethinking Sovereign Power and Resistance at the Border." *Annals of the Association of American Geographers* 102, no. 3 (2012): 685–99. https://doi.org/10.1080/00045608.2011.600193.

Jones, Tamsin. "Bearing Witness: Hope for the Unseen." *Political Theology: The Journal of Christian Socialism* 17, no. 2 (2016): 137–50. https://doi.org/10.1080 /1462317X.2016.1161300.

Jones, Tamsin. "Traumatized Subjects: Continental Philosophy of Religion and the Ethics of Alterity." *The Journal of Religion* 94, no. 2 (2014): 143–60. https://doi .org/10.1086/674952.

Jorstad, Eric. "A Theological Reflection on Sanctuary: Politics, Social Ministry, or Basic Mission?." *Christianity & Crisis* 43, no. 17 (1983): 404–7.

Josephus, Flavius. *The Wars of the Jews, by Flavius Josephus*. Translated by William Whiston. England: J.M. Dent & Sons, Ltd. E. P. Dutton & Co., 1915.

Kayaoglu, Turan. "Giving an Inch Only to Lose a Mile: Muslim States, Liberalism, and Human Rights in the United Nations." *Human Rights Quarterly* 36, no. 1 (2014): 61–89. https://doi.org/10.1353/hrq.2014.0004.

Keefe-Perry, Callid. "Schooling the Imagination: A Practical Theology of Education." PhD, Boston University, 2020.

Keshgegian, Flora A. *God Reflected: Metaphors for Life*. Minneapolis, MN: Fortress Press, 2008.

Koch, Dietrich-Alex. "Eucharistic Meal and Eucharistic Prayers in Didache 9 and 10." *Studia Theologica* 64, no. 2 (2010): 200–18. https://doi.org/10.1080 /0039338X.2010.517382.

Kolossov, Vladimir, and James Scott. "Selected Conceptual Issues in Border Studies."
    BELGEO (Leuven) 1, no. 1 (2013). https://doi.org/10.4000/belgeo.10532.
Kurt, Niederwimmer. *The Didache: A Commentary*. Minneapolis, MN: Fortress
    Press, 2016.
Kurzman, Charles, Rajesh Ghoshal, Kristin Gibson, Clinton Key, Micah Roos, and
    Amber Wells. "Powerblindness." *Sociology Compass* 8, no. 6 (2014): 718–30.
    https://doi.org/10.1111/soc4.12161.
Kwok, Pui-lan. *Discovering the Bible in the Non-Biblical World*. Maryknoll, NY:
    Orbis Books, 1995.
Kwok, Pui-lan. *Introducing Asian Feminist Theology*. Cleveland, OH: Pilgrim
    Press, 2000.
Kwok, Pui-lan. *Postcolonial Imagination and Feminist Theology*. 1st ed. Louisville,
    KY: Westminster John Knox Press, 2005.
Landy, David. "Talking Human Rights: How Social Movement Activists
    Are Constructed and Constrained by Human Rights Discourse."
    International Sociology 28, no. 4 (2013): 409–28. https://doi.org/10.1177
    /0268580913490769.
Latina Feminist, Group. *Telling to Live: Latina Feminist Testimonios*. Durham,
    NC: Duke University Press, 2001. doi:10.1215/9780822383284.
Lavariega Monforti, Jessica. *Latinos in the American Political System: An
    Encyclopedia of Latinos as Voters, Candidates, and Office Holders*. Santa
    Barbara, CA: ABC-CLIO, 2019.
Lemon, Jason. "Church Faces Backlash for Giving out Free Ar-15 During Sunday
    Service." *Newsweek*, 2020. https://www.newsweek.com/church-faces-backlash
    -giving-out-free-ar-15-during-sunday-service-1514113.
Lippert, Randy. "Rethinking Sanctuary: The Canadian Context, 1983–2003." *The
    International Migration Review* 39, no. 2 (2005): 381–406. https://doi.org/10
    .1111/j.1747-7379.2005.tb00271.x.
Lippert, Randy. "Wither Sanctuary?" *Refuge (Toronto. English edition)* 26, no. 1
    (2010): 57–67. https://doi.org/10.25071/1920-7336.30606.
Lorentzen, Robin. *Women in the Sanctuary Movement*. Philadelphia, PA: Temple
    University Press, 1991.
Lorentzen, Robin. "Women in the Sanctuary Movement: A Case Study in Chicago."
    PhD, Loyola University Chicago, 1989.
Loyola, Ignatius of. *The Spiritual Exercises of St. Ignatius of Loyola*. Translated by
    Elder Mullan. New York: P. J. Kennedy & Sons, Printers, 1914.
Lyon, Arabella, and Lester C. Olson. "Special Issue on Human Rights Rhetoric:
    Traditions of Testifying and Witnessing." *Rhetoric Society Quarterly* 41, no.
    3 (2011): 203–12. http://www.jstor.org.ezp-prod1.hul.harvard.edu/stable
    /23064463.
Lythgoe, Esteban. "Ricoeur's Concept of Testimony." *Analetica Hermeneutica* 3
    (2011): 1–16.
MacIntyre, Alasdair. *After Virtue: A Study in Moral Theory*. 3rd ed. Notre Dame,
    IN: University of Notre Dame Press, 2007.
MacIntyre, Alasdair. "Epistemological Crises, Dramatic Narrative, and the
    Philosophy of Science." In *The Tasks of Philosophy*, 3–23. New York:
    Cambridge University Press, 2006.
MacIntyre, Alasdair. *Whose Justice? Which Rationality?* Notre Dame, IN:
    University of Notre Dame Press, 1988.

Maxwell, E. Johnson. *Baptismal "Spirituality" in the Early Church and Its Implications for the Church Today*. Minneapolis, MN: Augsburg Fortress Publishers, 2015.

McCarthy, Colman. "The Sanctuary Movement in America." *Washington Post*, August 21, 1988.

McFague, Sallie. *The Body of God: An Ecological Theology*. Minneapolis, MN: Fortress Press, 1993.

McIntosh, Peggy. "White Privilege: Unpacking the Invisible Knapsack (1989)." In On Privilege, Fraudulence, and Teaching As Learning, 29–34. New York, NY: Routledge, 2020.

McKenzie, Bob. "Interview with Rev. Bob Mckenzie." By Eileen Purcell. *The Public Sanctuary Movement: An Historical Basis of Hope*. Berkley, CA: Graduate Theological Union, 1998.

Meeting, Chestnut Hill Friends. "Declaration of Sanctuary." February 10, 1985.

Mezzadra, Sandro. *Border as Method, or, the Multiplication of Labor*. A Social Text Book Ser. Edited by Brett Neilson. Durham, NC: Duke University Press, 2013.

Miller-McLemore, Bonnie J. "Five Misunderstandings about Practical Theology." *International Journal of Practical Theology* 16, no. 1 (2012): 5–26. https://doi .org/10.1515/ijpt-2012-0002.

Mills, Charles W. *The Racial Contract*. Ithaca, NY: Cornell University Press, 1997.

Mooney, Debra, and Cheryl Nuñez. *The Daily Examen for Diversity—Prayer Card*. Jesuit Resources, 2011.

Moore, Karen S. "The Impact of Covid-19 on the Latinx Population: A Scoping Literature Review." *Public Health Nursing (Boston, MA)* (2021). https://doi.org /10.1111/phn.12912.

Moschella, Mary Clark, and Susan Willhauck. *Qualitative Research in Theological Education: Pedagogy in Practice*. London: SCM Press, 2018.

Mullins, R. T. "Omnisubjectivity and the Problem of Creepy Divine Emotions." *Religious Studies* (2020): 1–18. https://doi.org/10.1017/S0034412520000220.

Myers, Jacob D. "Bearing Witness to God: Ricoeur and the Practice of Religious Testimony." *Literature & Theology* 34, no. 4 (2020): 391–407. https://doi.org /10.1093/litthe/fraa018.

Nancy, Jean-Luc. *The Inoperative Community*. Minneapolis, MN: University of Minnesota Press, 1991.

Navarro, Zander. "In Search of a Cultural Interpretation of Power: The Contribution of Pierre Bourdieu." *IDS Bulletin (Brighton. 1984)* 37, no. 6 (2006): 11–22. https://doi.org/10.1111/j.1759-5436.2006.tb00319.x.

Nelson, Lev Meirowitz, and Salem Pearce. *Mikdash: A Jewish Guide to the New Sanctuary Movement*. 2019. https://www.truah.org/wp-content/uploads/2019 /03/Mikdash-Handbook-Expanded-FINAL.pdf.

Nepstad, Sharon Erickson. *Convictions of the Soul: Religion, Culture, and Agency in the Central America Solidarity Movement*. Oxford, New York: Oxford University Press, 2004.

NguyRL, Ann Thúy, and Maya Pendleton, "Recognizing Race in Language: Why We Capitalize 'Black' and 'White.'" *Center for the Study of Public Policy*, 2020.

Nopper, Tamara, "The White Anti-Racist Is an Oxymoron: An Open Letter to 'White Anti-Racists.'" 2003.

Nordstokke, Kjell. "Christian Base Communities (Ceb)." In *Encyclopedia of Latin American Religions*, edited by Henri Gooren, 1–5. Cham: Springer International Publishing, 2014.

Nute, Betty R. "Sanctuary: New Challenge to the Conscience." *Friends' Journal* 29, no. 11 (1983): 5–6.

Office of the United Nations High Commissioner for Human Rights. "Frequently Asked Questions on Economic, Social and Cultural Rights—OHCHR Fact Sheet No. 33." Geneva, Switzerland, New York: Centre for Human Rights, 2008.

Osmer, Richard Robert. *Practical Theology: An Introduction*. Grand Rapids, MI: William B. Eerdmans Pub. Co., 2008.

Paik, A. Naomi. "Abolitionist Futures and the US Sanctuary Movement." *Race & Class* 59, no. 2 (2017): 3–25. https://doi.org/10.1177/0306396817717858.

Patricia, Stuelke. "The Reparative Politics of Central America Solidarity Movement Culture." *American Quarterly* 66, no. 3 (2014): 767–90. https://doi.org/10.1353/aq.2014.0058.

Pérez, Altagracia. "Latina/O Practical Theology: Reflections on Faith-Based Organizing as a Religious Practice." In *The Wiley Blackwell Companion to Latino/a Theology*, edited by Orlando O. Espín, 439–50. Malden, MA: John Wiley and Sons, Inc., 2015.

Pirie, Sophie H. "The Origins of a Political Trial: The Sanctuary Movement and Political Justice." *Yale Journal of Law & the Humanities* 2, no. 2 (1990): 381.

Purcell, Eileen. *The Public Sanctuary Movement: An Historical Basis of Hope*. Berkley, CA: Graduate Theological Union, 1998.

Qureshi, Waseem Ahmad. "Stemming the Bias of Civil and Political Rights over Economic, Social, and Cultural Rights." *Denver Journal of International Law and Policy* 46, no. 4 (2018): 289.

Rabben, Linda. *Sanctuary and Asylum: A Social and Political History*. Seattle: University of Washington Press, 2016.

Rae, Gavin. "Agency and Will in Agamben's Coming Politics." *Philosophy & Social Criticism* 44, no. 9 (2018): 978–96. https://doi.org/10.1177/0191453718771115.

Rambo, Shelly. *Resurrecting Wounds: Living in the Afterlife of Trauma*. Waco, TX: Baylor University Press, 2017.

Rambo, Shelly. *Spirit and Trauma: A Theology of Remaining*. 1st ed. Louisville, KY: Westminster John Knox Press, 2010.

Reddie, Anthony G. "Now You See Me, Now You Don't: Subjectivity, Blackness, and Difference in Practical Theology in Britain Post Brexit." *Practical Theology* 11, no. 1 (2018): 4–16. https://doi.org/10.1080/1756073X.2017.1404341.

Renny, Golden. "Sanctuary and Women." *Journal of Feminist Studies in Religion* 2, no. 1 (1986): 131–49.

Richard, H. Feen. "Church Sanctuary: Historical Roots and Contemporary Practice." *In Defense of the Alien* 7 (1984): 132–9.

Ricketts, Glenn M. "The Campus Sanctuary Movement." *Academic Questions* 32, no. 1 (2019): 81–93. https://doi.org/10.1007/s12129-018-9767-4.

Ricoeur, Paul. "The Hermeneutics of Testimony." In *Essays on Biblical Interpretation*, edited by Lewis Seymour Mudge. Philadelphia, PA: Fortress Press, 1980.

Rivera, Mayra. "Ghostly Encounters: Spirits, Memory, and the Holy Ghost." In *Planetary Loves: Spivak, Postcoloniality, and Theology*, edited by Stephen D. Moore and Mayra Rivera. New York: Fordham University Press, 2010.

Rivera, Mayra. *Poetics of the Flesh*. Durham, NC: Duke University Press, 2015.

Rivera, Mayra. "'Theologians Engaging Trauma' Transcript." *Theology Today (Ephrata, Pa.)* 68, no. 3 (2011): 224–37. https://doi.org/10.1177/0040573611416539.

Rosendale, Timothy. *Theology and Agency in Early Modern Literature*. Cambridge: Cambridge University Press, 2018.

Ruether, Rosemary Radford. *To Change the World: Christology and Cultural Criticism*. Kuyper Lectures. New York: Crossroad, 1981.

Russell, Letty M. *Church in the Round: Feminist Interpretation of the Church*. 1st ed. Louisville, KY: Westminster/J. Knox Press, 1993.

Safstrom, Jennifer. "An Analysis of Sanctuary Campuses: Assessing the Legality and Effectiveness of Policies Protective of Undocumented Students and of Potential Government Responses." *The Georgetown Law Journal* 106, no. 5 (2018): 1523.

Sánchez, Linda E., and Susan Bibler Coutin. "Insurgent Collaboration." *Departures in Critical Qualitative Research* 9, no. 1 (2020): 106–10. https://doi.org/10.1525/dcqr.2020.9.1.106.

Scharen, Christian. *Explorations in Ecclesiology and Ethnography*. Grand Rapids, MI: W.B. Eerdmans Pub. Co., 2012.

Scharen, Christian. *Fieldwork in Theology: Exploring the Social Context of God's Work in the World*. Grand Rapids, MI: Baker Academic, 2015.

Scharen, Christian. "Theological Ethnography and World Christianity: A Response." *Journal of World Christianity* 10, no. 1 (2020): 109–19. https://doi.org/10.5325/jworlchri.10.1.0109. https://doi.org/10.5325/jworlchri.10.1.0109.

Scharen, Christian, and Aana Marie Vigen. *Ethnography as Christian Theology and Ethics*. New York: Continuum, 2011.

Schmitt, Carl. *Political Theology: Four Chapters on the Concept of Sovereignty*. Cambridge, MA: MIT Press, 1985.

Schneider, Rachel C., and Sophie Bjork-James. "Whither Whiteness and Religion?: Implications for Theology and the Study of Religion." *Journal of the American Academy of Religion* 88, no. 1 (2020): 175–99. https://doi.org/10.1093/jaarel/lfaa002.

Schultz, Gustav. "Interview with Rev. Gus Schultz." *The Public Sanctuary Movement: An Historical Basis of Hope*. By Eileen M. Purcell. Berkley, CA: Graduate Theological Union, 1998. http://callimachus.org/digital/collection/p15008coll2/id/43/rec/3.

Sedgwick, Eve Kosofsky. *Epistemology of the Closet*. Updated ed./ preface by the author. Berkeley, CA: University of California Press, 2008.

Sedgwick, Eve Kosofsky. "Paranoid Reading and Reparative Reading or, You're So Paranoid, You Probably Think This Introduction Is About You." In *Novel Gazing: Queer Readings in Fiction*, edited by Eve Kosofsky Sedgwick, 1–38. New York: Duke University Press, 1997.

Seelye, Katharine Q. "God and Guns Were Part of the Foundation of This Country." *New York Times*, 2009. https://archive.nytimes.com/www.nytimes.com/imagepages/2009/06/26/us/26guns_CA2.ready.html.

Shah, Sonia. *The Next Great Migration: The Beauty and Terror of Life on the Move*. New York: Bloomsbury Publishing, 2020.

Sherman-Stokes, Sarah. "Reparations for Central American Refugees." *Denver Law Review* 95 (2019): 585–634.

Shoemaker, Karl. *Sanctuary and Crime in the Middle Ages, 400–1500*. 1st ed. New York: Fordham University Press, 2011.

Smith, Christian. *Resisting Reagan: The U.S. Central America Peace Movement*. Chicago, IL: University of Chicago Press, 1996.

Smith, Ted A. "Theories of Practice." In *The Wiley-Blackwell Companion to Practical Theology*, edited by Bonnie J. Miller-McLemore, 244–54. New York: Wiley-Blackwell, 2011.

Sojoyner, Damien M. "Another Life Is Possible: Black Fugitivity and Enclosed Places." *Cultural Anthropology* 32, no. 4 (2017): 514–36. https://doi.org/10.14506/ca32.4.04.

Sölle, Dorothee. *Theology for Skeptics: Reflections on God*. Minneapolis, MN: Fortress Press, 1995.

Sölle, Dorothee. *The Window of Vulnerability: A Political Spirituality*. 1st English-language ed. Minneapolis, MN: Fortress Press, 1990.

Spivak, Gayatri Chakravorty. "Can the Subaltern Speak?." In *Can the Subaltern Speak? Reflections on the History of an Idea*, edited by Rosalind Morris, 21–78. New York: Columbia University Press, 2010.

Squires, Jessica. *Building Sanctuary: The Movement to Support Vietnam War Resisters in Canada, 1965–73*. Vancouver, Toronto: UBC Press, 2013.

Stackert, Jeffery. "Why Does Deuteronomy Legislate Cities of Refuge? Asylum in the Covenant Collection (Exodus 21:12-14) and Deuteronomy (19:1-13)." *Journal of Biblical Literature* 125, no. 1 (2006): 23–49. https://doi.org/10.2307/27638345.

Stang, Charles M. "Giorgio Agamben, The Church, and Me." *Harvard Divinity Bulletin* (Spring/Summer 2020). https://bulletin.hds.harvard.edu/giorgio-agamben-the-church-and-me/.

Stewart, Kathleen. *A Space on the Side of the Road Cultural Poetics in an "Other" America*. Baltimore, MD: Princeton University Press, 1996.

Stoddard, Brad. "God's Favorite Gun: The Sanctuary Church and the (Re) Militarization of American Christianity." *Journal of Religion and Violence* 7, no. 3 (2019): 255–77. https://doi.org/10.5840/jrv202031171.

Strick, Simon. *American Dolorologies: Pain, Sentimentalism, Biopolitics*. Albany, NY: State University of New York Press, 2014.

Stuelke, Patricia Rachael. *The Ruse of Repair: US Neoliberal Empire and the Turn from Critique*. Durham, NC: Duke University Press, 2021.

Swinton, John. *Finding Jesus in the Storm: The Spiritual Lives of Christians with Mental Health Challenges*. Grand Rapids, MI: William. B. Eerdmans Publishing Company, 2020.

Swinton, John. *Practical Theology and Qualitative Research*. Edited by Harriet Mowat. 2nd ed. London: SCM Press, 2016.

Tanner, Kathryn. "Incarnation, Cross, and Sacrifice: A Feminist-Inspired Reappraisal." *Anglican Theological Review* 86, no. 1 (2004): 35–56.

Teel, Karen. "Can We Hear Him Now? James Cone's Enduring Challenge to White Theologians." *Theological Studies (Baltimore)* 81, no. 3 (2020): 582–604. https://doi.org/10.1177/0040563920960034.

Teel, Karen. "Whiteness in Catholic Theological Method." *Journal of the American Academy of Religion* 87, no. 2 (2019): 401–33. https://doi.org/10.1093/jaarel/lfz023.

Terrell, JoAnne Marie. *Power in the Blood: The Cross in the African American Experience*. Maryknoll, NY: Orbis Books, 1998.

Tertullian. *Tertullian's Treatises: Concerning Prayer, Concerning Baptism.* Translated by Alexander Souter. England: Society for Promoting Christian Knowledge Macmillan, 1919.

Thompson, Deanna A. *Crossing the Divide: Luther, Feminism, and the Cross.* Minneapolis, MN: Fortress Press, 2004.

Timpe, Kevin. "Cooperative Grace, Cooperative Agency." *European Journal for Philosophy of Religion* 7, no. 3 (2015): 223–45. https://doi.org/10.24204/ejpr .v7i3.113.

United Nations. General Assembly. *Universal Declaration of Human Rights.* Lake Success: United Nations Department. of Public Information, 1949.

Van Ham, Lane. "Sanctuary Revisited: Central American Refugee Assistance in the History of Church-Based Immigrant Advocacy." *Political Theology: The Journal of Christian Socialism* 10, no. 4 (2009): 621–45. https://doi.org/10.1558/poth .v10i4.621.

VandenBerg, Mary. "Redemptive Suffering: Christ's Alone." *Scottish Journal of Theology* 60, no. 4 (2007): 394–411. https://doi.org/10.1017/ S0036930607003717.

Vargas, Maria Elena. "Ghostly Others: Limiting Constructions of Deserving Subjects in Asylum Claims and Sanctuary Protection." *Journal of International Women's Studies* 21, no. 7 (2020): 77.

Velleman, J. David. "How to Share an Intention." *Philosophy and Phenomenological Research* 57, no. 1 (1997): 29–50. https://doi.org/10.2307/2953776.

Ward, Graham. *Cities of God.* New York: Routledge, 2000.

Ward, Pete. *Perspectives on Ecclesiology and Ethnography.* Grand Rapids, MI: W.B. Eerdmans Pub. Co., 2012.

West, Cornel. *Prophetic Fragments.* Grand Rapids, MI, Trenton, NJ: Eerdmans/ Africa World Press, 1988.

Wheaton, Philip. "Sanctuary Service Homily." Luther Place Church in Washington, DC, 1983.

Whitmore, Todd. *Imitating Christ in Magwi: An Anthropological Theology.* London: T&T Clark, 2019.

Wigg-Stevenson, Natalie. *Ethnographic Theology: An Inquiry into the Production of Theological Knowledge.* 1st ed. New York: Palgrave Macmillan US; Imprint: Palgrave Macmillan, 2014.

Wigg-Stevenson, Natalie. "From Proclamation to Conversation: Ethnographic Disruptions to Theological Normativity." *Palgrave Communications* 1, no. 1 (October 13, 2015): 15024. https://doi.org/10.1057/palcomms.2015.24. https:// doi.org/10.1057/palcomms.2015.24.

Wigg-Stevenson, Natalie. "Reflexive Theology: A Preliminary Proposal." *Practical Matters*, no. 6 (Spring 2013): 1–19.

Wigg-Stevenson, Natalie. "What's Really Going On: Ethnographic Theology and the Production of Theological Knowledge." *Cultural Studies, Critical Methodologies* 18, no. 6 (2018): 423–9. https://doi.org/10.1177 /1532708617744576.

Wild, Kara L. "The New Sanctuary Movement: When Moral Mission Means Breaking the Law, and the Consequences for Churches and Illegal Immigrants." *Santa Clara Law Review* 50, no. 3 (2010): 981.

Williams, Delores S. *Sisters in the Wilderness: The Challenge of Womanist God-Talk.* Maryknoll: Orbis Books, 1993.

Winner, Lauren F. *The Dangers of Christian Practice: On Wayward Gifts, Characteristic Damage, and Sin*. New Haven, CT: Yale University Press, 2018.

Woodley, Xeturah, and Megan Lockard. "Womanism and Snowball Sampling: Engaging Marginalized Populations in Holistic Research." *Qualitative Report* (2016): 321. https://doi.org/10.46743/2160-3715/2016.2198.

Woolf, Michael. "Holy Risk: Old Cambridge Baptist Church and the Sanctuary Movement." *Glossolalia* 6, no. 1 (2013).

Yancy, George. *Backlash: What Happens When We Talk Honestly About Racism in America*. Edited by Cornel West. Lanham, MD: Rowman & Littlefield, 2018.

Yancy, George. *Black Bodies, White Gazes: The Continuing Significance of Race*. Lanham, MD: Rowman & Littlefield Pub., 2008.

Yancy, George. "Is White America Ready to Confront Its Racism? Philosopher George Yancy Says We Need a 'Crisis.'" By Alex Blasdel. *The Guardian*, 2018.

Yancy, George. *Look, a White! Philosophical Essays on Whiteness*. Philadelphia, PA: Temple University Press, 2012.

Yancy, George, and Judith Butler. "What's Wrong with 'All Lives Matter'?" *The New York Times*, 2014. https://archive.nytimes.com/opinionator.blogs.nytimes .com/2015/01/12/whats-wrong-with-all-lives-matter/.

Yukich, Grace. "Constructing the Model Immigrant: Movement Strategy and Immigrant Deservingness in the New Sanctuary Movement." *Social Problems (Berkeley, CA)* 60, no. 3 (2013): 302–20. https://doi.org/10.1525 sp.2013.60.3.302.

Yukich, Grace. *One Family under God: Immigration Politics and Progressive Religion in America*. New York: Oxford University Press, 2013.

Zagzebski, Linda Trinkaus. *Omnisubjectivity: A Defense of a Divine Attribute*. Milwaukee, WI: Marquette University Press, 2013.

INDEX